Hancock

482-7921

REAL
TO
REEL

REAL
TO
REEL

DAVID COYNIK

McDOUGAL, LITTELL & COMPANY
EVANSTON, ILLINOIS

distributed to colleges and universities by
CANFIELD PRESS
A Department of Harper & Row, Publishers, Inc., San Francisco

FOR INEZ AND GABES
and all my students,
with special thanks to: Dr. Jack C. Ellis, Northwestern University; Mr. Gene Walsh; Mrs. Bernice Gregorio;
Dr. Edward Fischer; Mr. J. Paul Carrico; Bro. John Miller;
Bro. H. Raphael; Mr. James Wicklund; Mr. Sal Giarrizzo; Dr. Patrick Costello;
Mr. M. Jerry Weiss; Dr. W. Ann Reynolds; Dr. Phyllis Bogner; Dr. Seymour Metrick;
and a lot of other people.

I'll always be grateful to Bob Coleman, Paul Newell, Rob Orr, Jack Phalen, Bob Schiappacasse,
Mike Tabor, and many others who have taught me a great deal about film.
To these people, and to the many others from whom I've been
privileged to learn, I offer my sincere thanks.

PHOTOGRAPHY ACKNOWLEDGMENTS

Stills courtesy of Audio-Brandon Films, distributor, pages 16-17, 31 bottom, 100, 129, 143. Stills courtesy of Avco Embassy Pictures Corp., pages 9 bottom right, 9 top left, 27, 107, 158-59, 248. Stills courtesy of Cinema 5 Ltd., page 138. Stills courtesy Columbia Pictures, pages 78, 128. Stills courtesy of Contemporary Films/McGraw-Hill, pages 9 bottom left, 10, 12, 14, 23, 18 top, 19, 26, 28, 31 top, 47, 48, 49, 50, 56, 58 middle, 58 bottom, 62, 63, 64, 68, 69, 77 right, 79, 80, 82, 93, 95, 99, 110, 113, 114, 122, 124, 137, 151, 153, 155, 160, 171, 172, 173, 174, 177, 183, 184, 188. Stills courtesy of EYR Campus Programs, page 66. Stills from the Film Stills Archives Museum of Modern Art, New York, pages 2, 4, 52, 58 top, 104, 135, 150, 157, 187. Stills courtesy of Janus Films, pages 8, 13, 18 bottom, 25, 44, 59, 71, 106, 120, 124-25, 130. Still courtesy of Mayseles brothers, page 163. Still courtesy of Metro-Goldwyn-Mayer, Inc., page 96. Stills courtesy of Pyramid Films, pages 9 top right, 24, 29, 30, 35, 53, 168, 189, 190, 192-93, 203 top. Still courtesy of St. Bede Records, page 11. Stills courtesy of Summit Films, pages 22, 32-33. Stills courtesy of Twentieth Century-Fox Film Corporation, pages 108, 139, 141. Stills courtesy of Universal City Studios, Inc., pages 6-7, 74, 90. Drawing courtesy of Eastman Kodak Company, page 201. Photograph by Mike Tabor, page 164. Photographs by Robert V. Orr, pages 86, 87, 88, 89, 119 top left, 148. Photographs by the author, pages 3, 11, 38, 39, 40, 41, 42, 43, 83, 84, 85, 118, 119, 136, 180, 198, 203, 204, 206, 207, 209. Special thanks to: George Colburn Lab, Jack Behrend of Behrend's Inc., Conestoga College (Kitchener, Ontario).

ISBN: 0-88343-304-4

Editor: Stephan M. Nagel

Published 1976 by McDougal, Littell & Company
Box 1667, Evanston, Illinois 60204
Copyright © 1976 by St. Mary's College Press, Winona, Minnesota.
First edition © 1972 by St. Mary's College Press.

CONTENTS

1 THE SHOT 1

2 MOTION 23

Photo Essay: Preparing a Shot 38

3 EDITING 45

4 RHYTHM 57

5 LIGHT 75

Photo Essay: Shooting Indoors 86

6 COLOR 91

7 SOUND 105

Photo Essay: Making a Sound Film 118

8 THE DIRECTOR 121

9 GENRE 135

10 DOCUMENTARY 149

11 ANIMATION 169

12 NOW-FILM 181

13 FILMMAKING 199

Index 212

INTRODUCTION

Why study film at all? Mainly because film and television, which uses most of the same visual communication devices as film, give us more of our information today than ever before. And tomorrow they will give us more information than they do today. Since we base our decisions on what information we have, it's good to be able to understand communications from whatever channel they come.

And film is enjoyable. It moves. Motion is something that everybody enjoys, and movies seem to capture this universal feeling of delight.

By the time most people begin their first course in film, they have seen thousands of hours of movies and television, much more time than they have spent reading. When the thousands of hours that one student has already put in watching film is added to the thousands of hours that other students in class have spent, the total amount of film experience is enormous. Film study classes allow everybody in the group to pool his or her past experience through discussion with everybody else's experience.

Film study classes also allow everybody to share their immediate reactions to a film with other members of the group. Everyone has learned to appreciate and understand film to some extent. Some people, however, will notice certain things others do not notice. Some people will like certain films while others will dislike the same films. Discussion allows students to learn about film because everybody sees the same film differently, and discussion allows them to learn more about each other for the same reason.

A good film study discussion avoids the simplistic response of "I liked the movie" or "I hated the movie." Rather, the question of "*Why* did I like (or hate) the film" can led to important conclusions. What did the filmmaker say? How did he or she say it? These are questions that lead to discussions of *how* film communicates. Considering the questions of how a director (or some other creative person) has manipulated the tools of film to create a communication leads to an understanding of how film exists as a *language*.

During your film course, you will see a number of films. Some of them you will like, others you will dislike. You will not see every film mentioned in this book during class—there are too many different films mentioned. Other films mentioned here you may already have seen. Seeing films in class is the primary way you will learn about film. Discussing these films will let you know about the way that other people saw the same film; maybe you will change the way that you feel about a film as the result of a discussion. Perhaps you will understand it more. This book gives you a background for some of the techniques which filmmakers use to communicate with you—it tells you about film language, a new language that was first used around 1900.

In class you will see how particular filmmakers communicate using some of the parts of film language described here. You may see only a few of the films mentioned as examples here; but the films which you do see will use the same techniques as the examples we'll talk about in this book.

Film study is a group activity. For the most part, you are used to watching film and television as a private activity, not as a group activity. When you go to the movies, even if you go with a group, you usually don't spend much time afterwards sharing reactions to the film. In film study class, however, you will discuss your experience of the film with other people in your group. Sometimes it's hard to put into words how you felt during a film. Sharing your reactions with others in your film study group, however, requires that you learn to talk about how you felt. It may take practice, but it's worth the effort.

The last chapter tells you how to make your own film. Actually working on a film can help you to understand just what a filmmaker can do with the tools of film language. It's one thing to read about something you can do, it's one thing to see somebody doing it—but it's really something to try it yourself. Even though that chapter is last in the book, you should start thinking about making a film right now. As you see more and more films, you will discover more and more ideas about what you can do with film, what you can say to other people by means of film.

Film study is fun. Seeing film is fun. Talking and reading about film is fun. And the more films you see, the more fun it becomes. The more you see, the more you want to see more. And the better prepared you'll be for a world where, in the future, much of our communication will be done by film and pictures.

David Coynik

THE SHOT

Film is a form of communication. It is like talking to someone using an immense vocabulary of images, color, movement, light, sound, and more. And it is showing someone how you feel about something or seeing something the way someone else sees it.

Film communication starts with the **shot**, film's basic unit. A director talks to his audience by the way he creates the shots in his movie.

An early Russian film director, V.I. Pudovkin, remarked in one of his early works entitled *On Film Technique*, "To show something as everyone sees it is to have accomplished nothing." Pudovkin wanted directors to show things as they saw them, not as the event happened. Then the audience would see *more* than what happened; they would see the event as it affected the director.

To show things to his audience as he sees them, a director must carefully prepare his shots. Where a director puts his camera, what he includes and what he excludes, how he changes the way things in a picture relate one to another, all these are the methods by which a director can show how he sees something and what he thinks about it. One difficulty for the beginner is imagining all of the different techniques a director has at his disposal to create one shot. It is these many possibilities, how-

A single shot can communicate many different things. This still is from a famous shot in the 1923 silent film **Safety Last** with Harold Lloyd.

ever, which help make film the powerful communication medium that it is. Let's take a look at some of these techniques.

A director may spend hours preparing for a shot, setting up props, laying rails for the camera to run on, preparing the actors for what they are supposed to do. All of a director's efforts show up in what happens between the time he yells "Action!" and the time he yells "Cut!" The **shot** is what happens between those two yells. The movie itself usually consists of any number of different shots, created from different angles, cut, and joined together.

There are exceptions to the normal definition of movies as being composed of different shots joined together. Early films, like Thomas Edison's *The Kiss* or the Lumiere brothers' *Arrival of a Train at the Station* were so short that they consisted of just one shot.

In the 1960's, filmmaker Andy Warhol experimented with this early style of filmmaking, and some of his films, like *Sleep*, *Eat*, and *Empire*, consisted of only one shot. These films, however, last quite a bit longer than the early one-shot films did. While Edison's films lasted only a minute, *Empire*, a one-shot film of the Empire State Building, lasts eight hours. By using only one shot, Warhol was able to create particular effects for his audience.

Most films, however, consist of shots taken from various distances, with different lenses and camera angles and other techniques. The director,

or filmmaker as we shall sometimes call him, uses these various techniques because they allow him to make each shot different from any shot ever made, and to make this one shot communicate exactly what he wants it to communicate.

Some people have compared the shots in a film to the words in a sentence. This is a good comparison in as much as words, like shots, are basic units of communication. But comparing words to shots can be misleading in another respect. A good writer must search in dictionaries to find just the right words to communicate what he wants to say to his audience. But the film director does not have to *choose* words; he *creates* shots.

Authors have been inspired by the filmmaker's freedom to create "expressions" rather than only use what is given them. Some, like James Joyce, have written books in which they make up words, creating them for the occasion in the same way a filmmaker creates shots. In *1984*, George Orwell created a language called *newspeak* to describe ideas which other writers had never described before and for which no words existed.

A director need not rely on the past; an author, on the other hand, usually must use words which originated hundreds of years before his time. The director may use tools and techniques that other directors have used, but every time he creates a new shot, he has to start from scratch. That's why film is directed more to the present than literature is. Even when films show us the past, they show the past as if it were present now.

There's a better comparison than the one between the shot and the word: The way a director creates a shot for a film is quite similar to the way an artist creates a color on his palette. The artist can make his color lighter and greener, or darker and redder, anything he wants. The freedom of an artist mixing a color resembles the freedom of a director creating a shot much more than does an author choosing his words. But this is still a limited comparison because color is only one of a large number of tools a director can use.

Early films, like the Lumiere brothers' film **Arrival of a Train at the Station**, were short documents of actual events, consisting of only one shot.

THE LONG SHOT

Perhaps the first decision a filmmaker must make in filming a particular scene is how much he wants to *include* or, closely related to this, how much he wants to *emphasize* what occurs in that shot.

How much a filmmaker includes in a shot is determined partly by how far he places his camera from his subject. The including shot, or **long shot**, takes in the entire area of action. What the entire area of action is will depend upon what is being filmed. Suppose a particular movie takes place inside a courtroom. The entire area of action would be the courtroom itself, including the judge, jury, defendant, lawyers, and spectators. In another film, the director might wish to show cattle being rounded up for branding. In that case, the camera would have to be much farther away from the action in order to include the entire area.

The area of action can also change in different parts of a movie. In the film *Easy Rider*, for example, when Peter Fonda and Dennis Hopper are riding their motorcycles down the highway, the long shot has to be taken from very far away to include the entire area of action. But later on, when the two are sitting around a campfire talking, the long shot can be made a great deal closer and still take in the entire area of action.

Because the long shot takes in the entire area of action, it can be used as an **establishing shot** describing where the people or objects are located in a particular scene of a film. Perhaps someone may be talking to a couple of his friends around a campfire. Early in the scene, a director might take a long shot to establish the campsite for us. Then, if later the speaker talks to somebody on his right, we know to whom he's talking.

A director can communicate important information by using the long shot. For instance, at the

The information contained in a shot changes depending upon what the filmmaker decides to include in the shot. If a film sequence was about a group of boys climbing a hill, for instance, the area of action might be quite extensive. An extreme long shot (top) tells us quite a bit about the hill and very little about the boys. A long shot (middle) says less about the hill and more about the boys. A medium shot (bottom) focuses on the group of boys and says little about the hill.

Produced by Georges Méliès in 1902, **A Trip to the Moon** is one of the first examples of a story film. Read left to right, the stills on this page include every shot in the film. Note how every shot is a long shot and resembles a new scene in a stage play.

4/THE SHOT

beginning of his short film *Occurrence at Owl Creek Bridge*, director Robert Enrico used a long shot which included: dawn breaking, sentries in Civil War uniforms standing guard, burned branches against a bleak sky, trees with no leaves on them, a bridge isolated from the rest of the world and heavily guarded. With this single long shot, Enrico established the chronological hour, season, and historical period of his film; he also set a bleak mood and made his audience apprehensive of an ominous event on the bridge.

Many times a filmmaker employs a long shot to make ideas apparent to us. An example of this technique occurs in the short film *No Reason to Stay* at a point when Christopher Wood is arguing with his girl, Joan. Chris wants to quit school because he feels he isn't really learning anything, but Joan doesn't understand what he's trying to tell her. As the conversation progresses, the audience discovers that Chris's and Joan's ideas about education are moving them farther and farther apart. At the end of the conversation, Chris says, "Well, now I know exactly where I stand." Now, director Mort Ransen cut from the close shots of Chris and Joan he had been using to a long shot—and indeed the two are standing far away from each other. Their disagreement has separated them, and the director underlined this by a long shot, showing them standing much farther apart than a couple normally stand.

Director Orson Welles used a series of long shots in his feature film *Citizen Kane* for a similar reason. When Kane and his wife are newly married, they sit close to each other at breakfast. As time wears on, however, the closeness of their relationship wears off, and Welles indicated this by a series of shots of Kane and his wife having breakfast. The camera moves continually farther back as Kane and his wife grow further and further apart.

If this were 1910, we would have said all there was to say about shots. In the early days before film had developed as a language and as an art form, the long shot was the only shot that commonly existed for a director's use. The camera sat directly in front of the actors, who entered and exited from the frame much as actors do on the stage. As in the stage plays of the time, actors walked out of the right side of a picture and reentered from the left side in the next scene.

Early filmmakers had not really discovered the possibility of shots other than the long shot; few had ever thought about filming anything except the entire area of action. People thought of film only as a way to *record* action and not as a *language* which could be used to coordinate, subordinate, and emphasize thoughts and feelings. Cameramen were cautioned to include the entire area of action because directors were afraid that the audience would not pay the full price to see only half an actor.

When he has only long shots to work with, a director can't tell people how he feels about his subject or what part of a shot he considers more important than the other parts. He can only record what happens in front of his camera.

Fortunately, the early director David Wark Griffith and others experimented with new kinds of camera techniques. In films like *The Birth of a Nation* (1915), *Intolerance* (1916), and *Broken Blossoms* (1919), Griffith showed how film directors could better communicate their ideas in a shot by focusing on only a part of the area of action. In this way that part becomes as big on the screen as the entire area of action and seems more important than the parts the director does not show his audience. This is where communication, which is more than just recording, entered the film scene, and because D.W. Griffith's pioneering work extended the director's capability to say things with film, he is sometimes referred to as the "father of film language."

THE EXTREME LONG SHOT

Sometimes a director may choose to move his camera back farther than necessary to include the entire area of action. When he does this, he creates the **extreme long shot**. The extreme long shot is not just a longer long shot; it can be used by a director to convey ideas a long shot could not.

Suppose a director wished to impress his viewers with the vast scope of an event; it would be a good spot for the extreme long shot. In the short film *Corral*, for instance, there is a shot of a cowboy rounding up horses and driving them to a corral.

First, we are shown the roundup in a long shot to establish what is happening. The next shot, however, is an extreme long shot, showing the cowboy and the herd as minute details in a vast wilderness. The herd of horses is very large; in comparison with the vastness of the setting, however, it becomes quite insignificant.

Movie spectaculars use the extreme long shot to communicate grandeur, largeness, space. Indeed, many of the "big" and memorable shots from *2001: A Space Odyssey*, *Jaws*, and *Gone with the Wind* are extreme long shots.

THE MEDIUM SHOT

The usual distance for a shot is the **medium shot**. Because the distance from the camera to the subject varies depending upon the subject, the medium shot can best be described as an intermediate shot between the long shot and the close-up, or as a shot which allows the audience to get closer to the action than in a long shot, but not so close that it sees only part of the action. Narrative, or story, films use the medium shot with great frequency because it is the most effective shot to use when two people are talking to each other: The medium shot lets the viewer get close enough to the people to concentrate on what they're saying and not be concerned with where they are. A director can suggest the relationship between people by the way he places them in a medium shot. In the film *Occurrence at Owl Creek Bridge*, for instance, Robert Enrico wanted to emphasize the relationship between a condemned man, Peyton Farquhar, and the commander of the soldiers who is going to execute him. To do this Enrico used a medium shot which included both the commander and the condemned man. We see Farquhar, with the noose around his neck, standing on a plank above a river. The other end of the plank is held to the bridge only because the officer is standing on it. Enrico wanted to communicate the danger imminent to the condemned man and the fact that his life is in the hands—

The 1975 feature **Jaws** used various kinds of shots from the extreme long shot to the close-up. This is a still from a long shot including the action area.

Swedish director Ingmar Bergman uses the medium shot for dialog. Jof tells Mia about a vision he has just seen, in Bergman's feature film **The Seventh Seal**.

or feet—of the soldier. By using a medium shot, Enrico can show both men in the same shot and with one shot express the danger, the conflict, and the relationship between the two men. A long shot would allow the scenery to intrude on this event; other soldiers, visible in the background, would be distracting.

As another example, in the short film *Corral*, the cowboy enters a corral and attempts to saddle a half-broken horse. The audience sees only medium and close-medium shots. Although long shots might have been interesting to look at and might have added variety, the director deliberately uses only medium shots. Thus, the audience is confined to the corral with the cowboy and the horse he is trying to break, creating an enclosed feeling and communicating the intimate struggle between the man and the horse.

Even though the medium shot is the most common shot for filmmakers, it can be an effective

means of communication in the hands of an experienced director. Because it can isolate two people from their background and make the audience concentrate on them rather than where they are, the medium shot is sometimes called a **two-shot**.

THE CLOSE-UP

Another important shot for the filmmaker—and a communication device only film can offer—is the **close-up**. None of the other media allow such large-scale portrayal of only a portion of an action. The close-up magnifies an action or object and separates it from its surroundings. By making the object or action the entire content of his picture, a director also magnifies its importance.

The creative director can also use the close-up to communicate deep feeling or emotion. In *Occurrence at Owl Creek Bridge*, Enrico used close-ups of the condemned man's tied hands struggling for freedom. By isolating the hands and filling the screen with them, the director informs the viewers of Farquhar's suffering and conveys his strong desire to be free. Close-ups of the man's forehead beading up with sweat make the anguish of Farquhar's mental state apparent.

Many close-ups are of people's faces. The reason for this is that directors know that the human face is perhaps the most subtle instrument known for communicating emotion, ideas, and feelings without using words. Scientists, observing young children at play, have charted certain basic facial movements which allow young children to communicate to each other without using words. For example, one young boy may be quite happy with a toy. Another youngster steals the toy. Certain facial movements will occur as one child becomes the aggressor and the other the victim. Eyebrows, mouth, lips, even how many teeth are showing, are

nonverbal signals that tell each child how the other feels.

As we grow up, we use words to tell other people *exactly* how we feel, but the basic nonverbal signals of communication remain. We don't have the time to go into these, but we can look at one example. In small children, a defense mechanism against attack consists of raising the hand to the ear, preparing to "hit back." Many times if somebody accuses us of something or if we almost hit another car or if we get into some other situation where we are on the defensive, we unconsciously run a hand through our hair. This hand position is a vestige of the nonverbal gesture that we used as children.

Directors use close-ups to isolate these non-

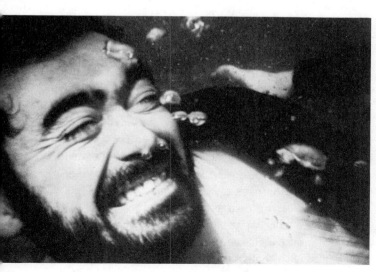

verbal signals of communication. Film critic Bela Balazs feels that the expressive qualities of the human face, lost as a result of so many years of depending upon printed words for communication, will again become a strong means of communication as a result of the film close-up. Hands, feet, sweat beading up on a person's head, all these signals suggest many things about a person. In Albert Lamorisse's film *The Red Balloon*, Pascal, a young boy, finds that he cannot ride a streetcar with a balloon he has just found. The director shows a close-up of Pascal's face, and in it we can "read" the boy's feeling of rejection.

We are used to picking up these nonverbal signs of communication. A disciplinarian might say, "I know that kid's lying. He couldn't look me in the eye." Filmmakers can enlarge the shifty eyes of somebody who is lying; no matter what he says, we know he is lying by the signs the filmmaker focuses on. The close-up is another technique a director uses to underline things for us. Just as the long shot can be called the establishing shot, the close-up can be called the **demonstrative shot** because it points out particular things for us to look at.

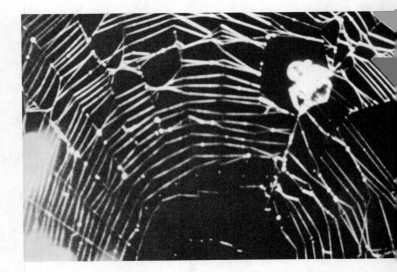

There are extreme long shots, and **extreme close-ups** exist as well. In these shots, the audience is permitted to see only a small part of the entire area of action. Such extreme close-ups can enlarge small things to monstrous proportions. Insects can dominate the screen, as viewers of horror films know. In *Occurrence at Owl Creek Bridge*, Enrico showed a series of extreme close-ups of insects when the condemned man first escapes from his captors. In the last few moments of the sequence, it is noticed that a spider has caught a victim in its net; the viewers know from this close-up that the condemned man has not eluded his captors yet.

THE EFFECTS OF DIFFERENT LENSES

If all the techniques the film director had at his disposal to create shots were choices of camera distances from extreme long shots to extreme close-ups, he would still have quite a range of possibilities for communicating. But the director has many different ways of creating his long shot, medium shot, or close-up.

For instance, a director can choose different lenses to make his point. Different lenses give a director a variety of perspectives to use in showing his audience how he feels about something.

Sometimes a director can use the **normal lens**. Things shot with a normal lens look as far away as they do in reality, with no distortion. Whenever a director wants his scene to look the way you would usually see it, he uses a normal lens.

A director can also express a feeling or idea by creating his shot with a **telephoto** or **long-focus lens**. Telephoto lenses make faraway objects seem closer, and with them a director can take shots of objects that cannot be approached by a cameraman. For example, extreme telephoto lenses help directors film shots of wildlife; cameramen, hidden behind blinds far away from the animals, can get close-up shots by using telephoto lenses.

Aside from keeping directors and cameramen safe from lions and tigers, telephoto lenses also have uses in film communication. When we view a scene with our two eyes, we see it in natural perspective and in three dimensions. A movie really has only two dimensions, length and width, but it can communicate a *feeling* of depth. It is this feeling of depth a director can alter with special lenses.

When a director uses a telephoto lens to create a shot, we notice that everything seems to be flattened out, bunched up. If you have ever watched a horserace or baseball game on television, you are familiar with the effect of a telephoto lens. As the horses take the far turn or as we see a shot of the pitcher in front of the batter, they seem much closer to each other than they really are. The director is using a telephoto lens; it magnifies the objects and makes them seem closer to us and it also makes the background appear close as well.

Suppose the director wants a shot of a highway to underline the fact that it is crowded. By creating the shot with a telephoto lens, he can make the cars seem more squeezed together than they actually are. The longer the lens, the more magnification it has, the more the bunched-up effect will be increased. A shot with a normal lens would have shown all the cars; the same shot, taken with a telephoto lens, conveys how the director feels about the cars. We experience the congestion in our imaginations.

Since a telephoto lens compresses distance, a director can also use this lens to make movement toward the camera seem to happen very slowly. A person running toward the camera can seem to run and run and make no progress. Robert Enrico used an extreme telephoto lens to create shots of the condemned man running to embrace his wife at the end of *Occurrence*. Enrico wanted to tell his audience how anxious the man was to be reunited

Telephoto shots separate a person from the background, by making any objects farther from the point of focus appear fuzzy.

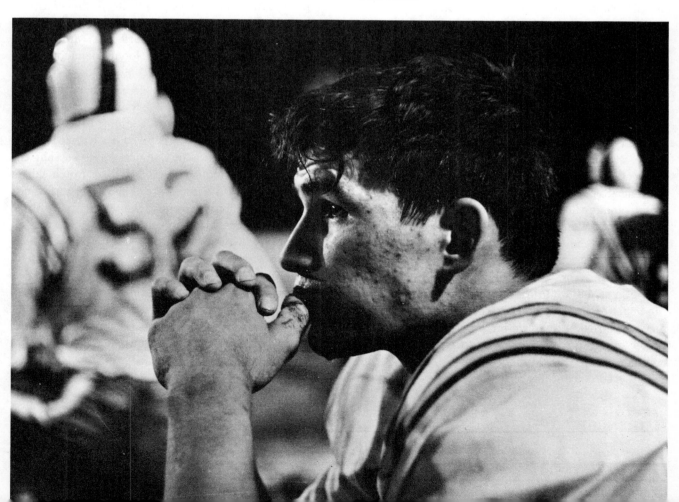

with his wife. By using an extreme telephoto lens to create the shot, Enrico makes the condemned man run as if on a treadmill; as fast as he runs, he seems to get nowhere. In this shot we sense how the man feels at the time; any length to run is too far.

Mike Nichols used the same type of telephoto shot near the end of his feature *The Graduate*. Benjamin Braddock is running to the church where his girl friend is about to marry someone else. Every moment may mean that he will arrive at the church too late to stop the ceremony. His race seems endless.

There's something else that a telephoto lens can do which makes it popular with directors. The telephoto lens has a **shallow depth of field,** which means that objects closer or farther away than the spot on which the lens is actually focused appear fuzzy. If background or foreground objects might distract from what the director really wants the audience to pay attention to, he will use a telephoto lens to make these other objects appear fuzzy and out of focus. Thus he can force the audience to look only at what he wants it to see.

At the beginning of his short film *No Reason to Stay,* director Mort Ransen used a telephoto shot of a school building. During the shot, he turns the focus of the lens so that the school goes out of focus: We realize that we have been looking at the school building through a wire mesh fence. Ransen wanted to tell his audience that this particular school is somewhat like a prison.

Many times a director will choose another type of lens to create shots with the opposite effect from those created with the telephoto lens. Lenses which have a wider angle of view than a normal lens are called **short-focus** or **wide-angle lenses.** Just as the telephoto lens can pinpoint a tiger from far away, the wide-angle lens can take a shot of a large number of people in a small room.

The creative effects of the wide-angle lens are also opposite to those of the telephoto lens. The wide-angle lens spreads objects apart, making them seem to be much farther apart than they really are. Perhaps a director wants a shot which suggests to the viewer that a person is standing on his own, cut off from everybody around him. The director might decide to create the shot with a wide-angle lens. By exaggerating the separation between this person and everybody else, the director would have made this idea apparent to his audience.

Just as the telephoto lens can make a person running toward the camera seem to be making no progress, the wide-angle lens can make a person moving toward the camera seem able to cover the distance so quickly he apparently takes giant steps. Thus if a director wanted to tell his audience that a man in his film was a very powerful person, he might have the character walk toward the camera in a wide-angle shot, letting him loom menacingly up to the camera.

In *Occurrence,* Enrico used a wide-angle lens to communicate an idea and feeling to his audience. Before the condemned man Farquhar is to be hung, a soldier prepares a noose for him. Enrico used a wide-angle lens and a low camera angle so that the noose and the soldier's hands appear much larger than they would be in reality. The noose and hands loom threateningly toward the audience. Enrico tells his viewers that the soldier's job of preparing the noose will be important in what follows.

The wide-angle lens has a **large depth of field,** allowing the director to have actions going on at various distances from the camera shown in sharp focus. This allows the director to design scenes in which two or more important actions are going on at the same time, all of them looking sharp and clear.

There are some lenses so wide in angle that they

photograph everything above, below, and to the sides of them, a full 180 degrees. Such lenses are called **fish-eye lenses.** Their use is more common in still photography than in movies, however, because they produce a circular picture rather than the usual rectangular one.

Some people confuse long shots with wide-angle shots and close-ups with telephoto shots. We have seen that a close-up may be created with a wide-angle lens or a long shot with a telephoto, if that combination enables the director to create the shot he needs to tell his audience what he wants to tell them.

The **zoom lens** allows the film director to change the focal length of his lens during a shot; rather than carrying around a whole bag of telephoto, normal, and wide-angle lenses, the filmmaker can use one zoom lens which he changes from wide-angle through normal to telephoto. And he can also make this change while he's filming, creating a feeling of movement inward or outward.

From a long shot including a great deal of area, the director can zoom in on any detail he wants us to notice during the shot. Moreover, the director may want to use a slow zoom, giving us a gliding, floating feeling. Or he may choose to startle the viewer and zoom in on an object or character quickly. In *Occurrence,* Enrico shows a medium shot

Many shots in Orson Welles's 1941 feature **Citizen Kane** were created with a wide-angle lens, giving a feeling of vastness and keeping near and far objects sharp.

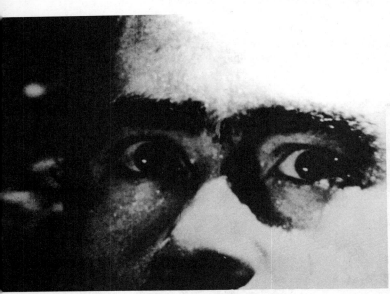

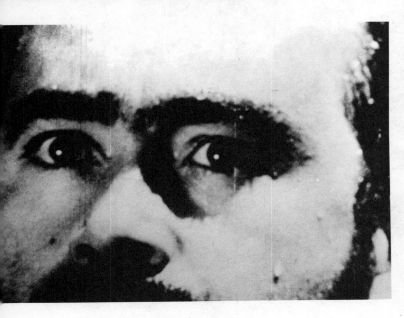

of the condemned man; then he zooms in quickly to the man's eyes just at the instant the man realizes he is trapped by soldiers. With this zoom shot, Enrico does two things: He creates a shock effect for his audience by the speed of the zoom and at the same time allows the audience to see a close-up of Farquhar's eyes at the precise moment when they express his fear.

Zooming is on things is a technique which has been quite overused by amateur movie makers. It's become super-easy on Super 8 to zoom in and out. Some Super 8 cameras even have electric motors to do the work of zooming; all a filmmaker has to do is push a button, and instantly the world becomes exciting! As with other film techniques, the secret to using the zoom lens well, however, is to zoom with a purpose, as Enrico does in the shot just mentioned. Rather than create a shock effect, Enrico uses the zoom to enhance a shock effect. Unless it is used with a reason, a zoom lens can create shots which drive an audience zooming out of the theater.

Slow zooms can add motion to shots that would otherwise be static. When used with care, with a reason, such zoom shots can create effective shots and exciting sequences. When used carelessly, a zoom lens can create motion sickness in a viewer.

During the summer after they graduated from high school, Bob Orr and Bob Schiappacasse got a contract to make a promotional film for a company that builds machinery to test soil. Engineers use these testing instruments to make certain skyscrapers don't sink into the ground they're built on. The filmmakers wanted to emphasize how important the firm's products were by showing shots of some buildings in Chicago's Loop. But stationary shots of buildings aren't exciting.

The filmmakers didn't want the shots to just sit there; they wanted their film to express the feeling a person can have looking up at immense buildings soaring above him. So using a zoom lens, they zoomed in toward the buildings; to give an upward motion, they tilted the camera upward as they zoomed. When they had collected a number of shots of different buildings in this way, they spliced them together. The conclusion of their film, *The First Foundation,* shows all of these zooms one after the other, and the viewer feels caught up in the motion inward and upward. All of these buildings, soaring as high as they do, rest on soil tested by the company's instruments. Zoom lenses allowed the filmmakers to tell this to their audience in an exciting film sequence.

Zooming in on an object isolates it from its environment, but it first discloses the object's environment. A zoom shot is like a long shot, medium shot, and close-up, all rolled into one.

Zooming works both ways; a filmmaker can also **zoom out**. From a close-up, he can zoom back to a long shot, to reveal the surroundings of an object. Zoom-outs, like the zoom-ins, can give a feeling of motion.

One short film, *Powers of Ten,* carries this zoom motion to fantastic extremes. The film starts with a man lying on a golf course. Copying the feeling a zoom lens provides, the film moves back from the man until it arrives at the farthest conceivable point in the universe; then it zooms inside the man to reveal a universe just as immense. *Powers of Ten* employs the feeling of motion that the zoom lens has accustomed us to.

Many times a director will wish to create the feeling of a zoom lens, but will not have an adequate zoom lens for the shot. At the beginning of *Catch the Joy—Dune Buggies*, cameraman Jim Freeman had the problem of zooming down onto a sand dune from 3,000 feet to 10 inches in ten seconds, a range too great for any zoom lens made. So he mounted his camera on a helicopter and took the shot descending rapidly with the helicopter.

CAMERA ANGLES

Where a filmmaker puts his camera means a lot, too. **Camera angles** can also tell us what the director feels about an object or person, whether or not we should look up to something or look down our noses at it.

Shots created with the level camera angle, or **normal angle,** are taken from the eye level of the subject. A director will use this normal angle to create shots when he wants to put his subject on the same level with his audience, so that we can look at the subject "face to face." This camera angle com-

A high angle in this shot from Edmond Sechan's **The Stringbean** makes the old lady seem all the more weak and downtrodden.

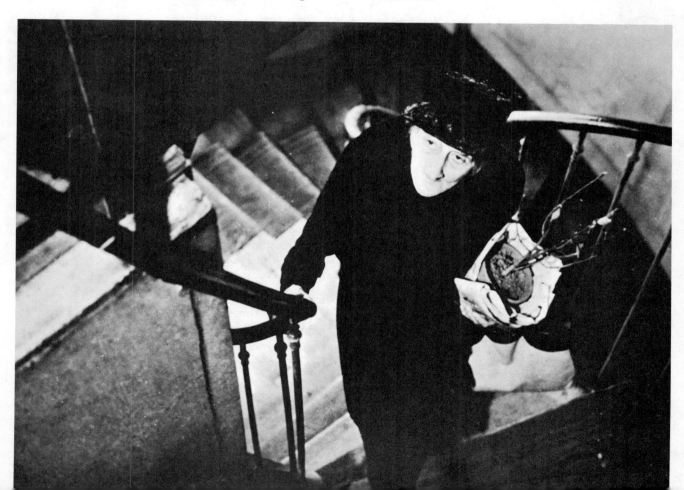

municates equality between character and audience. The eye-level camera angle also communicates a sense of honesty surrounding the person photographed because it allows the audience to look the person in the eye.

If the filmmaker wants to create a shot that will tell his audience that the subject is small and insignificant, a low person, a weak or broken character, he will probably choose to film his shot from a high angle, looking downward at his subject. This camera angle makes the subject seem smaller than he actually is. Many times, we refer to the feeling such a shot gives when we say a person "got cut down to size," and getting "cut down" makes a person "feel small." By deciding on a **high-angle shot**, the director makes us "look down" at whomever he wants us to.

A filmmaker doesn't have to get on a ladder to create a high-angle shot; the high angle is high only in relation to the object or person photographed. Elia Kazan used a high-angle shot of Terry Malloy near the end of his 1954 feature *On the Waterfront*. Terry has just been viciously beaten up for informing on the waterfront union's boss, John Friendly. Although the camera is only at normal eye level, it looks down at Terry, who is lying on the ground, and the audience looks down at him as well. The audience feels that he has been beaten more than just physically.

Many times a director who is using an extreme long shot to make people look small in relation to their environment will combine this technique with the effect which the high angle can give. Together,

the two techniques make people appear insignificant and unheroic.

The opposite effect of the high-angle shot is created by the **low-angle** shot, as might be expected. The camera looks upward at the subject. Since an audience sees what the camera sees, it looks up to the subject too. Such a low angle inspires awe and gives the subject power and authority. Western film directors many times signal which character is going to win a fist fight by using low-angle shots of the man who will win.

Just as the high camera angle gives a feeling we refer to when we talk about people, so does the low camera angle. We talk about "looking up to" somebody we respect; successful people are persons who are "getting up" in the world; judges sit on benches and kings on thrones so that people will

look up to them. These same feelings are evoked by directors in creating shots.

A director can also change his camera angle during a sequence to indicate that the viewer should change how he feels about a person. When we left Terry Malloy a minute ago, he was being shown with a high-angle shot, so that the audience could look down at him. But as this sequence from *On the Waterfront* continues, Terry is jarred back to his senses. If he can stand up and walk in defiance of Friendly's union, if he can make it to the door of the warehouse, he will have beaten John Friendly. Terry climbs to his feet and begins to walk. Now the camera is level with Terry; we wonder if he will make it or if he will fall over. But Terry does make it, and the other longshoremen have followed him. Kazan now shows Terry in a low-angle shot, because he is now "on top." To underline Friendly's loss of power, Kazan has an old man push him into the harbor; the camera angle, of course, is a high-angle, looking down at Friendly. He has been "put down" and we "look down" at him.

Seldom do we ever see a high-angle shot of Godzilla, Frankenstein, or King Kong. Not until the monsters are killed or vanquished do we look down at them. In *King Kong*, directed by Ernest Schoedsack in 1933, we look up to Kong, who is in power for the entire film. But at the ending, Kong stands upon the pinnacle of the Empire State Building. Misunderstood and mistreated for the entire film, Kong begins to get our sympathy. Airplanes strafe him, wounding Kong seriously. The camera angle changes. Now we look down at Kong; the change in camera angle shifts our feelings for him. The camera angle is unrealistic, one of the first unrealistic camera techniques in the film. What do you stand on to look down at a huge ape when he's standing on the pinnacle of the highest building in the world? Schoedsack, however, felt the high-angle shot was important to draw out our sympathy for King Kong.

Dictators as well as monsters like to be filmed from low camera angles. *Triumph of the Will*, a propaganda film Leni Riefenstahl made for Adolf Hitler in 1934, shows Hitler almost exclusively in low-angle shots. When she shows shots of Hitler in normal angle, Hitler has lowered himself to mingle with his people. But for most of the film, she uses the low camera angle to force the viewer to look up to Hitler.

One other camera angle deserves mention, although its use in film isn't common anymore. A director can tilt his camera sideways, so that the scene photographed seems to appear tilted on the screen, sloping diagonally off balance. This angle may be used by a director to disorient his audience, to make them feel that something strange is happening. Such a tilted angle is called a **Dutch angle**; Dutch angle shots regularly occur in episodes of *Flash Gordon* serials, as the soldiers of Ming the Merciless pursue Flash through the dizzying corridors of Ming's palace. But many directors today use other techniques to disorient an audience.

CAMERA MOVEMENT

Moving a camera left or right creates a **pan shot**, short for panorama shot. Pan shots are useful to directors. If he or she wants to show a large expanse of scenery which won't fit into one shot, the director can pan over the area and convey to us the vast expanse of scenery. A director may also use the pan shot to introduce a character as part of his environment.

If a director is taking a shot of something which is moving, he may follow the subject with his camera. This shot, a **follow pan**, was used by Enrico in *Occurrence*; since the audience cannot see the background, it seems that the character is running forward. And Enrico created the shot without moving his camera from one place; the actor ran in a circle around it. Such clever use of the camera allowed Enrico to give his audience the impression that Farquhar is running a great distance. At other times in the film, the actor actually ran past the camera, and Enrico followed him with a follow pan shot.

The pan shot is almost as overused by amateur movie makers as the zoom. If there's nothing exciting happening in a scene, many amateur movie

The Triumph of the Will includes low-angle shots of Hitler, while **Citizen Kane** uses Dutch angle shots.

makers wave the camera back and forth over the scene; their films are a *pan*demonium of shots. Carefully used, for a reason, the pan can be as fluid and as important as the zoom.

When an action moves up and down, the director can use a vertical pan called a **tilt** to create the shot. At the end of his feature *Lord of the Flies* (1962), Peter Brook shows Ralph running away from the other boys, who are going to kill him. Falling on the beach, he sees a pair of white shoes in front of him, and Ralph slowly looks up at the man. So that we can see things as Ralph does, director

Brook slowly tilts his camera up to the rescuer's face.

If an object is moving, a director might move his camera along with it. He will lay tracks and mount his camera on a rubber-tired vehicle and move it along the rails, creating a smoothly moving **tracking shot**. If there is a smooth floor, he can dispense with the tracks and simply have the camera pushed around a rubber-wheeled dolly, creating the **dolly shot**. Or he can simply put his camera on the back of a car, let some air out of the tires, and drive along with the subject he's photographing.

In *Occurrence*, Enrico had his actor run up to the camera mounted on the back of a car. As the actor nears the camera, the car starts, and the actor runs behind the camera. Such shots aren't as smooth as shots taken from tracks; but they're much easier to set up.

Constantly moving cameras give a feeling of motion, of excitement, to a film. The continual movement at the beginning of *Occurrence* keys up the audience, keeps them waiting for something to happen.

A director can eliminate the dolly and tracks and simply have somebody carry the camera around. Such **hand-held camera shots** are bumpy and jerky, but they seem real. Audiences are so used to seeing newsreels made with hand-held camera shots that when they see such shots in films, they feel such shots are "real." Stanley Kubrick used a hand-held camera to create a shot for his feature *2001: A Space Odyssey*. As the spacemen descend into a crater to observe a large black monolith, Kubrick uses a hand-held camera shot so that the viewer feels as if he were in the group.

Hand-held camera shots can also be used for creating **subjective camera shots**, which show what a character is seeing as though through his eyes. Mountain Rivera, a heavyweight fighter, is getting badly beaten up at the beginning of the feature *Requiem for a Heavyweight*. As he is being carried down to his dressing room, the camera follows him showing what he would see. The camera is hand-held, shaky, rapidly moving back and forth. A wide-

Robert Enrico filmed a follow pan shot in **Occurrence** by having his actor run around the camera.

angle lens exaggerates the sickening feeling of motion, and the audience gains an impression of Rivera's feelings.

One other important camera movement is commonly used by directors to create shots. Mounting a camera on a **crane** or **boom** to hydraulically raise or lower it creates powerful shots. Perhaps the most famous use of the crane shot occurs in Fred Zinnemann's 1952 Western feature *High Noon*. Marshal Kane is preparing to fight four gunmen who have come in on the noon train. Kane has been deserted by the townspeople and is forced to fight the gunmen alone. The scene starts with a medium shot of Kane as he walks down the street; a crane raises the camera—and the audience—higher and higher up until the entire street is visible. Now the audience can see for itself how absolutely alone Kane is at this moment.

All of these possibilities—lenses, angles, movement—exist for the director to create exactly the shot he or she wants for a particular sequence in a film. But they are only some of the possibilities. A director can choose to use them or decide to find different ways to create shots, new ways which haven't been tried before. In creating shots, in expressing his ideas or his reactions to events, the filmmaker is remarkably free.

ACTIVITIES

1) Still photographers, like filmmakers, use camera angles to control their viewers' attitude to their subject. In fact, advertising photographers consistently use camera angles and telephoto or wide-angle lenses to manipulate the feelings of viewers. Collect examples of low-, medium-, and high-angle shots from magazine or newspaper advertisements. Collect telephoto and wide-angle shots as well. Describe how the photographer uses camera angles, telephoto or wide-angle lenses, or combinations of these to create effects in the ads you have collected.

2) Many comic strips and comic books, like the Marvel Super-hero comics, are influenced by film techniques and use camera angles and long shots, medium shots, and close-ups much the same way that film does. Other comic strips, like the Peanuts strip, depend upon words for their effect and rarely change from an eye-level, medium-shot format for all their shots. Find and cut out examples of each type of comic strip. Look for low-, medium-, and high-angle shots, and long shots, medium shots, and close-ups. Label each shot and discuss the effects of camera angles in these comics.

3) In films you've seen recently, recall some shots that had an impact on you (you wouldn't recall the shots if they didn't have some impact on you). Describe the shot: Was it a long shot, a medium shot, a close-up, or an extreme close-up? Did the director use camera angle to increase the effect of the shot? Do you remember any subjective camera shots? Any Dutch angle shots?

4) Watch a five-minute segment of a theater movie on television. Then watch five minutes of a TV show or a made-for-TV movie. Which segment had more close-ups? More long shots? More zoom in or zoom out shots?

5) Here is a simple exercise that will show you how telephoto, normal, wide-angle, and zoom lenses work. Obtain a cardboard tube about the size toilet tissue is rolled on. Hold it about three inches from your eye and look through it. Notice how many objects you can see. Now, while looking through the tube, move the tube closer, to about one inch from your eye. As you move the tube, you can see a wider angle of view. Then move the tube so that it is a foot away from your eye. Keep looking through the tube and notice how you can zoom in on a particular object as the distance from the back of the tube to your eye gets larger and larger.

The distance from your eye to the tube is comparable to the *focal length* of a lens. When the distance from the lens to the film, the focal length, is short, the lens includes a wide angle of view, just as you did when the tube was close to your eye. Making the focal length longer creates a narrower viewing angle, as you zoom in to telephoto. Focal lengths of camera lenses are usually expressed in millimeters and engraved on the lens barrel. Check the lens barrel of a camera for the range of focal lengths the lens has. One zoom lens, for example, might have a range from 9 to 30mm; another lens, 10 to 60mm. Watch through the front of the camera as you zoom the lens in and out; you will see the moving groups of lenses within the lens that create the changing focal length.

MOTION

2

When someone invents a new medium, he immediately has a solution and a problem. New media extend our senses, make them more powerful, and that's an advantage. Telephones, for instance, allow us to talk over greater distances than we can yell; automobiles, to travel farther than we can run; television, to see farther than we can see with our eyes alone. There remains one problem, however: What do you call the new medium?

When the car was invented, nobody knew what to call it. People had never seen one before. But they *had seen* carriages pulled by horses. And since the first cars looked much like carriages, but didn't use horses, people called them horseless carriages.

The same thing happened with the radio. Nothing like it had existed before, but it did send messages just like the telegraph. The radio didn't have wires connecting it to wherever it got its messages though, and so people called the radio a "wireless."

When movies came along, people had the same problem. Movies, however, were similar to still pictures; the main difference was that the people in movies moved. So this new invention was named "motion pictures" in a manner similar to the horseless carriage and the wireless.

The point is that motion pictures was a good name. It stuck. Horseless carriages became automobiles and the wireless became the radio, but the name "motion pictures" has stayed with us. Sometimes we contract "motion pictures" into "movies" just as we have shortened "Coca-Cola" to "Coke," but even when we call them "movies," the idea of motion survives. Movies, it seems, just ought to move.

People have always liked to watch motion and to experience it. Movies remain the only art form which can capture motion and preserve it, which can change motion, and which can actually create it. It would be difficult to imagine a film which didn't have *some* motion; it would be even harder to imagine anybody staying around to watch it. Motion is the first word in motion pictures.

Film directors can use motion in a variety of ways in order to tell us things about their subject, to indicate motion we might have missed, or to allow us to enjoy a motion the director has created. The writer tries his best to copy the way film manipulates time and rhythm, but usually he fails. He may try using long words, rhythmic words, repetition of various sounds; he may try quickly shifting ideas, settings, places, all in an attempt to control rhythm. But a writer can't control how fast or how slowly we read what he writes, and so his control of time is very limited. A filmmaker, however, can control what we see, how fast we see it, and how long we see it, as precisely as he wishes. That's one of the major capabilities of film as a communication tool.

Tom LeRoi begins a somersault in the film **Ski the Outer Limits**, a film containing a great deal of motion.

Motion comes in many varieties. A cyclist is the subject of a motion shot in **Les Mistons** (top). Filmmaker Jim Freeman prepares to film a motion shot for his short film on dune buggies, **Catch the Joy**.

SUBJECT MOVEMENT

Many types of motion exist for a filmmaker's use. Perhaps the most common type of motion in film happens within the frame of the screen. Characters or objects can move within the frame, and it is easy for the camera to record their movements.

A filmmaker can inform his audience just by choosing the directions in which the subjects move within the frame of the screen. **Characters or objects can move across the screen.** If they move from left to right across the screen, they make our eyes move in a way that they are used to moving. Right now, your eyes are moving from left to right as you read these words. Filmmakers know that your eyes are accustomed to moving in this direction, and when they want to show something moving across the screen without disturbing the audience, they will usually have the person or object move from left to right.

In the beginning of *The Parable*, a short film directed by Rolf Forsberg and made by Fred A. Niles studios for the Protestant Council of the City of New York, a circus parade moves across the screen from left to right. The director wanted his viewers to feel that they are a part of this parade, and so he chose a left to right motion. Had he made the parade move from right to left, forcing the viewers' eyes to move in the opposite direction they are used to, they would feel that the parade is something dangerous, out of the ordinary, not a part of their normal experience. But since the director wanted the viewers to identify with the parade, to become a part of it, he chose a left to right motion.

On the other hand, whenever a filmmaker wants to make an audience feel that some person or object is out of the ordinary, he or she will probably make the object or person move across the screen from right to left, against the normal direction your eyes are moving right now. Because the viewer's eyes must move against this normal direction, the object or person will not appear as normal as it would if the direction were left to right.

In the feature film *The Seventh Seal*, whenever the character Death enters the picture, he usually enters suddenly from the right. Such move-

ments jar the viewers, and they feel that Death is an intruder in the frame.

Remember of course that these descriptions of how directors use motion to tell us things are not *rules*. There are no rules in film grammar because film is a young language, used to communicate feelings and emotions more often than ideas. But there are general descriptions of how directors have made use of motion to communicate and of how directors in the past have employed motion and other devices. A director can go against the usual practice of doing things, but he or she risks losing an effect that might easily have been obtained. As the French director Francois Truffaut observed, in film there are no rules, only risks.

Of course there are times when a director may

be stuck with using a right to left motion even when he doesn't want to use it to disturb his audience. For example if he wishes to show us a wagon train going west or a plane flying from New York to San Francisco, the wagon train will plod from right to left across the screen, and the plane will streak across the sky in the same direction; because we are so accustomed to seeing maps, when we see a right to left movement, we assume it is an east to west movement.

Most of the time, though, directors, consciously or unconsciously, will try to follow this conventional technique for screen directions. In *Runner*, a short film from the National Film Board of Canada, track star Bruce Kidd spends most of his time running from left to right across the screen; his movement is relaxing, rhythmic. In Robert Enrico's short film *Chickamauga*, dying Union soldiers crawl across the screen, changing into strange animals. Right to left? You guessed it. Murderers travel across the screen to kill a politician, and a car chases a man, trying to kill him, in the feature film *Z*. Again, right to left.

Movement away from the camera is also a common and useful movement for directors. It looks good: Movies are two dimensional, but when somebody moves toward or away from the camera, the scene appears to have depth. When characters or objects move away from the camera, we get the feeling that the character or object is leaving. You have seen this in Westerns. At the end, the hero rides off into the sunset. Movement away from the camera indicates that something or somebody will not be important anymore. In *Corral*, a short National Film Board of Canada film, a cowboy with his horse herds a bunch of half-broken horses into a corral. As he gets ready to saddle one of the half-broken horses, the cowboy unsaddles his old horse. For the rest of the film, the director wants us to concentrate on the process of saddling this new horse; the old horse is now "out of the picture." But how does the director get the old horse out of his movie? He could have the horse walk out the side of the frame, but instead the director has the

horse walk away from the camera, indicating that its part in the film is over. And in addition the shot gives a feeling of depth.

If you have ever seen a horror film, you know what a director can do with **movement toward the camera**. Besides the feeling of depth, such movement can shock an audience. Mummies, vampires, all kinds of enlarged insects and reptiles usually will move toward the camera in their shocking scenes. Ingmar Bergman utilized this motion for its impact at the beginning of his feature *The Seventh Seal*. Death moves toward the camera, and Bergman moves his camera toward the advancing figure. The combination of movements makes the figure all the more shocking. In the short film *No Reason to Stay*, the same technique is used for a particularly menacing teacher.

What kind of lens would a director choose to emphasize a movement toward the camera if he wanted to shock his audience: telephoto or wide-angle? Would he put his camera below the menacing object or above it? Probably the director would choose a wide-angle lens to make the subject loom up more quickly and a low-angle shot might be chosen to make the person seem large and powerful, forcing us to look up at it. These techniques would underline the impact of the movement toward the camera.

Objects and characters can move; so can the background. **Background motion** occurs frequently in cartoons where the characters move past the background drawn for them. But many films also include background motion for scenes in which people are talking in cabs, on horses, or in cars. Since these scenes could be boring without motion, filmmakers usually have windows through which scenery passes by, so that there is at least some motion in the shot.

At one point in the short film *Phoebe*, Phoebe is sitting on the beach and trying to decide how to tell her boyfriend Paul that she is pregnant. Paul is somewhat immature, and finding a way to break

Paul moves "out of the picture" for a section of the short film **Phoebe**, so that we can concentrate on Phoebe.

the news to him won't be easy. In the background, a group of people are enjoying the sun, having a carefree time. By showing us the carefree, happy events in the background, director George Kaczender underlines for us the problems of indecision that are going on in Phoebe's mind.

Sometimes directors decide not to have background motion in such shots because they are afraid that it might distract from the conversation. Elia Kazan didn't want us to miss a word of the conversation Terry Malloy had with his brother in the 1954 feature *On the Waterfront*. To avoid having to show the passing scenery, Kazan puts venetian blinds in the back seat of the car where the conversation happens. Kazan took the risk of boring his audience by not having motion in the scene, but his actors did such a good job of acting and the conversation was so important for the film that his risk paid off.

Using background motion to communicate to audiences isn't new by any means. In 1903 director Edwin S. Porter used it in *The Great Train Robbery*. The gunmen are holding a railroad clerk at

Motion creates a great deal of conflict in a shot from Mike Nichols' feature **The Graduate**.

gunpoint. Through the window we see a train approach and stop at the station. The shot creates suspense; it tells the audience why the gunmen are holding the clerk at gunpoint, and it explains where the train is in relation to the depot.

CAMERA MOVEMENT

The camera can also move over an area or object to create motion. The opening shots of *Occurrence at Owl Creek Bridge* use a moving camera to add motion to the scenes which establish facts about the setting. *Phoebe* begins the same way; the camera pans over the objects in Phoebe's room to establish what kind of a house she lives in, what her boyfriend looks like, what she reads. A group of still shots could be used, but **moving camera shots** add motion, and that's usually a good thing to do in an art form whose first name is motion.

Many directors employ a moving camera at

times. But one director uses it so often in all of his films, and so well, that it has become a trademark in his films. French director Alain Resnais introduces so much motion with his moving camera that his films make an audience uneasy and keep them watching the screen constantly. The beginning of Resnais' feature *Last Year at Marienbad* consists only of a moving camera traveling through the dark halls of a deserted baroque hotel. The same constantly moving camera begins another famous Resnais feature, *Hiroshima Mon Amour*. Both these films are difficult to understand, but *Marienbad* is especially confusing. In fact, film critic Pauline Kael has warned other directors to avoid "creeping Marienbadism." That is why *Last Year at Marienbad* is not found in most beginning film courses.

One of Resnais' short films, however, is less difficult to understand and displays his characteristic camera work. Before he had ever directed a feature film, Resnais made *Night and Fog* (1955). This is not a pleasant film to watch. It is, however, unforgettable, both for its subject and for the way in which Resnais uses the camera to heighten the impact of the film.

From various sources, Resnais assembled actual footage of Nazi concentration camps in action. Then he went to a concentration camp and took many shots of the buildings as they appear today. Always his camera moves in a wandering, restless manner. The viewer feels nervous, as if every camera motion might uncover some new horrible clue of what went on in the past.

Thus the audience moves with Resnais' camera: We move back in time, then forward again, as he shifts from the shots he has collected to the shots he has taken. The actual shots of the atrocities that occurred at places like Dachau, Auschwitz, and Belsen-Belsen are disturbing enough. But much of how Resnais' film affects an audience comes from the way he probes the peaceful-looking camp of today with his characteristic moving camera. For people who have seen other films by Alain Resnais, the moving camera is so typical that if Resnais' name was cut from the credits, it would still be possible to guess who had made the film.

Memorandum lacks the camera movement that characterizes films by Alain Resnais.

CAMERA SPEED

Besides choosing the direction of a movement, a director can communicate many things by the *speed* at which we view a motion. He can either speed-up a scene or slow one down. A director might do this to communicate something or to make the viewer feel differently about the motion.

It is easy for a director to play around with the speed of a motion. Projectors always show the same number of pictures per second. Theater projectors and 16mm classroom projectors that show sound films project twenty-four pictures per second. If the director sets his camera to take twenty-four pictures per second, then everything happens on the screen as fast as it did in real life.

But the director can also slow down his camera. For example, if he takes twelve pictures in a second, then it will take him two seconds to shoot twenty-four pictures. But the projector shows these twenty-four pictures in only one second. So two seconds of action are shown in one second; everything's twice as fast as normal.

Faster still? The director can take six pictures a second. In four seconds, he's got twenty-four pic-

Slow motion plays an important part in the short film **Moods of Surfing**.

tures. The projector will show twenty-four pictures in one second, as usual. Everything will come out four times as fast. And so on.

Speed in photography works both ways, of course. A director could take forty-eight pictures in a second. When the projector shows this film, it will take two seconds to show what the camera took in one second, and everything will happen at only one-half its actual speed.

Early comedies were often built around chases because chases are exciting on film: It's hard to have a chase without motion. To make them even more frantic, early film directors undercranked their hand-cranked cameras during chases. By turning the crank slower, cameramen took less frames in a second than normal, and the chases were speeded-up.

Today projectors run faster than they did when silent films were made, and so all silent films seem speeded-up to us: We show them at the twenty-four frames per second at which our modern-day projectors run, rather than at the approximately sixteen frames per second speed at which the films were shot. But in silent film days, chase sequences were faster still compared to the rest of the film. Very seldom did the Keystone Kops do anything at a normal speed!

Although speeded-up movements were most popular with silent film audiences, sometimes directors still use this technique in their films. Usually it has the same comic effect it did back in the old days. In *The Loneliness of the Long Distance Runner*, director Tony Richardson used speeded-up motion to create a comic effect while at the same time expressing how his characters are feeling. Colin Smith and his buddy have just committed a burglary. In leaving the scene of the crime, they walk away from the camera and go around a corner. A second or so passes, and they reappear, running toward the camera with highly speeded-up movements. We soon know why. Back at normal speed, a policeman slowly walks around the corner they had just turned. The speeded-up action is comic, but it underlines how scared Colin and his buddy are at that moment.

How far can a filmmaker go in speeding-up action? Take a look at the National Film Board of Canada's short film *Sky*. All the film shows is the sky during a day in western Canada. The day is typical, but the director has taken each frame of his film one-by-one with a time lapse between each frame. When this film is projected, the viewer sees twenty-four of these frames in a second. The clouds move quickly, rolling past each other on the screen, mounding up, frothing. Usually watching clouds go by sounds as interesting as watching the grass grow, but with time-lapse photography accelerating the action, a filmmaker is able to create enough motion for it to become exciting. *Sky* depicts fourteen hours of motion usually too slow to even notice in a ten minute film an audience can appreciate. With time-lapse photography, watching grass grow *could* be exciting!

Motions can also be slowed down for an audience to watch and appreciate. The "instant replay" many

Poetic movements in the sport of bullfighting are accentuated by slow motion in **Corrida Interdite.**

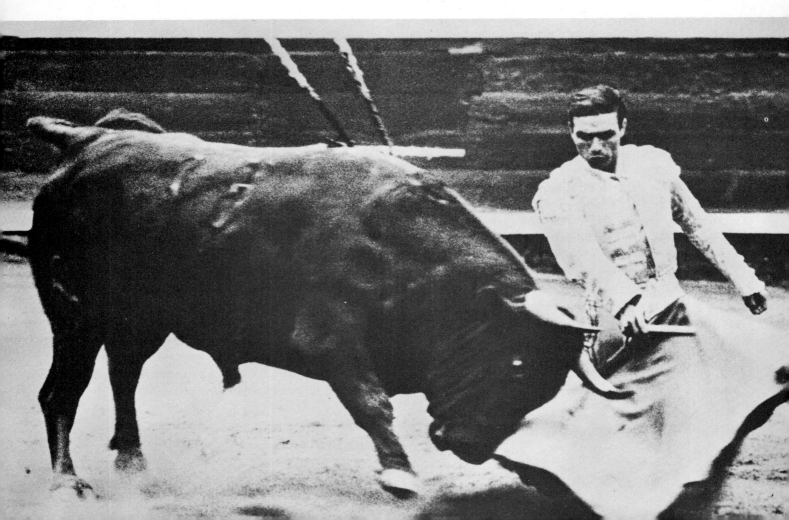

times slows down a sports play allowing us to appreciate the rhythm and precise motion involved in a completed pass or a successful double play. In the short film *Corrida Interdite*, for example, the sport of bullfighting is slowed down for this reason.

One of the classic examples of how slow-motion photography can slow sports action and create a new way of looking at the sport is the diving sequence from Leni Riefenstahl's documentary of the 1936 Olympics, *Olympia*. Often imitated, *Olympia*'s diving sequence remains one of the best examples of how to capture motion in photography. In *Olympia*, released in 1938, Riefenstahl had her cameramen follow divers through the air and underwater without a break. Cameramen followed the dive from their position at the surface of the water. When the diver hit the surface, the cameramen went underwater to see the end of the dive. Much practice was needed before the Games to perfect this technique, but the motion captured by it was incredible.

Kaleidoski, a documentary produced by the French Government to encourage people to ski in France, uses slow motion to capture the precise timing and rhythmic grace which a good skier can create. The slowed action allows the viewer to study the motions of the skier. Another ski film, *Ski the Outer Limits*, produced for the Hart Ski Company by Summit Films, uses a high-speed camera to literally freeze skier Hermann Goellner. As Goellner does a forward somersault at Jackson Hole, the

camera operates at four hundred frames per second. Watching this sequence projected at twenty-four frames per second, the action is slowed down more than sixteen times.

The movements of horses provide an interesting subject for Denys Columb de Daunant's film *Dream of the Wild Horses*. Sitting around watching horses move sounds only a little better than watching the clouds blow by or the grass grow, but unless you have seen *Dream of the Wild Horses*, you have never really seen horses' movements. Slowed down by photography, the animals become strange, unreal beings, suspended in space.

So far we've only talked about how slow motion can make things seem more graceful, more easily appreciated, and more rhythmic. But ugliness can be communicated and emphasized by slow motion as well. In his feature *The Wild Bunch*, director Sam Peckinpah, himself the son of an Indian chief, used slow motion to underline the ugliness of typical Western violence. In *The Wild Bunch*, bodies fall in slow motion, hit the ground; blood spurts slowly from the gunshot wounds, all through the technique of slow motion photography. Arthur Penn shows the death of Bonnie and Clyde in that film in slow

In **Zero for Conduct** (1933), Jean Vigo used slow motion to suggest the joy and excitement of a pillow fight.

Roger Brown, president of Summit Films, uses a moving camera to capture the motion of skier Billy Kidd.

motion in order to make the horror of the moment last longer and to have more of an impact on his audience. It works: So effective was this death sequence that when *Bonnie and Clyde* was shown on television, this sequence was shortened a great deal, presumably because it was considered to have an excessive impact.

In life as well as in movies, many things can seem to happen in slow motion. A dentist may feel that twenty seconds is a short time, but it may seem much longer for his patient. Filmmakers can re-create this feeling of suspended time by using slow-motion photography. Perhaps one of the best uses of slow-motion filming to capture the excitement of an action suspended in the person's mind is shown in the short film classic *Zero for Conduct*, directed by Jean Vigo in 1933. Boys in a school have made plans to embarrass the school by disrupting a special celebration. Elated, they begin

their rebellion with a huge pillow fight in the normally strict dormitory. As soon as the first feathers fly into the air, Vigo switches to extreme slow motion. The feathers float slowly in the air. The eerie, surreal effect suggests the joy of the boys and the excitement of the pillow fight.

In *If*, the feature-length film Lindsay Anderson made from the ideas in *Zero for Conduct*, there is no pillow fighting scene because the young men are playing for keeps and using weapons more powerful than feathers. But one similar scene remains. A younger boy notices an older boy working out on the trapeze. Anderson slows down the speed of the film underlining both the talent and coordination of the older boy and the admiration this causes in the younger, less coordinated boy.

AUDIENCE MOVEMENT

A variety of movements keep the motion in motion pictures—characters, objects, backgrounds, the camera, all can move. There's one more possibility left, an important one, but one we're not always conscious of. The audience can also move. By **audience movement** we're not talking about somebody walking out for a box of popcorn. Whenever a filmmaker stops his camera and moves it to a different position, he has in effect moved his audience as well because the audience sees only what the camera sees and from where the camera sees it.

Usually we are situated safely away from any stampeding herds of cattle, but in movies suddenly we are underneath one, the cattle are running over us. Now we are on a horse with a cowboy, trying to stop the stampede. Instantly, we can be on top of the ridge with the rustlers, watching the scene we were just involved in. When our vantage point changes, *we* seem to move as well. It takes us an instant to readjust our senses to a new position, and in that instant we feel we have moved. All the shots described could have been still shots, of immobile objects. And yet we would have felt we had moved.

At the Woodstock Music Festival, depending upon how lucky people were, they had either a close-up of the stage (very few), a medium shot of the stage (a few more), a long shot of the stage (a few more still), or an extreme long shot of the stage (everybody else). But viewers of the film *Woodstock* could jump from a close-up of the stage to an extreme long shot from an airplane, take a look at people in the audience, and come back for an extreme close-up of a performer, all without missing a single beat of the music. The financial success of the film *Woodstock* prompted many imitations, such as the films covering the closing of the Fillmore concert hall, a concert by Pink Floyd in an ancient temple or the concert for Bangladesh.

Such audience movement is an important part of the motion in motion pictures and one of the reasons film has become more popular than the stage play, where one is locked into a close-up, a medium shot, or a high-angle extreme long shot, depending upon the price of his ticket. At the movies, an audience gets all of these viewpoints for the price of one. Lately, stage plays have compensated for this disadvantage by involving the audience in their production. The audience movement possible in movies, however, has created a sort of rocket ship effect, in which the viewer is propelled over vast areas.

And if this isn't enough, directors can use the moving camera to create more motion. In *Kaleidoski*, the director chose a number of positions for the audience, most of them moving. The viewers follow a little boy, skiing behind him as he learns to ski. They fly through the air with a skydiver, watching a great area of landscape below. They ski with members of the French team, sometimes following them, sometimes leading them around sharp turns, through rocky passes. In *Ski the Outer Limits*, a cameraman skis down the Argentiere glacier with a movie camera strapped on, and the audience plunges down with him. In *Sky Capers*, a short film by Carl Boenish, and in the feature *The Gypsy Moths*, the viewer skydives with cameraman Boenish. In the short Canadian film *L'Homme Vite*, the camera is mounted in a race car. The viewers skid and chase along. In *Olympia*, Riefenstahl photographed the opening of the Games from the Hindenburg Zeppelin. Automatic cameras were set off in balloons, with instructions to the finder of the balloon to return the film to Riefenstahl.

LITTLE OR NO MOVEMENT

It's about time to repeat it. In film, there aren't any rules, only risks. There's no rule that says films *must* move. Certain early films by Andy Warhol, which he now refers to as experiments, take the risk by dispensing with audience motion and camera motion to concentrate on subject motion. *Eat* and *Sleep* are two examples; both films consist of only one shot, in which the subject moves. There is more motion in *Eat* than in *Sleep*; in *Eat* a man eats a mushroom again and again for forty-five minutes, but in *Sleep* the man doesn't move very much during the six hours of the film because he's asleep. Warhol took the risk of creating audience movement—out of the theater—when he created *Eat* and *Sleep*. But he considers this perfectly natural; audiences can come and go, return later to see more of the film. One film by Warhol, *Empire*, eliminates subject movement as well; it watches the Empire State Building for eight hours.

Such films return to the tradition of Thomas Edison's 1896 film *Kiss*, where two people kiss, or the Lumiere brothers' film *Train Comes into Paris*, another film with a self-descriptive title. In those days, audiences were so fascinated with motion that trains coming into Paris were exciting to watch. But today, most audiences like more action than that, and returning to this older style has its risks. Films like *Eat*, *Sleep*, and *Empire* do serve to remind us that many times we fail to really look at things in our world and introduce us to the concept of using the camera simply as a recording tool.

One French filmmaker, a member of the "new wave" of film directors in that country, tried an interesting experiment with motion. In his short film *La Jetee*, Chris Marker decided to use only still photographs to tell a science fiction story about a man who is transported back and forth in time from his underground prison camp in Paris, where everybody lives after the Third World War. Because images are particularly important in telling his story, Marker has only audience movement—the viewer jumps from place to place as he would in regular film but the images in front of him do not move—except for one shot, in which the subject's girl friend blinks.

Marker wanted to convey the idea that each of the images he is showing is like a fleeting instant captured in a man's mind and that the viewer should look at them very carefully. This particular style fits into the strange science fiction story Marker is telling, and the risk Marker took seems to have paid off.

Moments are frozen in the still shots from Chris Marker's film **La Jetee**.

Some directors like to stop all movement at some point during their films to force the audience to notice certain shots, as Marker does with his entire film. They can freeze any shot on the screen in the middle of a movement, hold it motionless for as long as they want the audience to see it, and then allow it to move again or move on to another shot. The entire beginning of Peter Watkins feature *Lord of the Flies* consists of still frames. In his feature film *The 400 Blows*, director Francois Truffaut shows the subject of his film, a young juvenile delinquent, running toward the sea. The boy has the option of committing suicide, but he does not. Nothing is left for him in life. As the boy turns to face the audience, Truffaut froze the frame so that no change can occur and ended his film. By eliminating motion entirely, Truffaut indicates that all hope is gone for this young boy.

In his feature *The Loneliness of the Long Distance Runner*, director Tony Richardson used a freeze frame at the conclusion in much the same way as Truffaut. Colin Smith is forced to do menial work as punishment for bucking the system. Colin has played the Establishment's game long enough and is not interested in doing anything to get himself out of the work detail. In the final shot of the film, director Richardson freezes Colin at work. He is informing the viewer that Colin is going to stay put down for the rest of his life, frozen in his way of life, because he has refused to do what the authorities want him to.

Motion, and how filmmakers use it or choose not to use it for a part of their pictures, can be the technique that makes or breaks a film. Motion, as we said before, is the first word in "motion pictures." You can see why the name stuck.

MOTION

ACTIVITIES

1) The practice of using right to left movement for "shocking" actions is one device movies inherited from stage plays. Because filmmakers have so many other effective ways of creating a shocking effect, they may neglect this method. Watch a movie on television and take notes. Do most "regular" characters move or enter left to right? Do most "shocking" or "bad" characters move or enter from right to left? Is this technique neglected by the director?

2) Using published film scripts, check and see if the director planned left to right or right to left movements for particular effects.

3) Describe a film sequence you have seen that uses slow-motion photography. Some TV commercials use this technique consistently. What type of sequence used slow motion? What effect did the slow motion give? Were any transitional devices, such as dissolves, used in the sequence?

4) Historical documentary films which contain still photographs have a problem: How do directors create motions in the still picture? In documentaries you have seen, how do directors use the camera to keep the audience moving?

5) *Freeze frames* are an effective device. Why do you think so many TV commercials use them? Are freeze frames in commercials usually long shots, medium shots, or close-ups?

6) Describe examples of speeded-up motion you have seen in movies, TV programs, or commercials. Which kind of filmmaking uses speeded-up motion most fre-

quently? What effect were the filmmakers most often attempting to create?

7) Watch a movie or a TV film and make note of any uses of background motion. Is background motion used for more than one reason? If so, what are these purposes?

8) How do comic books and comic strips add motion to their still frames? Cut out examples and bring them to class.

9) Certain artists have experimented with trying to create the illusion of movement by painting squiggly lines or different jagged lines. As you look at these paintings, your eyes tire, and the lines seem to float around the canvas. Find examples of this technique and bring them to class. Try the technique yourself.

PREPARING A SHOT

We follow a group of three filmmakers as they set out to create a two minute sequence for a 16mm film they are doing. In this sequence, a young boy is playing at night among some Indian burial mounds. The boy spots two seedy characters and hides behind one of the mounds. He sees the two digging up one of the burial sites and overhears them talking about how they plan to sell the Indian objects they find in the mounds. Accidentally discovered, the boy leads a hectic chase through the woods and manages to elude the grave robbers.

1) Film work begins early in the morning. Two weeks ago, one of the filmmakers found a suitable area and obtained permission to film. Two trucks of equipment, one trailing a generator, arrived early on a crisp fall morning.

2) A preliminary check in among some crew members by co-director Varo Krikoryan (sunglasses) begins the day. Plans are made and responsibilities are defined. Since the filmmakers are amateurs, responsibilities are not as strictly defined beforehand, as they would be if union personnel were working on the film.

3) Although necessary for the lights, the generator proves to be extremely noisy. Hiding it behind the van and covering it with blankets will be necessary. The platform above the van allows filmmakers to shoot high-angle shots.

4) Placing the generator far enough away from the scene to keep noise down has made extremely long cords necessary. Tests are necessary to see if all the wiring will work in the damp grass.

5) Some lights will light large areas and others will spot certain highlights. *Barn doors* on the sides of the lights will control the light, preventing it from spilling into certain areas. Co-director Paul Newell (army shirt) discusses lighting problems.

6) Sound men check the operation of the Swiss-made *Nagra* battery powered tape recorder. Because of the unexpected amount of noise from the generator, they will decide to use an extremely directional *shotgun mike* to record the conversation of the two robbers as they approach the burial mound.

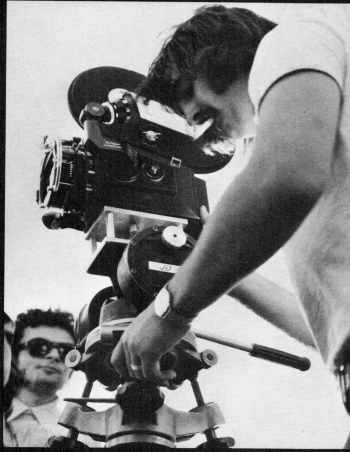

7) While other crew members continue working on the mounds location, the filmmakers select an area for the chase sequence and begin to set tracks. The camera will run down the cleared area. The little boy, chased by his pursuers, will run through the trees next to the camera.

8) With one section of the tracks assembled, crew members carry it to an appropriate spot. One crew member carries wooden shims to insure that the rails will be level.

9) The *dolly* that will carry the camera is carried to the tracks by Coleman and crew member Roger Korn. Such a dolly, with its rubber wheels, is an extremely versatile tool for filmmakers since it can be used on smooth surfaces without tracks if necessary.

10) Once the dolly is mounted on the tracks, it seems to run roughly. After careful inspection, one crewman notices that the previous renter of the dolly put one of the wheels on inside out. The problem is easily corrected.

11) Once the dolly is mounted on the track, co-director Coleman mounts the camera. The filmmakers have chosen the German-made *Arriflex BL* camera because it is a self-blimped, silently operating camera, capable of operating in synch with a tape recorder. The large set-screws on the dolly allow precise leveling of the pan and tilt head upon which the camera is mounted.

12) With the camera attached, the filmmakers place the lens on the camera. They have chosen a 12-120mm zoom lens for the chase sequence. The *matte box* (the rectangular bellows-like attachment in front of the lens) will prevent light reflections and glare from entering the lens.

15

16

17

13) To check on camera placement, instant developing still pictures are shot from each camera position. These pictures will give the filmmakers an idea of any problems the camera position might create, and will serve as handy ways to keep records of each shot as it is filmed. The 16mm camera is covered to protect it from the dust created by the digging.

14) The filmmakers have decided not to use a boom on this shot. They feel they can get enough mobility without it. Some dollies even have gas operated *hydraulic lifts*, to raise or lower the camera and cameraman during a shot.

15) The sun is starting to set. With lights set and camera positions ready, Coleman moves a few more shovelfulls of dirt and waits for darkness.

16) Night has fallen and it is quite chilly. Final lighting adjustments can now be made. One crewman uses a black cloth stretched on a frame and attached to a pole to cut off part of a light that is glaring into the camera lens. Such a light shield, called a *flag*, is effective in shielding lights but difficult to use in the windy conditions the filmmakers are now experiencing.

17) The filmmakers prepare for their first take of shot "2" which will show the little boy crouching behind the mound, standing up to see the grave robbers approaching, and crouching down again. It is now 10:00 p.m. The shooting sequence at this location will run until well past midnight, and then the filmmakers will move into the forest for the chase sequence. When the crew breaks up after shooting that sequence, most of them will have put in a 22 hour day. Early tomorrow, after a few hours sleep, some of them will have to repack the equipment.

EDITING

A film director, as we have seen, can communicate many things by where he decides to put his camera when he creates a shot, by what lens he chooses, and by how fast or slow he sets his camera speed. Each shot a director creates tells something specific about the subject. Close-ups, for example, can isolate certain portions of a subject for us; the larger a filmmaker makes something in a close-up, the more he or she forces an audience to see it as something important.

Once a director has created all of his shots, however, his job has only started: Now he must put all of these individual shots together. Putting shots together is a difficult task, but it is an important one because in this way a director can create new meaning from his shots. **Editing**, or the process of joining shots together, is at least as important a part of film communication as creating the separate shots. Some filmmakers believe it is even more important.

When an artist creates something, he starts with raw material. A painter might use canvas and oil paints as raw materials to create a painting. One sculptor might decide upon marble as a raw material for his artwork; another sculptor might choose clay. A filmmaker, however, must go through two steps in the process of creating a film. First

Conflict, often created by editing, can exist in one shot, as demonstrated in Orson Welles's **Citizen Kane**.

of all, he must create his raw material: a group of shots each of which has its own meaning. Once he has accomplished that, he still has only pieces of a film. To make a movie, he, or his editor, must arrange the shots into an order which communicates even more of what he wants to say.

Usually a director does not edit his own film. There are several reasons for this. A frequently mentioned one is that the skills which go into shooting a film and the skills which go into editing a film are different skills entirely: In other words, good directors don't necessarily make good editors. If a film is being made as a small-scale operation, however, like films made for small industries or by a student, the director may edit his or her own film. When a director chooses someone else to edit his film, however, he chooses his editor very carefully and works closely with him or her. A director knows that an editor can use his film to communicate to an audience, and he must be certain that he likes what the editor is saying. Robert Enrico worked so closely with Denise de Casabianca when they edited *Occurrence at Owl Creek Bridge* that both of their names appear on the editing credits. In fact, a skillful editor could have taken the same shots and produced *Occurrence* as a comedy, instead of the tense drama that it is.

An editor, besides what he or she can add to the film artistically, also simplifies filmmaking for a director. For instance, suppose a director wishes to show a sheriff walking into a saloon to stop a gunfight. The shot of the sheriff walking down the street might be filmed at a ghost town somewhere in Colorado. The shot of the sheriff inside the saloon, however, might be made in a studio in California. When the finished movie is viewed, however, the audience will not notice the switch in time and place because the two shots are joined together.

As another example, at the beginning of his feature film *2001*: *A Space Odyssey* in a section entitled "The Dawn of Man," director Stanley Kubrick wanted to show a group of man-like apes in an African wilderness. Kubrick collected shots of the wilderness he wished his audience to see. Then he costumed a group of actors as apes and filmed them in a studio. In viewing this sequence the audience places the apes in the middle of the trackless wilderness.

SELECTING SHOTS

One of the editor's first jobs is to eliminate obviously bad shots. Usually, a director will film many versions of the same shot, to make sure that one of his **takes** will come out exactly as he wants it. Even with the best planning, some takes include gross errors. A director may have attempted to create a shot from a low angle to make us "look up to" a person or object. But in several of the takes of this low-angle shot, something in the background might show up. Perhaps the low-angle shot reveals a distracting crack in the ceiling in an interior shot or a 747 jet flying overhead in a close-up of a Western marshal.

In editing the feature film *If*, editor David Gladwell included a shot of one of the main characters, Mick, shaving off his moustache. In 16mm prints, the shot includes Mick, a mirror, and most of a microphone dangling into the picture from the top. We can assume that all the takes of this shot included the microphone or editor Gladwell would have chosen a different take without it. In the 1971 feature *Billy Jack*, shots including a microphone occur even more frequently, indicating that the editor probably had fewer shots than normal to choose from.

ARRANGING SHOTS

After he picks out the best take, an editor places the shots he has chosen into a very general order. As we have mentioned already, shots created for a movie are usually not created in the order they are shown but rather in the order most convenient for the filmmaker. As an example, a movie might include a shot of a few thousand head of cattle stampeding through a valley. The next shot shows a couple of bad guys watching the stampede from the top of the hill. The next shot would be of the stampeding cattle again from a different angle. It is obvious that the director would not stampede the cattle for his first shot, stop the stampede, run up to the hill, take the shots of the bad guys, run down the hill again, and restart the stampede. Instead, he will create all of his stampede shots at once, while the cattle are running, and will film the bad guys sometime later. Possibly a director will assign a unit of filmmakers to go out and film the stampede while he works on the shots of the bad guys himself. The job of the editor, once he has eliminated the bad takes, is to assemble the takes he will use into a rough approximation of the order in which they will finally occur on the screen.

Sometimes an editor will join together shots in an order which will explain to the audience what should interest it at a particular time. The opening shots of Robert Enrico's *Occurrence at Owl Creek Bridge* offer a good example of how an editor can communicate with the order of his shots. The first shot in the film shows a sign nailed to a tree. The sign states that the punishment for interfering with the railroad bridge is immediate hanging. The next shots, long moving shots, are taken through the woods surrounding the bridge and indicate where the bridge is in relationship with its surroundings. Finally, the camera moves down to the bridge, to the soldiers in formation, to a soldier with a rope in his hand, and finally to the man who is to be hung.

To create this sequence, the editor had many decisions to make. He had to decide which shots to show, how long each shot should last, and in what order they should be shown. The first shot of the

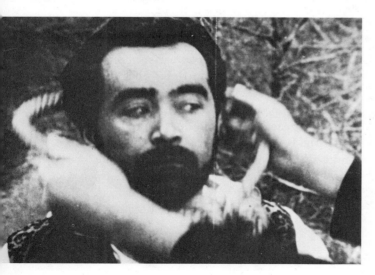

film, the shot of the sign, gives background information for the story. The editor must hold this shot just long enough for the audience to read what the sign says. The next shots, with the camera moving through the forest, can stay on the screen for a longer time without becoming boring; the camera's motion "keeps things moving."

The order these shots occur in is important. In *Occurrence*, the motion is through the forest down to the bridge and then to the man who will be the subject of the film. The editor has funneled the audience's attention to the man. And before seeing the man, the audience already knows what his crime is and what the penalty is going to be.

A film editor may often use this **funnel-like order** when he changes to a new scene. Usually, he will show a long shot to establish a location and identify where everything is in the area of action. Next, the editor may use a medium shot to narrow down the audience's attention, to center it on a smaller part of the action. Perhaps two people talking will be the area of action in this medium shot. Finally, a close-up may focus in on the person in the sequence on whom the editor wishes to concentrate.

Audiences are so used to watching films employing this funnel-like progression that all an editor need do is to change the order, and he can disorient his audience. Let's invent a scene which does this. Imagine a medium shot of Bad Bart talking to one of his fellow bandits in a saloon. Now a close-up shows Bart reassuring his partner that he won't double-cross him by telling their plan to the sheriff. After a close-up of his partner, nodding his head, there is another close-up of Bart; he continues to talk about his plan. The next shot is a medium shot, and in it Bart is now talking to the sheriff and not to his partner. Then a long shot shows Bart and the sheriff in the sheriff's office. During the close-up of Bart, the director switched scenes.

Normally after the scene of Bart in the saloon talking to his partner, there would be a long shot

In this sequence of shots from **Occurrence**, our attention is funneled from a long shot, through medium shots, to the close-up of the condemned man.

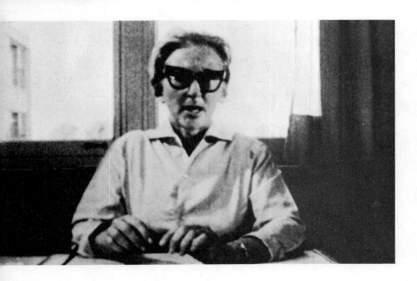

of the sheriff's office, and then a close-up of Bart as he talks to the sheriff. But editing covered up the change in scene by reversing the standard funnel-type arrangement of long shot, medium shot, and close-up, allowing the editor to underline Bad Bart's treachery. The audience experiences the same shock of Bart's treachery that Bart's partner will. Bart seems even more of a double-crosser because the editor has tricked the audience.

JUXTAPOSITION

In addition to this funnel technique, an editor can also join shots together in such a way that the ideas of the shots are emphasized. Advertisers commonly use this technique of **juxtaposition**, evoking a certain reaction to two shots by showing them together. "Before" and "After" pictures of men and women are often used demonstrating amazing weight losses through the use of certain dieting aids. When the two pictures are shown together, the "Before" picture looks much fatter and the "After" picture much more pleasingly slim than either would seem if the two pictures were shown in different ads. And the "After" pictures that muscle-building companies have printed in comic book advertisements make the men in the "Before" pictures seem incredibly more scrawny for the same reason.

Filmmakers have an advantage over advertisers in the use of juxtaposition. When an editor glues together two shots in a movie, he actually glues them together in our minds; the bond is much stronger on film than in still pictures. And filmmakers can "rub in" the comparison between the shots by cutting back and forth between them.

In his short film *Phoebe*, director George Kaczender joined shots together to emphasize the audience's reaction to each of them. Phoebe is lying on the beach trying to imagine what will happen at school when her dean finds out that she is pregnant. First, a shot of Phoebe lying on the beach is seen. Then director Kaczender shows a shot of Phoebe talking to the dean, a high-angle shot,

In the short film **Phoebe**, our impression of the dean is strengthened by juxtaposition.

lighted normally. The dean is helpful to Phoebe, quite understanding about her problem. The next shot is of Phoebe, rolling over on the beach. Kaczender is suggesting that there is another side to the coin, that things probably will work out differently at school.

Now a shot of the dean alone is shown. Kaczender used a low-angle shot to make the dean appear more menacing, more authoritarian. Rather than caring about Phoebe, the dean now talks only about "the ruling of the school board . . . leave this school at once . . . we have the other girls to think of . . ." By splicing these shots together, Kaczender has controlled the viewer's reactions to each of them. He has emphasized both the warm personableness of the dean in the first shot and her impersonal attitude in the second.

Besides using this technique of juxtaposition, an editor can stress an idea by **deleting** part of a shot. Simply by removing a portion of an action, an editor can suggest a great deal. In the film just mentioned, *Phoebe*, there is a shot of Phoebe sitting on a beach with her boyfriend Paul. They have a disagreement, and the next shot shows Paul starting to run off down the beach. Almost immediately a shot of Phoebe follows; she is trying to call Paul back. Now a long shot shows Paul; he is farther away than he actually could have run in that short time. By using editing to cut out parts of the shot of Paul running away, director Kaczender conveyed to his audience the strain that exists in Phoebe and Paul's relationship: Even a small disagreement separates them much farther than it would if their relationship was normal.

INTERCUTTING

In the 1920's, Russian filmmakers did a great deal of experimenting with editing and its possibilities. Cameras and film were expensive and in short supply for these directors, and sound had not come into use yet. For these reasons, directors experimented with different editing techniques to see what variety they could discover. One of the

Editing reveals how a young deaf-mute sees a dying soldier in Robert Enrico's **Chickamauga**.

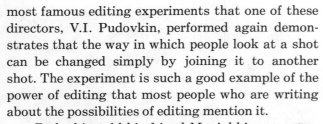

Joining these two shots together suggests to us that the woman and child are on the man's mind.

most famous editing experiments that one of these directors, V.I. Pudovkin, performed again demonstrates that the way in which people look at a shot can be changed simply by joining it to another shot. The experiment is such a good example of the power of editing that most people who are writing about the possibilities of editing mention it.

Pudovkin told his friend Mosjukhin, an actor, to stand in front of the camera and stare blankly into the lens. Pudovkin and his assistant took a number of feet of film in close-up of the actor staring into the camera. Then they collected shots of a plate of soup on a table, of a coffin with a dead woman inside, and of a little girl playing with a toy.

Pudovkin then edited the shot of the actor and the other shots he had taken together. First, he showed the actor; then he showed the shot of the plate of soup; then the actor again. Next he showed the actor's face and the shot of the coffin with the dead woman, and then the shot of the actor, followed by the shot of the little girl playing with the toy.

When he showed the film to his friends, they raved about the ability of the actor to express emotion simply with his face. They said they liked the heavy pensiveness of his mood over the soup. They said they were deeply moved by the sorrow the man expressed in seeing the dead woman. Was it his mother? And they admired the light smile on his face when he watched the little girl at play.

In each instance, the audience not only thought that the actor was looking at the various things that Pudovkin spliced into the shots of the actor's face, they also thought that they saw different expressions on the actor's face each time.

Many of the techniques used in editing are based on a special fact of filmmaking as evidenced in Pudovkin's experiment. It is that whenever two shots are combined, a bond is created between them in the minds of the audience. The audience then attempts to make sense out of this relationship. The National Film Board of Canada's short film *Cattle Ranch* demonstrates this bonding in a simple example. In this film the director wanted to present a different idea about cowboys. Instead of a cruel master of a herd of cows, the cowboy in *Cattle Ranch* is portrayed more as a shepherd, concerned for the welfare of the cattle he drives to market. Most of this is communicated using editing techniques. In one sequence, for example, the shots of a cow grazing and of a cowboy looking at him over his lunch are **intercut**. Every shot of the cowboy shows him watching the cow, underlining his concern.

The point is this: for convenience, the director of *Cattle Ranch* could have taken the shots of the cowboy and the shots of the cow on different days, perhaps thousands of miles away; if he had to, he could even have used "stock" shots of a cow and cowboy, taken from a library of standard shots, and intercut them. Because he had joined the two shots together on film, however, he would have also combined the subjects in the audience's minds. The audience assumes the cowboy is looking at the cow; in reality, they may never have seen each other.

Directors have used this uniting effect of editing in many ways throughout film's history. Nazi propagandist Leni Riefenstahl wanted her audiences to believe that there was a close bond between the German people and their leader, Adolf Hitler. In her propaganda film *Triumph of the Will*, she communicated this by repeatedly intercutting shots of Hitler with shots of cheering crowds. And later in the film, she assembled shots of high Nazi officials giving speeches at the Nuremburg rally; by splicing these shots together, Riefenstahl underlined the *unity* of all these leaders and emphasized the fact that they thought and worked as *one*.

MONTAGE EDITING

We have seen that editing can create these bonds of unity between the subjects of two shots, allowing the filmmaker the freedom to film various shots at different times. And in discussing the technique of juxtaposition, we saw how editing can emphasize ideas depicted in two shots. Filmmakers have another possibility for communication opened to them by editing techniques, however. This technique is called **montage editing**.

Another Russian film director of the 1920's, whose name is closely linked with the idea of montage editing, is Sergei M. Eisenstein. Joining together two conflicting shots, Eisenstein claimed, allowed their meaning to come out of the *synthesis*. In other words, piling shots one on top of the other like building blocks only allowed a filmmaker to create a pile of shots. If two shots conflict and they are joined together, however, a new meaning arises. One shot plus a conflicting shot equals a new meaning.

A sequence from Eisenstein's film *The Battleship Potemkin*, taken at the docks of the city of Odessa, shows how Eisenstein was able to use all kinds of conflicts to create new meanings by the use of montage. The people of Odessa have gone down to the docks of the city to give presents to the sailors of the battleship Potemkin, who have revolted. Suddenly, the soldiers of the Czar begin to march down the stairs of the city and attack the crowd. The entire sequence consists of conflicting shots: The soldiers move down the steps, conflicting with the upward direction of the people. The motion of the soldiers is disciplined, orderly; the people are scattered and running away. Back and forth, up and down, Eisenstein cut in shots of both groups. He adds a shot of a baby carriage, again adding to the conflicts, and creating an idea in the minds of the audience.

Eisenstein had discovered his ideas for montage by studying the picture writing of Japan. He knew that in Japanese picture writings, pictograms are combined to make new ideas. Eisenstein compared the pictures of picture writing with the way shots can be joined together in motion pictures and came up with his ideas on montage. For example, in Japanese, the picture-graph for *water* when written together with the picture-graph for an eye together mean "to cry"; similarly, the picture for *bird* and the picture for *mouth*, taken together, mean "to sing."

Montage editing became a powerful way to "say it with pictures." If Eisenstein wished to criticize a particular ruler in one of his films, he would show the character walking around and then show a shot of a peacock, strutting. Joined together, the two shots gave the idea that the ruler was a man with excessive pride.

As another example, let's imagine a film of a little girl enjoying her birthday party. She's got a clean, white dress on; her mother has made sure that everything has been fixed up just right for her party. The filmmaker has chosen a high camera angle to create his shot; the high angle places the audience above the little girl, and makes her seem smaller, younger.

Why is this shot simply a piece of raw material for the filmmaker? Because the viewer does not know how to react to this little girl and her party. By itself, this particular shot is neutral. The viewer may experience some of the happiness which the

little girl is feeling at her party; he may think that it's nice that she is lucky enough to have such a happy party.

But a filmmaker can easily *particularize* the viewer's reaction by joining this shot to another shot, informing the viewer about how he should look at it. Perhaps the filmmaker will choose to show the shot of the little girl at her party and then splice in a shot of a poor undernourished Indian girl, about the same age as the first girl, sitting in ragged clothing in the middle of a dusty street, eating garbage. By joining these two conflicting shots together, the filmmaker has created an idea that would not exist if they were shown separately. After seeing both shots together, it becomes obvious that although the girl's birthday party seems to be a happy occasion, it should be remembered that other little girls are not as fortunate.

To sum up our discussion of editing, we understand that the order in which shots are shown is important to their meaning. To learn this, we need only take another simple example.

Imagine that a director has given an editor four shots, but forgotten to tell the editor the order he wants to arrange them in. Here are the four shots:

1) A medium shot of a group of soldiers, showing the worried looks on their faces.

2) A long shot of a huge ape-like monster, trampling on a city.

3) A long shot of an explosion.

4) A medium shot of the same soldiers as in shot one, but this time with calm expressions on their faces.

If the editor puts the shots together in the order, 1,2,3,4, it would seem that the soldiers were worried about the huge monster, but that an explosion caused by a bomb they had planted had stopped the monster, and all is now safe. If the editor, however, shows the calm faces of the soldiers first, then the shot of the explosion, then the ape trampling the city, and then the worried faces in shot 1, it would be assumed that the soldiers were confident that the explosion was going to wipe

In Eisenstein's film **The Battleship Potemkin**, montage editing was used to create powerful reactions in viewers.

Film editor Dede Allen has worked with Arthur Penn on many of his feature films. Here they are viewing and discussing a scene from **Little Big Man**.

out the monster, but that their plan had failed, and the monster was still at large. And if the shot of the calm faces of the soldiers was shown first, then the ape, the worried faces of the soldiers, and the shot of the big explosion, it could be imagined that the monster had stepped on some dangerous explosive and blown up everything around, including the soldiers.

One more arrangement is still possible with these shots. Perhaps the worried faces of the soldiers were shown first. Then the explosion shot was used, and then the shot of the monster crushing the city, followed by a shot of the calm faces of the soldiers. It would then seem that the soldiers were worried that the explosion might hurt the monster, who was on their side, but that they were relieved to see that it had not, as the monster continued to destroy the city of their enemy.

From this one simple example it can be seen that an editor's ability to situate shots, to place the "right" shots together, can be decisive in communicating with film.

EDITING

ACTIVITIES

1) Study the comic strip you collected for the first chapter's exercise. Does it use the order long shot, medium shot, close-up? If not, why not? Look for a sequence that does and cut it out. Look for a sequence that reverses the order; if you can find one, cut it out as well.

2) Recall sequences from films that you've seen recently. Do any of them reverse the LS, MS, CU order of editing? Describe a sequence that does. Why did the director use the reverse order?

3) Select an advertisement that uses juxtaposition to create an effect. Describe the juxtaposition and its effects on your perception of each shot.

4) Create a juxtaposition by mounting two photographs together. Perhaps you could also experiment with two photos of different shapes or with a black and white photo juxtaposed to a color photo, or a comic book drawing juxtaposed to a photograph.

5) Practice *reverse scripting*. Watch a television show for five minutes, preferably a movie on television. Describe each shot to an assistant who will write it down. For example, you call out, "Shot number one, long shot, high-angle, wide-angle lens, inside of a western saloon." Your assistant, using abbreviations, writes, "1. LS, HA, WA, in saloon." This technique is an excellent way to study how professional filmmakers can use editing techniques.

6) Write a script for a short sequence of a simple action. For example, a person walks into a room, sits down, and opens a can of soda. Use the funnel-like order of shots. Remember to indicate directions for camera angles, choice

of wide-angle or telephoto lens if necessary. Then write a script for the same action, but reverse the funnel-like order. In our example, you would start with the can sitting in the room.

7) Use a still camera or a movie camera to actually take each shot for each of the scripts you wrote in the previous activity. Or draw each shot on an index card (using stick figures if necessary).

8) Obtain shooting scripts for a feature film or for another movie. Describe how directors use the long shot, the medium-shot, the close-up, camera angles, and lenses. View the sequence you have studied, if possible, and discuss how the director's choice of techniques helps convey his or her message.

RHYTHM

A film director communicates many ideas and emotions to his audience by how he cuts and joins the shots he has created. The meanings of each shot, as we have seen, can be changed or emphasized by juxtaposition. A director can also communicate, however, through the **rhythm** of the shots he or she edits into a film and through the rhythm created by editing itself.

Rhythm and editing are closely related; both are created by cutting and joining shots. Cutting can create new rhythms, isolate and contrast rhythmic motions within shots, and speed up or slow down the pace of actions occurring in the shots. While juxtaposition and montage editing affect the *meaning* of a shot or sequence, rhythmic editing creates the *feeling* of a shot or sequence. Both unite in the final film to communicate just what the director wishes to have his viewers experience.

Most of us identify the word *rhythm* with music. Rhythm, however, simply refers to a *repetition* of an object or action; rhythm can be created by repeating a form or color, as it is done in painting, or by repeating a sound, as in music. Film offers the possibility of creating rhythms with these art forms and others besides: with sound, with objects, with color, and with motion.

Much of the excitement of a short film like **Timepiece** is due to the fast rhythm of its editing.

RHYTHMIC MOTION WITHIN A SHOT

Sometimes a film director will create a shot which includes a great number of similar things—trees, people, lines, objects. If there is an orderly pattern among these objects, the shot itself can have a rhythmic feeling. Many of the shots in Leni Riefenstahl's Nazi propaganda documentary *Triumph of the Will* contain rhythmic repetitions of Nazi flags, upraised hands in the Nazi salute, large numbers of tents, and other groups of repeating objects. Filmmakers share this type of rhythmic structure with still photographers and artists.

Filmmakers, however, can go quite a distance beyond simple repetition of objects. They can capture rhythmic movement which occurs in moving objects and isolate it on the screen for the viewer to see. Many filmmakers have used **naturally cinematic objects** in their films to create this kind of rhythm. **Naturally cinematic objects** are objects that have an interesting rhythm of their own, which a photographer can capture on movie film. Objects such as water, horses, clouds, have long been popular with filmmakers because the rhythmic motion of such objects can add interest to a film. Albert Lamorisse's short film *White Mane*, for example, derives much of its interest from the fact that it includes horses and water. And Denys Columb de Daunant's short film *Dream of the Wild Horses* concerns itself only with water and horses and

their rhythmic motion. *Corrida Interdite*, also one of Daunant's films, captures the gracefulness of bullfighting, another rhythmic naturally cinematic subject.

Trains have also been a naturally rhythmic subject, popular with filmmakers through the entire history of film. Editing has often been combined with this subject to create a heightened rhythmic effect. *Night Mail*, a documentary by John Grierson, covers the movement of a fast mail train and adds the interest of rhythmic editing to match the movement of the train itself. *Pacific 231* also tries to capture in editing the rhythmic effect of watching a train; and *Castro Street*, a modern experimental film by Bruce Baille, uses editing along with other techniques to capture the same nostalgic feeling many people have for trains.

Sometimes the rhythm of an action is so pronounced that editing would interfere with it, and so a filmmaker may choose to show the entire action from one point of view, without using cutting to add another rhythm. In Charlie Chaplin's film *The Rink*, Chaplin has gone to a roller skating rink where he meets up with a bully who's been pursuing him all through the film. The bully may be bigger than Chaplin, but on roller skates, he's no match. Rather than allow cutting to interfere with the rhythm of the event, the entire event is shown with Chaplin's movements creating all the excitement.

Sometimes a filmmaker may decide to use other types of rhythm to create a feeling of excitement on the part of his audience. During one scene from his feature film *Bonnie and Clyde*, director Arthur Penn showed the Barrow gang sitting in a house. Suddenly, the police attack. From the beginning of the attack until the Barrows escape from their motel room into a field, the audience witnesses a scene of fantastic excitement and horror. Instead of creating the excitement by cutting each shot short, Penn simply used shots that have an incredible amount of motion within them. The rhythm

Rhythms, the repetition of patterns, characterize Leni Riefenstahl's **Olympia** (top) and **Triumph of the Will** (middle, bottom). More complex rhythms are found in a shot from Bergman's **The Seventh Seal**.

of the scene quickens to an almost unbearable rate, not because of the rhythm of the editing, but because of the rhythm contained in each shot. And no static close-ups break the clamoring rhythm of this scene.

EDITING FOR RHYTHM

Even when a naturally cinematic or rhythmic subject is filmed, most of the rhythm of a film is determined by the manner in which the director edits the shots of the subject. If he edits the shots so that each has a slow, equal length, the audience will experience the relaxing, rhythmic feeling one might feel by rocking in a rocking chair. Such a regular rhythm would make the viewer experience a feeling of relaxation, order, calmness.

If the director edits his shots, however, so that each shot lasts a short time on the screen, his viewers will probably feel excited. They will know that the tempo of the action has picked up and will expect an important, dangerous, or fast-moving event.

For example, if four men are sitting around in a saloon sequence from a Western, the director may decide to make every shot last a long time on the screen to reflect the feeling that a card game is an activity with a very slow rhythm. If one of the players accuses another of dealing from the bottom of the deck, however, the tempo of the events around the table will speed up. Matching this speed-up of the rhythm of events, the filmmaker will most probably increase the tempo of the editing. Instead of the long slow shots he has been using, he will switch to short-lasting shots, and the rhythm of the sequence will pick up. Maybe one of the antagonists will go for his gun, and a fight may start. The editing will reflect this by very quick shots. When the fighting is over, the director will again let each shot last longer on the screen, creating a slower rhythm.

Whenever a director speeds up the rhythm of his editing, he is not utilizing some unnatural device

This still from Fellini's 1957 feature film **Nights of Cabiria** demonstrates conflict within a shot, as a confused woman confronts another in a religious frenzy.

to make his audience experience the excitement of the event on the screen, but rather he is reflecting the normal human reaction to excitement. If something dangerous or exciting happens to us, our bodies naturally react to it by speeding up their rhythms. When we are in danger, our pulses speed up, our heart rhythms increase, our breathing rhythms become quicker. When a filmmaker speeds up the rhythm of the sequence by cutting down the length of each shot, he is signaling to our minds these same quickenings and excitement.

Movies which attempt to capture the thrill of fast moving objects usually consist of a number of short-length shots to communicate the fast rhythm of the event. The National Film Board of Canada's short film *L'Homme Vite* attempts to capture the excitement of a car race. Quick editing of short shots in *L'Homme Vite* conveys the rhythm of the subject. Other films dealing with auto racing use the same technique of short shots to create the feeling of fast motion. *The French Connection* and the racing sections of Claude Lelouch's feature film *A Man and a Woman* contain shots edited quickly to convey a mood of excitement.

To create a feeling of developing excitement, a filmmaker may start a sequence with long shots and progressively shorten each shot so that the rhythm of the sequences increases. And perhaps one shot in this group is held longer than the others to create suspense. In one scene from Lelouch's *A Man and a Woman*, drivers wait to run to their cars at the beginning of the twenty-four-hour Le Mans race. The shot of the drivers waiting for the clock to strike the hour is held on the screen longer than the other shots to create a feeling of suspense, of waiting, on the part of the audience. Everything else is happening quickly, but there is that agonizing wait for the clock to signal the beginning of the race.

Toward the end of his film *No Reason to Stay*, director Mort Ransen wanted to convey all of the pressures building up on Christopher Wood because of his school. Ransen used extremely fast cutting of a number of shots which recall the entire movie in a short time. The fast pace of the shots builds up into a faster and faster rhythm, until Chris "breaks" and runs off down the corridor

away from his classroom. The cutting of the shots produces a rhythm so fast that the viewer himself experiences the forces which are pressing in on Christopher.

As we have mentioned in discussing naturally rhythmic subjects, every object which moves has its own rhythm, and usually a filmmaker will harmonize his editing rhythm with the rhythm of the object on camera. When a filmmaker chooses a rhythm which is different from the rhythm of an object, he does this to indicate something. For example, smoke billowing out of a factory smokestack usually has a slow, rhythmic motion of its own. But if a filmmaker wants to communicate the fact that this smoke is polluting our atmosphere,

Smoke pollution is a fact of life in the short Canadian film **Day after Day**.

he may choose to show quick cuts of a number of different smokestacks, all billowing their noxious gases into the air. What is usually seen as a rhythmic motion can be translated, by editing, into a monstrous attack on the atmosphere.

Shots which are held on the screen much longer than normal force the audience to look more carefully at the object on the screen. Filmmakers can also communicate a feeling of uneasiness, can irritate their audiences, by letting a shot remain on the screen much longer than such a shot usually would last. At the beginning and end of the National Film

Board of Canada's short film *The End of Summer*, there is a particular shot of one of the characters, Celine, standing in the snow and looking into the camera. This shot remains on the screen for an incredibly long time without anything happening. By letting this shot run as long as he did, the director allowed his audience to feel the same boredom with winter which his character on the screen was experiencing.

Beginning filmmakers sometimes ask how long a shot should be held on the screen. The answer is that a shot should remain only as long as is necessary for it to give its information; then it should leave the screen without wearing out its welcome. Practically speaking, this means that long shots, with lots of information, usually have to remain on the screen for longer lengths of time than medium shots. Close-ups, with their quicker impact and smaller quantity of information, usually require the shortest screen time of all. Experienced filmmakers can create slower rhythms by making their shots last longer than usual, but beginning filmmakers probably are best off by cutting each of their shots

to the minimum length necessary for it to deliver its information.

Capturing rhythmic movement which is out of rhythm can produce the same effect as holding a shot longer than it would normally be held. One filmmaker simply decided to record a marching band rehearsing its maneuvers for the first time. Since the rhythmic motions of a marching band are usually quite precise, the effect of seeing them out of rhythm produced a funny film. This technique underlines the fact that we usually expect certain things to move with a particular rhythm.

The Death of One, a short film, shows the death of a seagull from pollution. Instead of the rhythmic movement which is usually associated with seagulls, a dying bird is shown limping along on a beach, hardly able to walk. The change in rhythm from what is normally expected creates the powerful effect of the movie; the film's slow rhythm is like a funeral procession for the bird.

Summer is a leisurely enjoyable time; the slow rhythm of shots in **End of Summer**, a short film, reflects this.

THE CUT AS A JOINING DEVICE

The way in which a filmmaker chooses to join together his shots makes a great difference in how the audience perceives the rhythm of his film. The simplest joining device in film is the **cut**. When a filmmaker **cuts** from one shot to another, there is no connection between the shots except the fact that one replaces the other on the screen. The *cut* unites the two shots because the viewer sees them one after another, and it divides the two shots: When the second shot appears on the screen, the first is gone.

In his short film *Chickamauga*, filmmaker Robert Enrico described the fantasy world of a little boy who is a deaf-mute. The little boy has difficulty separating reality from fantasy. During one sequence, the young boy sees dying soldiers retreating from the battle of Chickamauga. For him, the dying soldiers are like toys. Enrico showed the reality of the scene, the horror of the massacred soldiers, and then cut to the fantasy in which the boy sees

the men. The **cut** divides the shots because it takes two different shots to show the scene, but it unites reality and fantasy in the film.

A filmmaker may also decide to cut together seemingly unrelated shots into a quick succession of images which, taken together, means something. Filmmaker Jim Henson decided to unite quickly changing images in his short film *Timepiece*. Within *Timepiece* events happen quickly: A man swinging on a vine becomes an olive, falling into a martini; while dining in an expensive restaurant, the man finds his own head served to him on a platter. Cuts join each shot together, and the quick rhythm of the film creates a strange, *surreal* world.

Directors can choose different types of cutting to create the rhythm which they need for their subject. If the pictures on the screen are meant only to illustrate the story a narrator is telling, as in some documentary films, a director most often will use **compilation cutting**. The order and the rhythm of the shots in compilation cutting are not important since the film is tied together by the narration.

Travelogs, newsreels, and other such films many times use only compilation cutting.

In **continuity cutting**, a filmmaker follows one person or group of persons continuously and details what happens to them. Although a filmmaker will usually choose a number of different types of shots in continuity cutting, the idea is to concentrate on one action or subject rather than to move back and forth between actions.

In his 1970 feature *Butch Cassidy and the Sundance Kid*, director George Roy Hill used continuity cutting to follow Robert Redford and Paul Newman as they are pursued by a posse which intends to capture them dead or alive. Because only Redford and Newman are seen, and not the posse, the audience identifies with the two men.

Most directors, however, would not use continuity cutting for a chase sequence but rather would choose **dynamic cutting**. This means that they would cut back and forth from the pursuers to the pursued. The back and forth cutting would create a rhythm, add variety to the sequence, and allow the director to emphasize the conflict between the two groups. Probably as the chase became faster and more furious, the action in the shots would speed up, and each shot itself would become shorter and shorter. Dynamic cutting allows a director practical means for increasing the rhythm of the editing in his film; it offers him different shots to cut to when he wants to increase the speed of a scene. Dynamic editing provides the audience with such intense excitement that Alfred Hitchcock refers to the chase as the final expression of film art.

Parallel cutting allows a director to build up the same excitement and suspense as dynamic editing. Parallel cutting includes two actions going on at the same time; the director cuts back and forth between them, just as he does in dynamic editing. The difference is that in parallel cutting, the actions usually don't have the same close relationship between each other as they do in dynamically edited chase scenes.

For example, toward the end of his short film

Cuts are used to divide reality and fantasy in Robert Enrico's film **Chickamauga**, part of a trilogy on the Civil War.

The Golden Fish, filmmaker Edmond Sechan used parallel cutting to create a great deal of suspense. A young boy has just won a goldfish, and he hurries home from school to see it. In his apartment, however, a black alley cat is busy trying to attack the fish. Sechan cut back and forth between the boy walking home and the action in the apartment. Will the boy arrive in time to save his fish? He stops in a pet store. The cat continues his sly deed. Parallel editing increases the suspense. Parallel cutting is sometimes called "meanwhile-back-at-the-ranch" editing, which gives a good idea of the difference between it and dynamic editing. Dynamic editing concerns itself with one event and shows that event from different viewpoints. Parallel cutting is concerned with two different actions, which themselves will be related only later in the film. Two entirely different actions, the baptism of a child and a murder, are edited together at the end of *The Godfather*. Director Francis Ford Coppola used parallel editing, cutting his shots shorter and shorter as both actions reach their climax, to create an exceptionally dramatic effect.

Extremely complex parallel cutting can occur when a director tries to tell more than one story at a time. In his 1916 film *Intolerance*, for example, D.W. Griffith told four simultaneous stories of intolerance, from the fall of Babylon to modern times. More recently, George Lucas followed Griffith's pattern in his film *American Graffiti* (1973), which told four simultaneous stories, joined by parallel cutting.

Sometimes a director will use a **cut-in shot** to change the rhythm of a scene. In his one-minute-long experimental film *Not as Yet Decided*, filmmaker Jeff Dell shows two little girls, one white and the other black, playing happily in a park. They seem happy and friendly. Suddenly a few frames of racial violence are cut into the scenes of the little girls at play. The violent scenes are still pictures of adults displaying racial hatred. As the film continues, Dell cut more and more of these flashes of adult racial violence into the peaceful world of the little girls. Finally the white girl tries to kiss the black girl; the black girl pulls away; and motion is drained out of the scene until it also becomes a still picture, like the shots of the adults.

The quick cut-in shots spoil the gentle rhythm of the little girls at play and produce a jarring interruption of the slow rhythm of the scene.

By using the cut-in shot, Dell informs his viewers that although these two little girls are happy now, they probably will not be able to escape the example of their parents and will end up hating each other out of prejudice. The cut-ins are quick, violent, to convey the violence of the adult world which is impinging upon their lives, thrusting new complications into their simple relationship. Similar quick cut-in shots of the character Death in J. Maynard Lovin's lyrical 1970 short film *Threshold* are repeated to interrupt the one last afternoon of love and peace granted the film's main character. By the end of the film, Death has entered the man's life for good.

A director can **cut away** from an action for many purposes. If something ugly is happening, a director can spare his audience the shock of watching it by using a **cut-away shot**. In the 1922 version of *The Hunchback of Notre Dame*, a cut-away shot is used to show the flogging of Quasimodo. First the hunchback is shown bound tightly to a platform. Then the flogger raises his whip. Instead of the whip hitting the hunchback, however, different cut-away shots are well used to show people's reactions to the violence. Later in the same film when Jehan stabs Phoebus, the shot does not include the actual stabbing. Jehan prepares to stab Phoebus, but immediately a cut-away shot of the hunchback inside Notre Dame cathedral, blowing out a candle, is shown. When the scene returns to the garden, Phoebus had been stabbed and Jehan has fled. The cut-away allows violence to occur without the audience having to witness it. A quick cut-away allows the director to change the rhythm of a sequence and to increase its impact.

Cut-aways also allow a director to guide the audience's reaction to something on the screen. If an action occurs that might be funny or tragic, a director may cut away to an observer. If he laughs, the viewers know that they should laugh too; if he

An action can be funny or violent in a film, and a director can cut to an observer to tell his audience which way he wants them to react.

is shocked, the viewers feel that they should feel shocked as well.

A **jump cut** breaks a normal feeling of rhythm in a sequence. If a character is standing on the right side of the screen in one shot, and then suddenly appears on the left side of the screen in the next shot, it is disturbing to an audience. Or a character may be far away in one shot, close up in the next. Filmmakers avoid jump cuts by inserting **cover shots** between the jumps. Thus, if a character is shown on the right side of the screen, the filmmaker may cut in an unrelated shot, such as another character watching the action, and then show the shot with the first character on the other side of the screen. The cover shot in the middle "cushions" the jump. If a filmmaker decides to go from a long shot of a character to a medium shot or a close-up of that same character, he will probably move the camera to a different angle to avoid the apparent jump forward.

Filmmakers can use the jump cut to create an interesting rhythm in parts of their films. In *Phoebe*, Paul and Phoebe are shown in a series of silhouettes, dancing in a semi-completed building. They stand in stationary poses and in a series of jump cuts appear to dance around the screen. The rhythm of the jump cuts provides an interesting effect and gives the impression that Phoebe and Paul were once happier together than they are during the course of the film.

In the cartoon film *Les Escargots*, a farmer is walking in his field, trying to decide how to make his crops grow. Instead of pacing back and forth, he walks in one direction, and then repeats his action; a jump cut brings him back to his starting point.

The jump cut can make objects seem to appear and disappear as well as jump around the screen. Early French filmmaker George Méliès is said to have discovered the jump cut when he was filming a shot of a street scene. Melies stopped cranking his camera for a second; when he projected the film, he noticed that a cart that had been on the street seemed to jump around. Melies experimented with this technique and began using the magic effect in his films, making people appear and disappear at will.

OTHER JOINING DEVICES

The **cut**, of course, is not the only device which enables filmmakers to join two shots together. Filmmakers can **dissolve** two shots together, that is, make the shots melt into each other. This technique changes the rhythm of the sequence. Rather than creating a sharp division between two shots, as does the cut, the dissolve softens a cut; the shots blend and one disappears.

Traditionally, the dissolve was used by filmmakers to tell their audiences of some change in time or place. In this way, a shot could be shown of New York and dissolved into a scene in Paris. Usually credits on films also dissolve into each other.

In his feature film *A Man for All Seasons*, director Fred Zinnemann wanted to tell his audience that Sir Thomas More spent a year in prison. He could have cut to another shot and put a title "A Year Later" on the screen, of course, but Zinnemann preferred to show his audience this information rather than tell them. Thomas can see out of a single window in his cell. Zinnemann showed the view from the window and dissolved together shots so that the scene is constantly changing from spring through summer, fall, and winter. When we return to a shot of Thomas More, we know that a year has passed.

Director Robert Rossen wanted to include a pool game shot in his film *The Hustler*. Rather than show the entire game, however, Rossen showed various parts of the game, connected together with dissolves. Rather than using a series of cuts, which might have looked like shots from different games, Rossen joined all the shots together with dissolves, indicating that one particular game is shown. The dissolves prevent the rhythm created by a number of cuts from distracting the viewer.

Filmmakers can also make objects seem to fade away from a scene by dissolving two shots of the same scene together. One shot will have the object in it, and the other shot won't. If a filmmaker dissolves these two shots together, the subject will seem to fade away. Director F.W. Murnau used this technique to make the vampire fade away after being struck with sunlight in his 1922 German vampire film *Nosferatu*.

Interesting examples of the dissolve occur in

A giant snail chases townspeople in a sequence from the French short animation **Les Escargots**.

Leni Reifenstahl's Nazi propaganda film *Triumph of the Will*. Because the dissolve allows objects to melt together, it makes bonds of unity seem to occur between various objects. In *Triumph of the Will*, for instance, church steeples melt into the tents of the Nazi youth camps, giving the impression that the churches are offering their blessing to the camps.

Because dissolves can soften cuts and allow a filmmaker to create a soft rhythm, they find their way into sequences of love, of tenderness, and of sorrow. Slow, lingering dissolves can be combined with lyrical slow motion sequences to create a poetic effect.

In one sequence of *The First Foundation*, an industrial film, dissolves allow the filmmakers to create a rhythmic scene without having to worry about a secondary rhythm created by cuts. In this sequence, machines and their movements are synchronized to the tempo of a piece of music. Using dissolves rather than cuts in this sequence allowed the filmmakers to concentrate on the motion and rhythm of the machines without having to worry also about the rhythm created by a series of cuts.

If he decides that it is important, a filmmaker can create a complete stoppage of the rhythm of his film with a **fade-out**. The screen gradually becomes totally black, interrupting the rhythm of the film and allowing the filmmaker to change rhythm, time, or place for his audience. The fade-out, followed by the **fade-in**, are often used by filmmakers to inform their audiences that a major change in time or place is occurring. Films which have a fast pace, such as *Phoebe* and *No Reason to Stay*, do not interrupt their rhythm with fade-outs. And a film like *Occurrence at Owl Creek Bridge*, in which the story happens in a very short span of real time, would also be harmed by fade-outs. Most films begin with a fade-in and end with a fade-out, to cushion the shock of going from total darkness to color and vice-versa.

The fade-out and fade-in are much like the period at the end of a sentence: The filmmaker uses them to interrupt the rhythm or statement of his film and to turn his audience's attention to a new area of interest.

Fragments of a Day, an advertising film promoting Beloit College in Wisconsin, begins with a

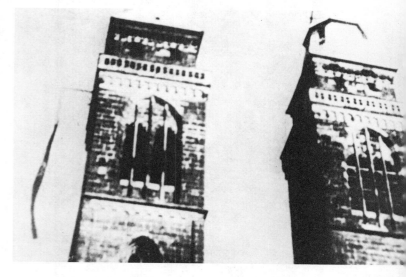

The dissolve merges the church steeples with the camps of Hitler's youth in the Nazi film **Triumph of the Will**.

series of images of the college quickly fading in and out; fade-outs and fade-ins separate various parts of this short film and help to section it into areas of concentration—sports, studies, recreation.

In one section of his short film *The Red Balloon*, director Albert Lamorisse used a fade-out to tell his audience that a day had passed. Instead of using a fade-in to begin the next scene, however, Lamorisse showed a new picture moving up the screen from the bottom. The audience suddenly realizes the shot is from the inside of a store in Paris; its owner has just raised the night curtain

covering the window, and it is early morning. Lamorisse used the fade-out to end a day and an imaginative new device to bring light onto his screen again.

Other devices exist for the filmmaker to create special rhythms in joining together his shots. The filmmaker can use the **wipe** to create a special type of rhythm in editing. In a wipe, one shot pushes, or wipes, the preceding shot off of the screen. A wipe can move up, down, or diagonally across the screen. Although the wipe was quite popular in early films, only recently have directors returned to the wipe as a means of joining shots together. Japanese director Akira Kurosawa used the wipe many times in his samuri Western *Yojimbo*. As the hired sword of one of the fighting families in the town, the bodyguard walks triumphantly across the screen, and the next shot wipes behind him as if he were leading it onto the screen.

In the 1971 horror film *Willard*, the wipe is used regularly to change scenes; the unnatural effect of the wipe fits well into the tone and rhythm of the film. And Dalton Trumbo used a half-wipe in his 1971 feature *Johnny Got His Gun*. During one scene of this film, the hero is thinking of his girl friend while he is at war. The shot of his girl friend wipes halfway onto the screen, and both of them are shown in the same shot. In this way, the wipe lets the thought of Jim's girl friend intrude onto the picture just as it intrudes into his mind. Thus the wipe is able to capture the rhythm of the movie at that moment.

One of the devices that pioneer filmmaker D. W. Griffith used to join shots together was the **mask**. Portions of the screen become dark, as in a fade-out except for one area which remains light to focus interest on a particular detail. For example, a shot might be showing a woman in a courtroom, wringing her hands in worry over her husband. A mask would come in and darken the entire screen except for her hands, which would linger for a few seconds and then fade out in preparation for the next shot. Today, filmmakers seldom use the mask,

Although it is not often used in modern films, the wipe was popular in early films as a means of joining shots and creating meanings.

although director Francois Truffaut used it in his 1970 feature *The Wild Child*.

In working with a group of images, a director can employ all of these devices to create a particular rhythm or to achieve a reaction in his audience. The next step for filmmakers has been to use multiple images and multiple screens in order to show more than one movie at a time. In this manner, various images can exist at the same time, each with its own rhythm. Such multiple image films

A classically oriented director like Francois Truffaut may use wipes and masks, as in **Jules and Jim**.

have an extremely complex rhythmic structure, and perhaps signal the way that film will go in the future, with as many as six moving images and seven still inserts shown simultaneously on the same screen. Whatever may happen, editing creates the pulse of film and remains the heartbeat sustaining it.

RHYTHM

ACTIVITIES

1) Rhythm within shots occurs in many photographs. Look for examples in magazines and cut out shots that show repetition of similar objects or shapes. Architects frequently use rhythmic repetition of shapes, and nature photographers also capitalize on the repetition of structures in their pictures.

2) Recall films that use *naturally cinematic objects*. Water, for example, possesses rhythmic movement and sparkles, making it naturally appealing for the motion-picture photographer. Describe sequences from movies you have seen recently that effectively use naturally cinematic objects.

3) List ten naturally cinematic objects. Describe how you might use as many of them as possible in a film. For example, you might describe a film showing horses running through water with a fire floating on the water, to be called *A Dream about Wild Horses*. Try to plan a more original idea than this example.

4) *Reverse scripting* is probably the finest method for learning about rhythmic editing. Obtain some television commercials from a studio or advertising agency. Examine one film and list each shot as long shot, medium shot, or closeup; describe each shot and indicate the length of each shot in frames and seconds. You can time each shot either by actually counting frames (good for short shots) or by measuring each shot with a ruler or yardstick (one foot of 16mm film, the size film TV stations use, contains forty frames). Once you have measured each shot, convert the length of the shot to seconds. Each second of 16mm sound film requires 24 frames. A close-up for instance, might be 2½ feet long. Script it as, "Man's face, smiling, CU, 2½ feet (100 frames, about 4 seconds).

Indicate all transitional devices between shots (fade-in, fade-out, dissolve, wipe, etc., using abbreviations: FI, FO, DZ, WP)

When you're done, compare your scripts with other people's and verify the general statement that long shots, with more information, usually last longer on the screen than close-ups. Also look for rhythmic editing. Read each script and then screen the commercial from which it was made.

5) Watch a TV commercial or film clip and pay attention to transitional devices like fades, cuts, wipes, etc. When are dissolves used? Time each dissolve by counting "One thousand-and-one" for each second of the dissolve. Compare the rhythm of commercials and regular filming. Do commercials use shorter length dissolves and faster rhythms than regular films? Why?

6) Have you seen any films recently that use the transitional device of a wipe? Describe the sequence.

7) Scripts are available for many feature films that use rhythmic editing; obtain a script and study shot lengths. Select an appropriate sequence and describe its use of transitional devices and shot rhythms.

LIGHT

The film director creates shots out of nothing, arranges them, keeps them moving. He does all of this to tell us things, to let us enjoy what he has captured on film, to irritate or to arouse us. And much of what a director uses to communicate to us, his audience, comes to us through our eyes.

This means that one of the tools a director can use to communicate to his audience visually is light. Of course a certain amount of light is necessary to make any movie, and the director must be sure he has at least a sufficient amount of light for exposing his film. Once beyond this lower limit, however, he can start creating with light, using light to communicate. The director may add many lights in various areas, tell his subject to move nearer to the light or further away from it, place screens over lights to soften them. The best filmmakers are aware of the many possibilities light offers for communicating with the audience. In effect, these filmmakers are able *to paint with light*.

Director Stanley Kubrick was able to tell his audience a great deal in his film *2001: A Space Odyssey* simply by the way he arranged his lights. Throughout the entire space journey to Jupiter, the film poses many questions about man and his relationship to machines. In one particular shot,

When a film is competently directed, lighting can add interest, beauty, and emotion. High-key lighting lends starkness to this scene from Alfred Hitchcock's **Psycho**.

Kubrick used light to sum up many of the problems he is concerned with.

The colored lights from the instrument panel of his spaceship reflect off the face shield in David Bowman's space helmet, creating a complex pattern of colors. Bowman's face is almost obscured by these multiple light reflections. Kubrick is emphasizing for his audience how the machine Bowman operates had begun to overwhelm him as a man; the vast amounts of data transmitted by the lights almost obscures Bowman's face.

So effectively did Kubrick use light in this one shot that it became one of the most famous single shots of the entire film, finding its way into most of the advertisements in the movie's selling campaign. Without the careful positioning of actor and lighting to achieve these multiple reflections, a shot which became a symbol of the entire film would have been only a simple close-up of a man in a space helmet. Such careful use of the technique of lighting to communicate ideas and feelings to an audience is one of the marks of a talented filmmaker.

PAINTING WITH LIGHT

To make a movie interesting to an audience, a filmmaker knows he must carefully control the light he uses on his subject. The Russian feature film *Ballad of a Soldier* has many exceptional ex-

amples of thoughtful use of light. In one sequence
of shots, a young soldier comes to the realization
that he loves the girl he has just left and that the
train he is on is carrying him farther and farther
away from her. The director shows a shot of the
soldier gazing out the window of the train. Covering his face is the reflection of the wilderness outside. The loneliness of the forest in the reflection
underlines the sorrow the boy experiences at that
instant and helps communicate that feeling to the
audience.

When it comes to painting with light, perhaps
no one is more respected than the Swedish director
Ingmar Bergman. Working with skilled cameramen, Bergman has been able to achieve remarkable
effects with light and shadow, changing the mood
of his films by precise uses of light. In *The Seventh
Seal*, the feature film which served to propel him

Bright, high-key lighting illuminates the happy parts of
Ingmar Bergman's **The Seventh Seal** (above). Dark, low-key
lighting is used for Death (below, right).

into international prominence, Bergman created
cheerful sequences by using bright, happy, sunny
lighting, as in the sacramental scene between Jof
and Mia and the Knight in which they share straw-
berries and fresh cream. Bergman's use of light
makes the audience feel the happiness of the Knight
in his momentary respite from Death. Jof and Mia
are simple people, glad to be alive, and so they are
brightly lighted, even overbright; the entire scene
is sparkling and open, and there are no dark backgrounds. Photographers use the term **high-key** to
refer to shots that contain mostly bright light and
light tones.

Whenever Death appears, however, Bergman
used different lighting. The scene at once becomes

dark and gloomy, as if a cloud were passing over. Shots of Death show contrasting deep blacks and ghostly whites; with this **low-key lighting** Bergman makes his audience experience the ominous feelings of his characters.

A use of light similar in some ways to Bergman's occurs in Robert Enrico's films. In *Occurrence at Owl Creek Bridge*, Enrico switches from the sharp, harsh, cold light of dawn when Peyton Farquhar is on the bridge, to warm, sunny light when Farquhar seems to escape. And as the end of the film brings Peyton Farquhar nearer his home, shadows lengthen, and the viewers know it is evening; Enrico is telling his audience that Farquhar has walked for an entire day.

In *Chickamauga*, Enrico's second film of his Civil War trilogy, he used light to influence a change in the audience's feeling as the movie progresses. At the beginning, a seven-year-old deaf-mute boy plays near his home. The shots are bright and happy, much like the shots of Jof and Mia in *The Seventh Seal*; they reflect the joy the boy has in his home life. After being rebuked by his mother, however, the boy wanders into the forest to play at war games and falls asleep. When he awakens and begins to head home, he is unaware, because of his deafness, that a battle has been raging nearby. And as he continues to play in his fantasy world, he finds himself in the middle of the Union Army's retreat after the battle of Chickamauga.

In this section of the film, Enrico lighted the scene sparingly, creating a dark, somber, low-key feeling for his audience. What had been playing for fun now becomes playing for keeps, as soldiers are dying around him. Although the little boy is unable to separate fantasy and reality and so uses the dying soldiers as part of his play, the audience knows that the game has become real because Enrico used somber lighting to create a feeling of death.

When the boy finally returns to his home to find it in flames and his dead mother blankly staring at him, Enrico holds the same mood with light. Standing in contrast with the bright scenes of the

Robert Enrico's careful use of high- and low-key lighting and of types of lighting adds interest to **Chickamauga**.

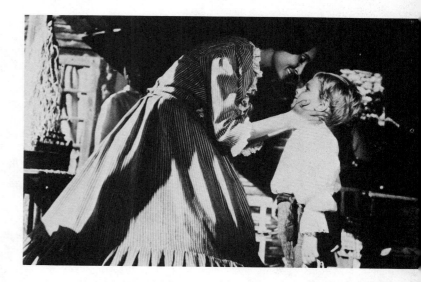

boys' home life at the beginning of the film, the tragedy of the scene is emphasized. Enrico then shows a close-up of the young deaf-mute, his face lighted by the flickering flames of his burning home. This time the lighting suggests that, although he cannot understand it yet, the young boy will never again have the same life he had before. The flickering light stresses both the uncertainty of his future as well as the tragedy of the moment. All this Enrico does with the technique of light.

A director can also use light to keep his audience "in the dark" about a particular event. At the beginning of *Mockingbird*, the third film of his trilogy, Enrico employs lighting techniques both to make his viewers experience what the character is feeling and to hide the identity of a dead man.

Private Graylock, a sentry in the Union army, is keeping watch. The night is dark, and the forest is filled with mystery and danger. By using very little light, illuminating only parts of objects in the scene, Enrico is able to give the audience a feel for the suspense, fear, and confusion Private Graylock feels. Hearing a noise, Graylock fires into the darkness. He kills the intruder but cannot find the body. Enrico creates much of the mood in this sequence by his carefully controlled use of light; he adds to the effect with a carefully orchestrated sound track.

In the middle of the film, when Graylock is thinking of his childhood, Enrico changes to bright, happy lighting to describe the joy of Graylock and his twin brother at play. But soon we see a shot of

their mother, her head on a pillow. The mood of the shot, dark and somber in its use of light, hints to us that something is wrong. The camera pulls back revealing that their mother is lying in bed, dead. From this time on, Enrico never again uses the bright, sunny lighting. In the last part of the memory scene, the twins separate from each other in a sequence lighted very coldly, reminding one of the bridge scene in *Occurrence*. Again Enrico, through his use of light, is suggesting to the audience a grim truth.

LIGHTING TO COMMUNICATE

Some directors employ lighting in ways which become characteristic of their directing style. Arthur Penn, for example, many times uses light to direct his characters, or to blind or confuse them. This lighting technique is used consistently in all of Penn's films. Two automobile headlight beams begin Penn's feature film *The Chase*. Bubber Reeves, an escaped convict, darts away from these searching lights. Light leads Bubber to his hometown; a lighted sign tells Bubber he has made it to "Val Rogers Properties"; a lighted back porch leads him to a house where he can steal food. Sheriff Calder uses a flashlight to try to rescue Bubber. Calling our attention to Penn's use of light as a guideline, Sheriff Calder yells out to Bubber, "Can't you see my light?"

Other Penn films reveal this same lighting technique. In *Bonnie and Clyde*, after the members of the Barrow gang are ambushed by the law while eating dinner, headlights blind them as they try to escape, but the headlights also show them the way to the road and freedom. The first time Jack Crabb sees General Custer in *Little Big Man*, Custer's face is directly in front of the sun, and the light is so dazzling that Crabb cannot see Custer clearly. Later Custer leads the still-blinded Jack and his troops into the Battle of the Little Big Horn. Finally, Penn himself has described his first feature *The Left Handed Gun* as the spiritual journey of Billy the Kid from light into dark.

Arthur Penn uses the harsh lighting of car headlights in a scene from his feature film **The Chase**.

Penn, of course, controls light in his films in ways other directors do. Whenever Bonnie and Clyde are inside, the lighting is dark, and the rooms seem to be inappropriate places for them. The only inside shots which are brightly, happily lighted are the ones in which the Barrows are robbing banks, stores, and the like. Outside where the light is bright, Bonnie and Clyde seem happy, relaxed. Even when they are ambushed and killed, it is outside which seems an appropriate place for the pair to die.

The Summer We Moved to Elm Street, a short film produced by the National Film Board of Canada, also uses light to suggest reactions and feelings to the audience. The father of the family is an alcoholic, and the film focuses on the effect this has on his family, primarily on his daughter. To stress the difference between his home life and his tavern life, the director uses dark, brownish light to show the father in the frequent tavern scenes and uses drab, dull, uninteresting light inside his home.

In one sequence, the director wants to stress the unhappiness the father's alcoholism causes his children. Inside the house, his little girl eats a hurried meal, and the dull, unexciting light indicates that her house is not a happy place. The little girl immediately runs over to a neighbor's house for another lunch. Here, in a home without an alcoholism problem, things are happy, bright, with light illuminating everything. A lunch in the neighbor's garden, compared with the lunch just seen, underlines the drabness and the tension in her own home.

Thus, by careful use of light, the director can emphasize how much unhappiness the father's alcoholism causes.

At the beginning of Francis Ford Coppola's film *The Godfather*, similar use is made of the contrast between the inside of the Godfather's house, where the business of crime is being transacted, and the outside of the house, where a party is being held. Inside the house, lighting is sparse, and heavy brown tones prevail. Outside the house, light, happy, high-key lighting emphasizes the contrast between two parts of the man's life.

Creating a mood, letting audiences know how they should feel, making objects look abnormal, all are effects of light a director can employ. In his feature *The Wild Child*, director Francois Truffaut

Compare the two top shots from Serge Roullet's feature **The Wall** and the two bottom shots from Jean-Luc Godard's film **Alphaville** to see different effects of background light. Director Sembene Ousmane used harsh, high-key lighting for realistic effects in the 1969 film **Black Girl**.

used light to underline the relationship Victor, the "young savage," has with water. For Victor, water was one of the pleasures which reminded him of his freedom. Whenever water appears in the film, Truffaut was careful to have light play on the water brightly, reflecting the happiness Victor is feeling. And when Victor runs away, Truffaut switched to a drab, grayish light to stress the unhappiness of Itard, the boy's teacher.

Sometimes "the harsh light of reality" is the best

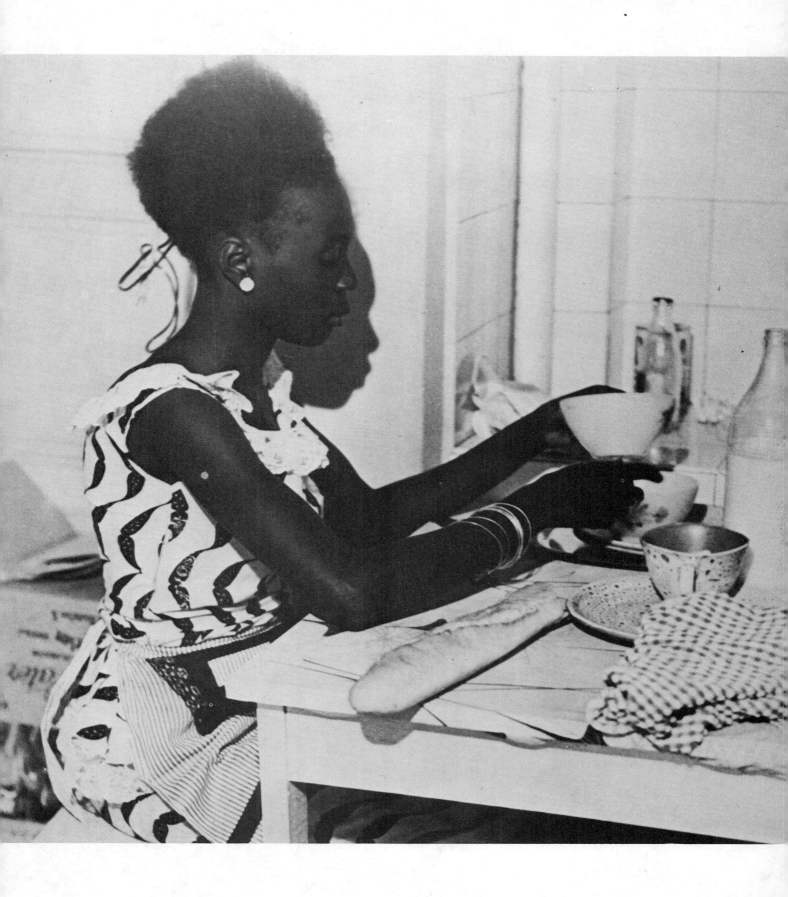

light for describing to an audience what people are really like. Documentary filmmakers frequently use this unchanged, harsh light because adding lights would often make it impossible to film people unobtrusively. But non-documentary filmmakers occasionally use realistic light to capture the believable, newsreel quality of documentaries. British director Peter Watkins used realistic, harsh lighting to add the feeling of reality to his film *The War Game*. Italian director Gillo Pontecorvo used the same technique of realistic lighting so well in his feature *The Battle of Algiers* that he had to remind his audience at the beginning that none of the film was actual documentary footage. Watkins and Pontecorvo made their audiences feel that what they were watching was really happening by avoiding the "pretty" effect that lighting can have. Rather than paint with light, these directors chose to record with it.

Other filmmakers avoid fancy lighting for the same reason. In fact, the practice of using crude light in movies to capture reality goes back to the Italian neo-realist filmmakers who made films in Italy immediately after the Second World War. Working on limited budgets, some with film they had stolen from the Nazis, directors had no desire—and many of them had no equipment—to paint with light, but preferred to use harsh light to make their films reveal the sufferings in Italy after the War.

Directors like Roberto Rosselini, in *Rome, Open City*, Vittorio DeSica in *Shoeshine* and *The Bicycle Thief*, and later Luchino Visconti in *The Earth Shakes*, all used this hard, realistic light. Throughout these remarkable films and others like them darkness and light seem indistinguishable. In their places, a uniform grayness, a drab cloudiness, presides. Watching these films today, from our comfortable surroundings, we can still feel the drabness, the depth of suffering, that the people in a war-ravaged country go through.

Many filmmakers use light to evoke particular feelings in an audience. In *Corral*, a short film from the National Film Board of Canada, the director

Light can be used for its uncomplimentary effects, as in Godard's **Alphaville**.

The flat lighting used for snapshots with instant impact is usually undesirable for filmmaking purposes.

positioned his camera so that the face of the cowboy is obscured in shadow. Since the audience cannot identify the cowboy as a particular cowboy, it is more conscious of what he is doing than of who he is. The director wanted his viewers to feel that they were watching a *ritual*, something in which what is done is more important than who does it.

In the short film *Rainshower*, the director simply wanted to capture how light before and after a rainfall can change reality. Filmmakers are always conscious of this evocative use of light, and entire films have been made simply recording the play of light on soapsuds washing down a parking lot.

Andre Bazin, the late French critic, talked about photography as a molding, a relic, taken by the manipulation of light. He underlined the importance of light in creating a valuable experience for the audience of a motion picture. Light, then, can be an important tool for the director in suggesting to his audience how to react at a particular time, in setting a mood for his scenes, and in underlining the response desired. Motion picture photography remains true to the original meaning of the Greek words *photos* and *graphos* from which it came: "to write with light."

LIGHT

ACTIVITIES

1) *High-key* and *low-key light* are tools of the still photographer as well as of the cinematographer. Collect examples of each in photography magazines and mount them. Collect examples of "documentary," or uncontrolled lighting, as well.

2) Changes in light quality have been used by directors to control audience feelings. Recall films you have seen. Describe how the director used changes in lighting to signal changes in mood or timing. Could other methods have been used to signal the changes in mood or time? Would they have been as effective?

3) The following exercise can help you learn about the way directors control lighting. Practice lighting on a person's face. Have your subject sitting down in a darkened room. Have an assistant hold a flashlight or use a reflector light on a stand or use a light you can aim easily, as your main or *key light*. (Don't confuse the term "key light" with "high-key" or "low-key." The key light is simply the light in a shot that supplies the majority of the light hitting the subject.)

Aim the light head at your subject from the same height as his face. Notice how flat and two-dimensional the lighting is. Keeping the light at eye level, move the light (or the subject, whichever is easier) slowly so that the light hits the subject from the side. Stay in front of the subject yourself and watch the changes in lighting as the light progresses to the side. Notice how the person's face loses its flatness and gains a three-dimensional appearance with *side lighting*. Keep moving the light around back. Note how extreme side lighting, or *rim lighting*, creates an interesting effect, and how *back lighting* forms a "halo" separating the subject from the background.

Now repeat the experiment with the light shining *down* from a 45 degree angle above the subject onto his or her face. Put the light *underneath* the subject for a horror film effect. Aim the light directly down at the subject and notice the effect of *top lighting*.

If you have two lights, you may want to experiment with a *fill light*. When you moved the main light around your subject, you noticed that although the shadows it created gave the subject a three-dimensional appearance, some of the shadows were too dark and proved to be distracting. When the light was aimed down at a 45 degree angle to your subject's face, for example, you probably noted that the eyes were in shadow. A fill light, placed about twice as far away as the main light, can brighten up these dark shadows without eliminating them. For example, a fill light at eye level almost head on, can lighten up, without erasing, the shadows created under a subject's eyes by a main light aimed down at a subject. Experiment with a fill light to determine where it could be helpful in controlling the problems created by a main light.

4) If you have a still camera, or a movie camera, you may want to take pictures of each of these lighting experiments. Label and display each shot.

SHOOTING INDOORS

Shooting a film indoors can give a director much greater control over certain aspects of filmmaking. This crew of filmmakers is shooting a 16mm color instructional film on the use of the library for a large educational film company.

1) Camera angles are important in any film. The director prepares to shoot an over-the-shoulder zoom shot of the student's work. He has attached an electric motor to the zoom lens to create a smooth zoom-in.

2) Zooming the lens to telephoto to create a shallow depth of field, the director plans to create a shot where the focus will change during shooting. One area in the frame will go out of focus and another will come into sharp focus. His assistant uses a grease pencil to mark each of the two points the director needs on the focus scale.

3) During shooting, the director's assistant turns the focus ring of the lens between the two grease marks he has made to create the shift-of-focus shot.

4) Indoor shooting requires lights. Each different camera set-up will require moving of existing lights and possible addition of new ones.

5) A dolly with a boom attached gives the director mobility. He has chosen the French-made Eclair NPR 16mm camera, a self-blimped, relatively silent camera, and a 12-120mm f.2.2 Angenieux zoom lens.

6) Lighting presents two problems to a director. He's got to have enough light and light must "look good". Because the library he's filming in is brightly lit by ceiling lights, the director is using them as his *main light* (the main light is the light source that provides the *quantity* of light needed for shooting). The lights he sets up will simply be *fill lights* to create an appealing *quality* of light and to fill in some of the "problems" created by the main light.

7) Measuring the quantity of lights is necessary since few professional cameras have built-in light meters. An *incident light meter* such as this one, when held at the subject's position and aimed back at the camera, measures the quantity of light *falling on* a subject.

13

COLOR

It's a colorful world. Color is everywhere, all around us, and more than that, we're surrounded by colors that tell us things, communicate ideas to us, make us feel different. Red lights tell us to stop, gray clouds suggest a storm, yellow signs warn us a curve is ahead on the road, blue rooms relax us, green rooms are cool, black clothes remind us of mourning, and white is traditional for a bride.

A filmmaker can choose to use the effects color has on us, or he can choose not to. Color, this natural part of our lives, is another tool in the hands of the creative film director.

When films first started, only black and white film stock was available; that was all directors could use. But even early filmmakers were intrigued by the reality that color could provide and wanted to be able to employ color. One method of producing color on the screen was to paint each frame of the movie by hand, a difficult task. Even so, many filmmakers did this, as far back in film history as 1902. They hand-colored a frame of film as small as one inch by one and a fourth inches, doing it about sixteen times for each second of film. This kind of effort suggests how badly filmmakers wanted color for their films.

Inventors soon developed new color processes for film. In 1908 the British came up with a cumbersome color film method called Kinemacolor, but the color was so distorted that the process was not used for very long. In America a forerunner of the Technicolor process was developed and was first used in Douglas Fairbanks' film *The Black Pirate* (1926). Sound arrived just about this time, however, and people became so excited at hearing movies that they forgot about the joy of looking at them, and interest in color died out. By 1935, though, people were accustomed to sound and were looking for something new.

In that year, Hollywood director Rouben Mamoulian made *Becky Sharp* in the new Technicolor process. This first attempt at color film might have been a disaster. Garish costumes, with attempts to use every color at least once in every shot, would be what you would expect. (When 3-D was first developed in the early fifties, one of the first directors chosen to use the process had only one eye. He couldn't see or appreciate the stereo effect of what he was directing. As a result, the technique was overused in his films.)

Color, however, was used successfully in Mamoulian's film *Becky Sharp*. At one point, Mamoulian wanted to prepare his audience for the bloody battle of Waterloo, which was the next scene in his film. He used a party scene, with bright, blood-red capes and cloaks. This creative use of red to foreshadow a bloody battle was a classic example of how color could be used in film communication.

Color is an expected part of most modern feature films, such as the 1975 feature **Jaws**.

THE USE OF COLORS

The excitement of early directors for color is not surprising. A good director can use color in many ways to communicate with his audience. Even when talking, we often refer to the feelings which particular colors generate in us. We say, "I feel blue today," "She's green with envy," "He's red with rage," "He's in a black mood," "I'm feeling in the pink." Such statements refer to the psychological effect which colors have on us. Yellow, for example, is a "hot" color, reminding people of fire; but it is also a "sour" color because it is associated with the tangy flavor of lemon. And yellow also conveys the feeling of cowardice; people call somebody "yellow" for refusing to do something daring.

Advertisers also use colors to generate feelings in people. They choose colors very carefully for their merchandizing campaigns to capitalize on natural feelings. Cigarettes flavored with menthol are sold in packages with blue or green colors to emphasize that the product inside is so cool that the buyer need take only a puff, and it's springtime. Some beer companies wish to emphasize the idea of cooling refreshment and, for this reason, stress cool colors in their ads, claiming for instance, to come from a land of sky-blue waters. Mouthwashes which cool one's throat and have a cool mint flavor are usually colored blue, just as are antifreezes and summer coolants, which do the same job for your car's radiator. Every magazine contains many examples of advertising which uses cool colors like blue and green, hot colors like red and yellow, or other colors to communicate feelings to us.

We speak in such phrases about the feelings a color represents, but a filmmaker can use the actual color to create the same feeling directly.

Directors found ways to communicate the feelings specific colors engender even before color film was invented. Along with handcoloring film, early directors would also tint the copies of their movies that were shown in theaters. By dipping the films in tinting chemicals, a director could produce almost any color he would want to use. Black and white movies, like the ones we see today, were almost never used in the days of silent film. Direc-

tors used tints of red, blue, yellow, green, and lavender to communicate the feelings of these colors.

When an early director wanted to suggest night in his film or a cold feeling, he would tint his film blue. More recently, Roman Polanski used this same technique in his short film, *When Angels Fall*. When his film shows an old woman going about her job in a public lavatory, the black and white film is tinted blue. The viewer experiences the coldness with which people treat the old lady.

Red and reddish colors were used for fire sequences by early silent film directors because they knew red produces a feeling of excitement and danger in people. D. W. Griffith hand-colored the costumes of the Ku Klux Klan members a pink color for his 1915 film *Birth of a Nation*. This strong use of color intensified the emotional impact of the scene: The Klan is racing to save a young Southern girl from dishonor. The use of bright costumes for the Klan, plus the tinting of the flames of the fire around which the Klan met, allowed Griffith, a Southerner, to express his admiration for what he considered the heroism of the Klan. One film historian believes this sequence of *Birth of a Nation*, heightened in emotional impact by its strong use of color, contributed a great deal toward making heroes of the Klan members and was even a factor in the revival of the Ku Klux Klan not long after *Birth of a Nation* was shown throughout America. That is a lot to say for color, but the emotional impact of color is deeply ingrained in all of us.

Russian director Sergei Eisenstein shot his famous silent film *The Battleship Potemkin* in black and white. But that didn't stop him from using color as an important signaling device in his film. At the climax of his movie, another battleship approaches the *Potemkin*, which has been taken over by the revolutionaries. Tension builds up. Are the sailors of the approaching ship friendly to the cause of the revolution, or are they still loyal to the Czar? Eisenstein cuts back and forth between the ships to build up tension. Finally, the strange ship unfurls a red flag; they are friends. Eisenstein had to shoot the film with a white flag and color it red on each copy of the film he showed. Although artists using special stencils usually performed this exacting job of hand-coloring, Eisenstein was so excited

about seeing the red flag on the first copy of the film that he took red ink and colored the flag in himself.

Because we are always surrounded by color, we sometimes seem blind to the effect that color can have on us. It might be that we must step outside our environment for a while before we can really notice color. Watching our environment enlarged on a movie screen can separate us from our day to day surroundings enough to help us see color. An example of a film that controls the environment for the maximum effect of color is the short film *The Big Shave*.

The Big Shave is a bloody account of a man shaving. Because the color red is important in his film, the director deliberately made red more apparent. Everything in the setting of his film, a bathroom, is white, colored with a tinge of cool blue. Much of the impact of the blood, when it finally starts to flow, is due to the fact that the director has used only white and blue colors earlier.

Federico Fellini was careful to use enough red in his 1971 film on circus clowns, appropriately named *Clowns*. Because red is a color people associate with clowns and circuses, Fellini controls the red shadings so that they come out extremely bright and deep.

Light brown, or **sepia**, is an important color for filmmakers because it usually reminds audiences of old photographs. Before scientists discovered processes to make photographic prints permanent, photographers used to tint their prints with brown tones to make them last longer. Today, directors can use these same toners to attain an old-fashioned look in their films. Directors can film sequences in black and white, and then tint them brown and white. Often, when magazines print old photographs, they use brown ink to get this same old-fashioned effect.

Edmond Sechan, directing his short film *The Stringbean* (1964), employed both color and this brown and white tint to tell his story. To impress his viewers with the drabness of the life of an old lady in her home, Sechan used black and white film. But to express her happiness and freedom when she goes out to the Tuileries Gardens near her home, Sechan filmed in color. Sechan then tinted all except a short section of the black and white sequences to make them brown and white. In this way he stressed the fact of the woman's old age.

The Stringbean is somewhat similar to the story in Polanski's *When Angels Fall*, but in important aspects it is a very different film. The coolness of the blue and white tinted sequences of Polanski's film is replaced in *The Stringbean* by a feeling of age, of aloneness. Could Sechan's film have been as effective, toned in the blue color Polanski chose for his film? Probably not. Polanski's film deals with rejection, with the coldness with which people treat an old lady. Sechan's film, on the other hand, deals with an old lady who is attached to a stringbean plant she grows in her home. Brown tints express the warmth the old lady in Sechan's film feels for something she has grown. The one film uses blue to express coolness; the other film uses brown to express warmth, growth, as well as old age.

In his feature film *A Man and a Woman*, director Claude Lelouch provides another example of the careful use of color in communicating with his audience. Viewers who watch the film on black and white television sets miss most of the effects that

Lelouch employed. When the man and woman of the film first meet, the director used black and white film tinted cool blue to tell his audience that their love relationship hasn't developed yet; they're still cool to each other. As the film continues, Lelouch used several colors and various tints of black and white film to express how the people on the screen feel. In one scene, Lelouch uses black and white film tinted bright yellow to help the audience experience the warmth of their relationship. But suddenly, the woman remembers her husband, who has died. In a flashback, she is rolling in the snow with him, laughing happily; this shot is in bright, garish color.

When the flashback ends, the yellow and white photography has changed to cool blue and white. Simply by changing colors with tinting, Lelouch was able to tell his audience that although the woman feels a real warmth for the man, the happiness she knew with her husband puts a chill on this romance.

BLACK AND WHITE VERSUS COLOR

Sometimes, we might hear it said that a person "lives in a gray world." When such phrases are used, they refer to the feelings that directors can give us directly by using black and white film. In fact, directors many times have made use of the different effect from color film that black and white has on an audience.

In choosing their type of film, directors have come to realize that color generally gives an audience a feeling of happiness and black and white makes it experience depression or harsh reality. Not long ago, directors would use black and white film when they wanted to make "serious" films, or films that dealt with dull, depressing topics. *The Seventh Seal*, Ingmar Bergman's treatment of death, would be hard to imagine in color, as would most of his other films. *Billy Budd* was shot in black and white, director Peter Ustinov said, to make it more real. The 1974 film *Lenny* was shot in black and white to gain the effects of reality and

Color is used in parts of the short film **The Stringbean** to communicate the old lady's joy at being outside.

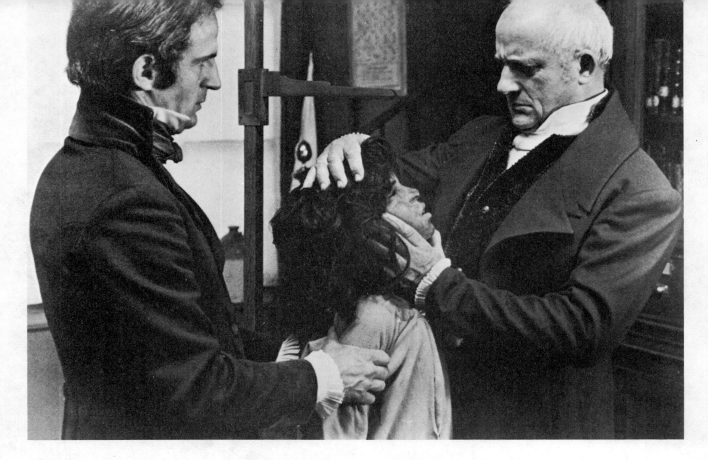

depression in the life of Lenny Bruce. *The Wild Child*, created in a historical setting, was filmed by Francois Truffaut using techniques meant to remind his audience of the 1915 style of director D.W. Griffith, and like Griffith's films, *The Wild Child* is a black and white film. Director Peter Bogdanovich shot *The Last Picture Show* and *Paper Moon* in black and white to capture a particular feeling.

The association of black and white with reality is something we have become accustomed to by exposure to black and white news photographs, black and white newsreels, and black and white photographs in many news magazines. We even say, "Show it to me in black and white." And although the phrase refers to printing, it still evidences the fact that things in black and white seem more real or truthful to us.

Director Peter Bogdanovich has said that black and white is less real because life is in color. But black and white, he says, seems more real because people grow up with black and white news photographs and associate the tough, harsh look of black and white with reality. Color, Bogdanovich notes, often looks "pretty." Orson Welles claims that one

Wild Child, by Francois Truffaut (left in photo above) was filmed using 1915 techniques and black and white.

of the mysterious truths of the movies is that actors give better performances in black and white than they do in color.

There was another reason, not long ago, for the director to use black and white film, especially if he planned to make a serious film. Serious films weren't very popular; not many people would go to see them. And since black and white film was quite a bit cheaper than color, these movies were filmed in black and white.

A movie which uses both black and white and color film offers viewers a unique opportunity to understand how the two modes of photography affect an audience differently. By viewing a film which uses both kinds of photography, an audience can compare its reactions to the various sections of the film and realize more clearly why a director might choose one or the other mode for shooting an entire film.

Roman Polanski, in his short film *When Angels Fall*, used both color and black and white film. As mentioned earlier, *When Angels Fall* tells the story of an old lady who works in a public lavatory in Poland. Her existence is ugly and boring, as could be expected from her job. Polanski underlined this for the audience by using black and white film and harsh realistic lighting to communicate the depression of her life and the stark ugliness of her surroundings.

From her sub-street situation, she hears and sees things which remind her of her childhood, when she was happy and beautiful. Flashbacks depict various events in her past life. Polanski chose to employ color in these flashbacks, thus distinguishing them from the harsh reality of her present life. With this technique, Polanski informs the audience which part it is viewing and how it should react.

Chromophobia, a short animated film, demonstrates how directors can use black and white tones inside a color film to communicate particular ideas to their audiences. A black-and-white clad army marches through the film, draining color from everything, changing people to prisoners clothed, like the army, in black and white. The standardization of the army, expressed by their lack of color, suggests visually how a desire for conformity can destroy individuality. The director of *Chromophobia*, Raoul Servais, then used color to show how individuality can overcome conformity. One little girl has saved a red flower from the army. This spark of color serves as the beginning of a rally; the people beat back the dull army of black and white conformity and restore their color-filled world.

Many people have trouble understanding the color techniques used in Lindsay Anderson's film

Black and white helped Ingmar Bergman communicate the depressing feeling of Death in **The Seventh Seal**.

If (1970). Scenes in *If* change from color to black and white and back again without apparent reason. Some critics have explained these puzzling changes by saying that Anderson wanted to remind his audience that the whole film is a fantasy, and by changing back and forth he keeps his audiences from becoming too involved in the movie.

There is another explanation, however, for the use of color and black and white in *If*. Although the fantasy explanation is probably true, another reason is that Anderson ran short of money during the shooting of *If* and still hadn't filmed certain long shots inside a large cathedral. Rather than spend the large amount of money necessary to rent lights and generators and make the entire cathedral bright enough to shoot color film, Anderson decided to film these shots in black and white. With black and white film, he could get away with much less light. And because these shots by themselves would stick out, he also selected other shots to film in black and white.

Is It Always Right to Be Right?, a 1971 Academy Award winning short film, also uses both color and black and white film in its presentation of a generation gap. Two generations are presented in the film as two worlds, growing farther and farther apart. As they do, color drains from each of them. Finally, both sides admit that each of them may possibly be wrong, and immediately color returns.

The habit we have of identifying black and white with reality more than color is changing. Roman Polanski, director of *When Angels Fall*, told Gene Siskel, film critic for the *Chicago Tribune*, that color is a part of life and that the notion that black and white films are more realistic and earthy is the result of an accident: Photography began with black and white film. Actually, Polanski pointed out, black and white images are unimaginable until they are seen.

For the present, however, the choice between using black and white and color film is limited for a director. Audiences, aware of the higher prices they pay for color television and for color photo film, feel cheated when they see a black and white movie, as if the director didn't care enough to use the best equipment. Consequently, directors have

had to find methods of communicating with color film the drabness and unhappy feeling which black and white film can communicate so effectively. If a director is trying to shoot an unhappy scene and he is using bright, happy colors, he's only working against himself.

If he is careful, a director *can* achieve drabness in color film, and thus make his audience experience depression. Only recently has this technique been in practice, however; earlier it was easier for the filmmaker to use black and white film in the first place, rather than to try to work with subdued colors. The reason for this was that many hands touch a color print after the film leaves the director. If a director had planned a subdued color sequence, it might be so in the first copy. Later copies of the film, however, produced perhaps by an over-ambitious printer who liked to show how bright he could make prints, would turn out to be bright and garish. Only lately, moreover, has the color process itself been sufficiently controllable.

One early example of the use of drab, naturalistic color photography to set a mood for a story may be familiar to viewers of late-night television movies. Director Nicholas Ray's 1955 feature starring the late James Dean, *Rebel Without a Cause*, used the Warner color process, which was able to create a world picture drab enough for this story of senseless death.

COLOR'S ADVANTAGES

Modern filmmaker Roger Corman prefers to use color film for his movies. Corman likes to turn out films quickly, with low budgets. And he prefers to work on location, rather than in a studio. With black and white film, Corman has said it is necessary to cast a certain number of shadows to give an impression of depth in a scene. But with color film, a director need only contrast the color of his subject with the background to create depth. This saves the filmmaker time and therefore money. Corman also believes that because of this color

British director Peter Watkins chose black and white film to give a newsreel feeling of reality to his make-believe documentary **The War Game**.

films seem more realistic: In order to create shadows for depth, filmmakers sometimes had to use overly dramatic styles of lighting. Color, on the other hand, can be lighted flatly, easily, like a normal room.

One famous movie in which color is well controlled for its impact on the audience is Albert Lamorisse's short film *The Red Balloon*. In this film the main character is a large, bright red balloon, possessing many human characteristics. To give the audience the impression that the balloon is from another world, the world of fantasy, director Lamorisse photographed his movie in drab colors, with many grays and browns. This lack of color stresses the fact that the only brightness in the life of the young boy who owns the balloon centers on the dazzlingly bright red toy.

Since there is no dialog in the film, Lamorisse was forced to communicate the drabness and dullness of the boy's life, and the beauty of the fantasy world which the balloon brings to the boy, by visual means alone. *The Red Balloon* demonstrates successfully how color, in the hands of an experienced director, can communicate both feelings and ideas to an audience. The final sequence of *The Red Balloon* shows Pascal, the young boy, finally leaving the everyday world for the world of fantasy. In this scene colors finally rush into the boy's life, for Lamorisse has withheld color in his film until it really mattered.

Could *The Red Balloon* have been made in black and white, with the feeling of reality which black and white usually gives? Or would the reality we associate with black and white have overpowered the fantasy of the film? This question would be only a matter for discussion had Lamorisse not filmed the same story eleven years earlier in black and white. In *White Mane*, a young boy, tied to the everyday world, acquires a powerful white stallion. The reaction of the routine world is the same in both films, as is the ending. It's interesting to note, however, that *White Mane* is in several respects less a fantasy film than is *The Red Balloon*.

Carefully controlled colors add much to the effect of Albert Lamorisse's short film **The Red Balloon**. The bright color of the balloon lights the boy's world.

Larry Yust, who produced *Dr. Heidegger's Experiment* for the Short Story Showcase of Encyclopedia Brittanica Educational Corporation, wanted to capture in his color film the feeling of age which Nathaniel Hawthorne wrote into the story originally. Because it's an old story, about old people, Yust was very careful to use color to underline the feeling of oldness in the film. To achieve this, Yust used extremely brown tones in his photography and brown objects decorating the set. Since he was working with color film, Yust had to control the lighting and the processing of his color film to make sure that what started out as a very brownish film wasn't "fixed up" along the way by a printer.

Later on, Yust made another film for the series, *The Princess or the Tiger?* Yust added as much color as he could to this fantasy tale. He shot with color film, black and white film tinted various colors, negative color film in which peoples' faces look orange, like the negatives from color snapshots, and other strange effects to underline the fantasy in his film.

As more and more people acquire color televisions, and as newspapers print color news photos as regularly as they do black and white, the general attitude people have toward the added reality of black and white films will fade. Until it does, however, filmmakers who want to use color for realistic sequences usually must be careful to control the color well. With control, color film can be realistic, rather than the "Oh, look at that beautiful sky!" kind of color that distracts from reality by calling attention to itself.

In all these situations, we can see the importance of color in the language of film. A talented director will control color in his film as carefully as he controls time and light, to "color" his audience's response. One famous Italian director was so concerned with color in a film that when shooting a scene in a park, he felt that the grass wasn't the correct shade of green. So he hired painters to spray paint the entire park until the grass was the shade of green he wanted. Although it might be judged excessive in this case, such care for exact color suggests how important many directors feel color can be.

COLOR

ACTIVITIES

1) If you are scientifically inclined, find out how color film reproduces color. *Color as Seen and Photographed*, Eastman Kodak's Data Book #E74, (E74H in hard cover) is an inexpensive source of the principles behind color photography. Give a short lecture or explain the basic principles to others who do not understand them.

2) Carefully collect magazine advertisements and confirm the way in which some photographers use colors. The following checklist may help.

Blue, for primitive man, was the color of night, the time when he had to return to safety and could not hunt. Gazing at blue relaxes the viewer, reducing his blood pressure, pulse, and respiration. Blue is the color of loyalty ("true blue"). Dark blue is recommended as the best color for meditation.

Green is the cool color of the forest and as such represents permanence and resistance to change. It is also the color of envy ("green with envy") and can actually be perceived as an astringent, a "pucker up" color. It is the color of a healthy plant but an unhealthy person ("His face looked green" and of inexperience ("a green recruit").

Red is an energy-expanding color, speeding up the pulse and respiration, and increasing the blood pressure. It is the color of blood and danger and fire, the color of red lights and stop signs, the color of erotic desire.

Violet is a mixture of red and blue, retaining some of the properties of both colors. Needless to say, the feelings of two colors are hard to blend, and violet is the mystical color of enchantment, merging the relaxing surrender of blue with the hot conquest of red.

Yellow is bright and radiant, the color of the sun and the signal for primitive man that daylight had arrived and he could leave his cave and hunt. Yellow is a happy, light color, found in painting as the color of halos. Green ambition pursues prestige and importance; yellow pursues happiness and adventure. Yellow is the color of cowardice because of this: A person with a "yellow stripe" would rather pursue happiness than danger.

Brown is the color of the earth, of relaxation at home, of roots and family comfort, of down-on-the-farm hospitality. Greens, when teamed with brown, lose their "pucker-up" feeling and become natural, agricultural, organic.

Much research needs to be done on color and its effects on us. Color is not yet an exact science. But the filmmaker and communicator can be aware of possibilities and utilize them.

3) Look in the library for a book on the psychological effects of color and discuss your findings with others.

4) Write an outline for a simple film you would like to do and describe how you would use colors to enhance or create meanings. Imagine doing your film idea in other colors. How would this affect what you are trying to communicate in your film?

5) Are you color blind? Are any of your friends? Find a color blindness test card set and check yourself and your friends. You may be surprised. What colors are most color-blind people color blind to?

6) Colors influence our taste buds as well as our emotions. Make some flavored drinks with sugar water and flavoring extracts from the kitchen. Add some safe food colors and challenge a test panel to pick out the correct flavors. Use strange colors. You might want to color your lemon water red and your cinnamon water yellow, or your chocolate green and your mint brown. Does color have an effect on how you taste things?

SOUND

7

In one way or another, sound has been an integral part of the film experience since movies were first discovered. Some people talk about the great days of the silent movie. Movies, however, never were silent. Every theater in the days before sound films had some sort of sound-making device, ranging from pianos and organs to full-fledged orchestras. Today when we watch "silent" films without musical accompaniment, we are not viewing these films as they were meant to be viewed.

When most people talk about silent films, then, they are actually referring to the **non-dialog movie**, a movie in which nobody talks. Such films are of course still with us in the form of short, wordless films like *The Red Balloon, The Stringbean, Sky*, and many others. Films like these trace their history back to the non-dialog films of the early part of this century, to films such as the Charlie Chaplin shorts in which Charlie never speaks and which did not use titles between shots to simulate speech.

DIALOG

The **dialog films** also trace their history back to the story films of the early 1900's. And when

Before dialog was added to movies, D. W. Griffith explored an important social problem in his complex film **Intolerance**. Assisted by his able cameraman Billy Bitzer, Griffith filmed scenes of elaborate symbolism.

most people refer to sound films they are talking about the dialog film, in which the audience sees and hears people talking at the same time.

The possibilities of making a dialog film intrigued filmmakers from the very beginning. If people in films could talk, without needing to rely on titles inserted between shots to communicate their words, filmmakers knew that whole worlds of filmmaking possibilities would open up. And dialog films do offer the filmmaker greater possibilities for communicating with his audience: If characters can talk, they can tell people what they're thinking about. Films with dialog can explore new areas that non-dialog films simply cannot handle. Many ideas and concepts need the built-in precision of words for their expression.

From the very beginning of dialog, however, filmmakers ran into at least one problem: What do you do with the camera when somebody's talking? What do you show? If the filmmaker simply records the face of the person speaking, the visual part of the movie quickly becomes boring.

For a few years after the introduction of talking pictures, filmmakers did not have to face up to this problem of what to show their audiences while a person was talking. Audiences were so fascinated by the invention of **talkies** that they were easily satisfied. But when the thrill of seeing somebody talk wore off, their interest in talkies became more sophisticated. Once talkies were old hat, people

demanded that movies solve the problem of sound in creative ways.

One big secret that the filmmakers of the thirties discovered was that **talkies** need not be *all* talkies. Movies could show dialog scenes and then show audiences visual sequences for the rest of the film, sequences which did not have dialog.

Another difficulty which has perplexed filmmakers is that speaking has its own rhythm. If a character is talking, a filmmaker must wait until he is finished before he can change scenes. This problem of dialog still troubles filmmakers today. Dialog too frequently becomes the deciding factor in the rhythm of a sequence, and not the rhythm of the shots.

We can see that dialog is a mixed blessing for the filmmaker. It expands the world he or she can portray and provides the opportunity to communicate in a second medium. But a filmmaker must control the dialog in a movie to be sure that it doesn't become the master of the situation.

Most of the early dialog films turned back the clock to the time when film was simply a recording instrument, rather than a communication tool. Even today, some filmmakers fall into the trap of letting dialog do all the work, telling the audience their stories. Television programs, for example, too often depend upon dialog to do most of the communicating.

Dialog adds a new dimension to film. With words, a filmmaker can discuss deep philosophical issues in his or her films, as Ingmar Bergman does in **The Seventh Seal**. Knight Antonius Block talks with Death.

When is dialog useful in films? It is useful when a filmmaker chooses dialog scenes carefully, when with it he or she can provide an audience with information which it would not gain from the pictures, when dialog opens new dimensions to a filmmaker. When dialog *complements* the pictures which the filmmaker shows to an audience, then it is successful.

Sometimes a filmmaker will use most of his pictures to show his audience the *reaction* to a portion of dialog. When a filmmaker does this, he is allowing the pictures and the sound track to do different jobs. Instead of watching somebody speak, the audience hears the speech and sees how various people are reacting to the words. In this way, the filmmaker is using both the pictures and the words to communicate with us. He is also underlining the fact that an audience at a movie is usually more interested in the reaction to something than it is in the action itself.

In Lindsay Anderson's feature *This Sporting Life*, he shows the hero, David Hemmings, lying on a bed. Hemmings is wondering if he will be able to stay in the rooming house he has been living in.

Someone is heard walking up to him, but Anderson kept his camera focused on David Hemmings' face. A woman's voice tells him that he can stay. Footsteps are again heard going away. Instead of cutting to a shot of the woman who runs the boardinghouse, Anderson never showed her. He kept his camera focused upon the face of the person whose reaction the audience should be most interested in.

Dialog can also be used as a bridge between two scenes. In *No Reason to Stay*, Christopher Wood goes to his mother's office building to tell her that he has decided to quit school. As he approaches the building, his voice is heard talking to the receptionist even before he enters the building. The dialog bridges the gap between the two scenes. Earlier in the film, the same sort of sound transition is used to join a shot of Chris standing outside the school with a shot of him in a poetry class.

In the feature film *Downhill Racer*, a young skiing champion goes home to see his father, who is a farmer living out in the middle of nowhere. Robert Redford, the son, has been all around the world during the winter, competing in races and developing his skill. From the shots of the two people, the viewer knows that the father and his son live in two different worlds, and the possibility of communication between them is quite limited. But it is not until they finally attempt to talk to each other that we understand the barrier which exists between them: Redford's life as an athlete is a world where he wins one victory only to have to win another.

Redford tells his father about all of the places in Europe where he competed during the last season. His father is unimpressed; he asks his son when he's going to start earning money. Finally, he asks his son why he keeps up his practicing, if it doesn't earn him money. "To be a champion," says Redford. But his father is still unimpressed. "World's full of them," he replies.

This short scene tells much which pictures alone will not or cannot express. Pictures of Redford skiing are shown all through the film. The audience begins to wonder perhaps what drives him to do all that he does. The dialog scene gives the answer: He wants to be the best. But the dialog scene also suggests that "being the best" is a need that only people who want to be the best can understand.

Words in movies can convey exactly what a person feels, as in this shot from the film **The Graduate**, directed by Mike Nichols.

Words cannot express everything in films. Sometimes a filmmaker must rely on expressions and gestures, as in the 1970 feature **The Great White Hope**, with James Earl Jones.

Redford's desire to be a champion is lost on his father.

This scene is a good example of dialog well used because it communicates ideas about the people on the screen which pictures could not. The idea, however, is expressed only in a limited way by the words. To understand what "being the best" means, the shots of races and practices are needed also. For this reason, the scene ends immediately when Redford's father tells him that the world is full of champions; there's nothing more that dialog can say.

One of the classic examples illustrating the limits of dialog occurs in Elia Kazan's 1954 feature *On the Waterfront*. Terry Malloy is trying to explain to Edie his part in her brother's murder and to make excuses for himself. But words can't explain away hurts like these, and so director Kazan com-

pletely muffles Terry's explanation with the sound of a ship's horn. Not a word of the explanation can be heard by the audience or by Edie: She holds her ears to stop the pain.

Director Dalton Trumbo used the same technique in his 1971 film *Johnny Got His Gun*. Jim is trying to explain to his girl friend that he will come back from the war safely. She doesn't believe him, however, and his explanations, like Terry Malloy's, are covered up by the noise of a train pulling away from the station. In both examples, the noise came from an object naturally in the picture, which did not call attention to itself. In both cases, words, dialog, have reached the limit of expression.

NARRATION

Narration can suffer the same problems as dialog in films. If a filmmaker uses narration to describe something the audience already knows, the viewers will usually feel insulted. People expect narration to be more sophisticated than the Dick and Jane commentary and expect a narrator to use a type of **counterpoint** with the picture. An example of a failure in this counterpoint technique offers some insight into what audiences expect. *Cattle Ranch*, a short film produced by the National Film Board of Canada, was produced to acquaint viewers with the way life goes on at a big ranch. The structure of the film is seasonal; sections of spring, summer, fall, and winter are presented. Some of the narration, provided by a woman's voice, adds a great deal to the pictures. But some of it simply repeats what is already known from looking at the screen. After the sections of the film on spring and summer, a long shot is shown of a hill covered with trees. The trees are covered with autumn leaves, and the leaves are falling to the ground. After this shot, the narrator states, "It is fall." Narration such as this, which simply repeats what everybody in the audience already knows, adds nothing to a film.

Although counterpoint between sound and shots is a desirable match and will be mentioned again in connection with music, narration which conflicts in rhythm with the shots creates an undesirable effect. Filmmakers know that when viewers go to see a film they are there primarily to see it, to watch it, and only secondarily are they there to hear the film. When filmmakers must deal with shots which are extremely rhythmic, they may try to reflect the rhythm of the shots with a poetic commentary of some sort. Pare Lorenz tried to mirror the rolling of the Mississippi in his 1937 documentary *The River*. Lorenz's shots had a pronounced rhythm of their own; so he tried to write a poetic commentary for the narration. The rhythm of the shots predominates, however, and the narration is only a poor accompaniment to the visuals. In listening to efforts like *The River*, it is evident that the words are being *forced* to match the pictures, and it's a case of the square peg in the round hole.

Night Mail also attempts to synchronize a poetic commentary with the rhythmic motion of a steam engine. Again, the rhythm of the shots is much too pronounced to allow the filmmaker to do anything but to try to force the words of his commentary into the rhythm of his images, and the strain shows. Poet W.H. Auden, as another example, wrote a commentary for the short film *Runner* which depicts the life of track star Bruce Kidd. Auden's commentary tries to add a new dimension to the pictures, and at times when the pictures do not have strong rhythms, he partially succeeds. For most of the film, however, when the visuals do have a strong rhythm, his commentary becomes a glaring failure to fit the rhythm of words with the rhythm of images.

If a filmmaker wishes to use a commentary which has its own rhythm he should choose pictures which will not conflict with the rhythm of the words. Working in the other direction, approaching a unity of rhythms working from pictures to words is a more difficult proposition. When Les Goldman wanted to produce a film based upon Maurice Ogden's poem *The Hangman*, he realized that visuals which had a strong rhythm would conflict with the rhythm of the poem. So he selected drawings which would not move and used them as accompaniment for the reading of the poem. Because the still drawings could be cut and dissolved together to fit the predetermined rhythm of the poem, Goldman was successful in combining pictures and poetic words.

Many times narration can be used to inform an audience of things which it would not know by watching the pictures on the screen. In his short film *Good Night, Socrates* student filmmaker Stuart Hagmann, who later directed the feature *The Strawberry Statement*, wanted to describe for his audience the destruction of part of Chicago's Greek neighborhood during the construction of a new university. The pictures center on one little boy and the effect that the destruction of his home and way of life has on him. The story is told, however, by the boy as an adult reacting to the events of his childhood shown on the screen. By using narration and pictures which occur at different times in the boy's life, director Hagmann was able to avoid the duplication of picture and sound. When Hagmann used a somewhat rhythmic poetic narration, he

chose visuals which do not have heavy rhythms; when he used rhythmic editing and pictures, he wisely switched to music rather than words for his sound track.

The sound track of a movie can sometimes crystallize the viewer's reaction to the images on the screen. The film *The Critic* shows a group of abstract images as visuals. The sound track, however, consists of remarks an old man in a theater is making to the visuals. Here, the narration informs the viewer what his reaction to the pictures on the screen is supposed to be.

Near the beginning of his feature *The Battle of Algiers*, director Gillo Pontecorvo shows a young man arrested for a crime. While he is being brought in by the police, a narrator states the man's name and his criminal record. Pontecorvo uses the narration to mention things the visuals could not. Again, the narrator adds information which helps the viewer to form his opinion of this character.

Sound itself can be extremely important in setting a mood for a scene. At the beginning of his film *Mockingbird*, Robert Enrico shows us a Civil War soldier watching his post on an especially eerie night. The sounds of the forest become as frightening to an audience as they are to the soldier. Unfortunately, *Mockingbird* was never meant to be shown as a separate film but as part of a trilogy with *Occurrence at Owl Creek Bridge* and *Chickamauga*. This scene in *Mockingbird* begins the film, and usually audiences are not as settled down as if they had been in a theater for an hour. Seen and heard properly, however, this scene communicates terror as much with sound as with visuals.

MUSIC

Music seems to be a more workable sound for filmmakers than words. Possibly the fact that film is more like music than words has something to do with this: Both music and film can be broken down into certain measurable units. For example, filmmaker Janos Vadasz collected a large number of shots of time-lapse pictures of the development of

Still pictures do not distract from the rhythm of Maurice Ogden's poem **The Hangman**.

a chick embryo with a microscopic camera. After he had collected the shots, Vadasz decided to find a piece of music which would match the rhythm of his pictures. He selected Beethoven's "Egmont Overture," a piece of music which seems to convey a feeling of triumph, of the development toward a strong finish which could be seen in his pictures. Vadasz carefully edited the shots he had collected to fit the mood and tempo of the music; quiet parts of the music matched restful movements of blood cells, faster movements of the embryo's heart fit with the developing intensity of the music. His film, *Overture/Nyitany*, represents a successful combining of two strong rhythmic patterns into one film. Rather than straining to blend the two rhythms, as is apparent when poetic narration is fitted into rhythmic visuals, *Overture/Nyitany* easily combines the two.

St. Matthew Passion stands halfway between the world of narration and the world of music. Filmmaker Tamas Cozny started with a singing rendition of St. Matthew's Gospel and edited images taken from films of the Nazi persecutions of the Jews in Germany prior to World War II. The rhythm of the music and the meaning of the words combine with the pictures to produce a film which says one thing and shows quite another. The audience tends to believe the pictures rather than the words. Experiencing the two together, however, usually produces a stronger effect upon audiences. A new meaning arises from the conflict of the sound and the pictures, just as Eisenstein claimed would happen when two shots conflict.

Carl Foreman was able to utilize this conflict between sound and picture in his 1962 feature *The Victors*. On the sound track an old recording, "Have Yourself A Merry Little Christmas," is playing. The song is light-hearted and happy. The picture which Foreman used, however, is quite different in emotion. A soldier who has deserted is being executed by a firing squad, and other troops have been marched out into the snowy field to witness the punishment. The moods of the two scenes conflict; rather than softening the horror of the visuals, however, the sound track makes the visuals still more horrible.

The Inheritance is a feature-length documentary which traces the rise of the labor movement in America. During one particular section of the film a familiar song is heard: "This land is your land/ This land is my land/From California/To the New York harbor." The pictures, however, depict a particularly violent chapter in the history of American labor, a time when laborers were being attacked and beaten in the streets. The conflict between what is heard and what is seen only increases the impact of the pictures.

The important thing a filmmaker must remember in choosing music for his film is that it somehow must *fit* the movie that he is making, even if it is used to create a conflict. The music in *On the Waterfront*, for example, is a very rich and dramatic sound, while the visuals in the film are drab and dull, reflecting the poor dockside surroundings. Taken together, the two do not seem to fit, and the conflict produces no meaning. The music from *Lawrence of Arabia*, however, does seem suitable for the dramatic surroundings of the movie. The "heavy" music of *2001: A Space Odyssey* is so well known and recognized that it has become a cliché, appearing in student films and even in a television commercial for a stomach antacid. When *2001* was made, however, the mood of the music fit the subject matter well.

When he was halfway into making his feature *The Graduate*, director Mike Nichols still had not decided what kind of music to use. At that same time, his brother came to visit him and happened to bring a Simon and Garfunkel album. Nichols felt that Simon and Garfunkel sounded like what he imagined Benjamin's voice to be; so he hired them to write new songs for the picture. In the end, however, Nichols decided to use music they had already written because it seemed to fit much better than what they wrote specially for the film. The words of "Sounds of Silence" sounded like what Nichols felt the film was about.

Glass, a short film by Bert Haanstra, shows us a factory where handmade glass is produced. To him the process of hand-blowing glass resembled the playing of musical instruments. So for most of his film, Haanstra cut the pictures he had collected to fit a light jazz-type score: As a saxophone sounds, an old man is puffing on a pipe inserted in a blob of molten glass. For another section of his film, Haanstra showed how machines produce large numbers of similar bottles. During this section, electronic, mechanical sounds are played.

Many times music will grow out of a film itself. In *Mockingbird*, one of the connecting threads of the entire movie is a particular melody which two young boys teach to their pet mockingbird. Here the music originates from the story itself and is not added to accompany the film.

A director may choose to let a piece of music determine his pattern of editing to a very precise level. Toward the end of his short film *Occurrence at Owl Creek Bridge*, Robert Enrico used the rhythm of his music to create an editing pattern for the sequence. Peyton Farquhar is running toward his wife. A shot of her through the trees, walking down from her house, is shown. Enrico used with it four measures, four beats apiece, of the "Living Man" theme heard earlier. Then comes a shot of Farquhar and only silence with it.

Enrico then began an intricate plan of shots, based entirely on the music. First, a shot of Abbie, walking toward her husband, is accompanied by two measures, four beats each, of the "Living Man" theme; but Enrico cut the shot at the end of the seventh beat, so that on the eighth beat of the music, there is a shot of Farquhar. The shot of Farquhar continues for one measure, four beats, of the countermelody to the "Living Man" theme. At the end of the four beats, the shot of Abbie returns for seven more beats of the melody and is cut in the same place as before. Again and again, Enrico repeated this same pattern, using the music to determine a careful pattern in his sequence. The same editing rhythm is followed even after the music fades out. The shot of Farquhar and Abbie together ends on the seventh beat of the rhythm established by the music; at the eighth beat, he is back at the bridge.

This technique of using music to determine the rhythm and time of the pictures occurs in many films, though not always in such a precise way as in Enrico's film. Fitting pictures to music seems

The sequence of shots suggests the intricate pattern based on music that Enrico uses in **Occurrence**.

to be a successful way to marry the two means of communication. Efforts to cut words to the tempo of visuals, or visuals to the tempo of words, usually are much less successful.

Grant Munro used a combination of music, silence, and noises in his animated film *Toys* to guide his audience in its reactions to various parts of his film. At the beginning of *Toys*, children are pushing against the glass of a store window filled with toys. The delighted murmurs of the children are mixed with a happy, fast-moving piece of music. Suddenly a group of war toys comes alive. Immediately the happy music stops, and there is only silence. Then the soldiers begin fighting a war, and the actual sounds of combat fill the sound track. Even though the war is being fought by toys, the sound track suggests that the experience is quite real for the children, whose faces are intercut into the sequence. At the end of the film the war also ends; other toys appear again, and the music from the beginning of the film returns. But now, it

sounds different. The happiness fails to reassure the audience that everything is all right again.

NOISE

Noise can also be an important communication tool for the filmmaker. If it comes from *within* the frame, such as in a situation when a noise is made by someone on the screen, noise adds reality to the pictures. If noises come to us from *outside* the frame, however, a filmmaker can describe two things at once: What's happening in the frame and also things which cannot be seen.

At the beginning of his feature *2001: A Space Odyssey*, director Stanley Kubrick uses the noises of animals from outside the frame surrounding a group of apes. Although the animals are never seen, they are heard. From their noises, it is evident

Toys, a short Canadian film, combines noise and music to section off different parts of the film.

that the family group of apes is being threatened by these animals, against whom they have no defense. At the end of his feature, Kubrick shows spaceman David Bowman in the bedroom of a cage in a zoo for humans. While Bowman is being investigated and reconstructed by superpowers, only the strange laughing sounds of the superpowers are heard; the audience is aware of their presence only by the sounds they make.

George Stevens' 1959 feature *The Diary of Anne Frank* uses noises that come from outside the frame to indicate various facts to the audience. While the Van Danns and the Franks hide from the Nazis in an attic above a spice factory, only pictures from inside the attic are seen. Noises from downstairs warn the characters that someone may have discovered their hiding place. Noises like the ringing of a telephone, the pounding of feet and fists on a door, and finally the frightening sound of a police siren, becoming louder and louder as it approaches their hiding place, suggest what is going on outside. Using this technique, director Stevens has imprisoned the audience in the attic along with his characters.

Filmmakers many times use noises to help them set the mood of a sequence or an entire film. The war noises in *Toys*, for example, help express much more horror and violence than are in the pictures.

In the 1970 feature *Downhill Racer*, several shots of a skier performing a swift downhill run are seen. Only those sounds are used which tell something about what's happening on the screen. Sounds of heavy breathing suggest how exhausting the race is, sounds of skis leaving the ground and touching it again indicate the precision body control necessary to ski in such a manner. At times, only silence is heard; at other times, the beeping of the timing clock reminds the audience of the split-second timing necessary to win the race—or at least make it to the bottom of the hill alive.

During many sections of *Downhill Racer*, only the cold wind is heard whipping through the trees. The sound of the wind communicates the feeling of isolation that a person can feel on the top of a mountain. Throughout all of the sound track of David Lean's feature *Lawrence of Arabia*, the same sound of wind is used, emphasizing the loneliness of the terrain in the pictures.

For many of his experimental animations, Canadian filmmaker Norman McLaren creates his own sound tracks by drawing directly onto the film. Since the sound track of motion picture film creates sound by optical means—altering the amount of light that can shine through a piece of film—McLaren draws a sound track for his films simply by painting various shapes in the area where the sound track should go. Electronic sounds which fit his pictures thus appear on the sound track. Films like *Blinkity Blank*, *Boogie-Doodle*, *Dots*, and *Loops* are good examples of this technique, and the documentary film *Pen Point Percussion* describes how McLaren creates his sound tracks with pen and ink.

Sound and picture merge in Francois Truffaut's feature film *The Wild Child*. Victor, the "wild child" who has been brought up in the forest and has never learned to talk, is being educated by Citizen Itard. Itard tries over and over again to teach Victor to talk; when he finally utters the word *lait* (milk), the sound seems to be as exciting for the audience as it is for his teacher, because we have waited so long to hear it.

SILENCE

Silence may sometimes be the most effective type of sound. Now that films have learned to speak, they can sometimes speak eloquently with silence. *Ballad of Love*, a short Russian film about a deaf-mute girl, uses silence extensively to communicate the feeling of silence that the girl in the film experiences constantly. In *Ballad of Love*, the use of silence allows the audience to enter into the world of a deaf person; as a result, during the portions of the film when sounds are heard, they seem different.

Although sound is usually secondary in importance to pictures in the total movie experience, taken together the two channels of communication can tell the audience a great deal. The universal languages of pictures and music, merged with the specific and intellectual language of words, combine to form the movie as we know it.

SOUND

ACTIVITIES

1) Sound can be effective in many ways. Recall and describe examples that you remember of effective uses of narration, of music, of sound effects, of dialog, of silence.

2) Directors of television commercials spend great amounts of money to create effective theme songs and music for their films. Sometimes, the music is more memorable than the product. Interview a film composer, either by telephone or letter, to find out the special problems film composers have and how they solve them. Perhaps the composer will have a sample reel of his or her work. Find a composer in any big city's Yellow Pages under "Music— Arrangers & Composers." Or get the address of a composer from an advertising agency.

3) Published film scripts, available in paperback for many "classic" films, offer excellent sources for study of how filmmakers get around the problem of dialog. Pick a dialog sequence, study it, and report: What does the camera show while the speaker is talking: the speaker? the listener? somebody else? something else?

4) Learn how to splice and edit ¼-inch reel-to-reel audio tape. It's a fairly simple technique, described elsewhere in this book. Specific instructions for splicing tape usually come with the tape splicer. For practice, interview someone for two minutes on tape. Play the tape. Then edit out all the questions, leaving only the words of the person you interviewed.

5) Select a short film or commercial which has no dialog. Watch the film a few times with the sound on the projector turned off. Then create two different sound tracks for the film. You may use dialog, narration, music,

noise, or any combination of sounds you choose; but try to make each of the two sound tracks unique.

6) Watch a movie or made for TV film and note the different kinds of sound the director has selected. How many sounds are included and what is the effect of each?

7) Make a sound show. Collect sounds and edit them into a sound performance. Maybe you'll want to make a radio show by the seashore, complete with slapping waves, whooshing wind, and splashing water. Or perhaps a Lone Ranger episode or similar type story interests you. Produce thunder by rattling a sheet of metal. Produce horses hooves by using coconut halves on a desk. Or purchase a sound effects record and create a really effective radio show. Sound effects records can usually be purchased from a large record store. Radio stations may even give you old 78 rpm sound effects records. Whatever you do, use lots of effects. Insert a commercial in the middle of your show if you want. Do a good job.

8) Collect some old tapes or records of some of the classic radio shows that existed in the days BTV (Before Television). In these BTV years, suspense and comedy shows reached great heights of sound creativity. Today, collections of these early shows are available on record and tape. Study an episode and play it for the class. Interview people who would remember the shows using your tape recorder and edit their remarks into a tape. Do some research on your own and add a commentary to their remarks.

MAKING A SOUND FILM

Sound is an integral part of a modern film. In conjunction with the visuals, sound adds an entire new channel of communication to a film. Producing a final print of a film involves various steps.

1) If a narrator is required, his or her voice must be recorded and cut to fit the visuals.

2) Editing sound and pictures together provides a great opportunity for film communication, but editing sound can be more restrictive than editing visuals alone. The editor uses a *work print* of the pictures, an exact copy of the original film.

3) Synchronous sound editing is easiest on an editing table, although other methods are used. The picture is visible on the screen in front of the editor and comes from the picture roll threaded nearest to the screen. This editor is threading the second roll of sound on to the second magnetic tape head. Thus, he can run picture, dialogue, and narration synchronously to see if any need to be changed.

4) Once each track is in synch and marked, the filmmaker goes to a sound studio and has the various tracks adjusted in volume and balance and mixed into one track which will match the edited visuals on the work print.

5) While watching the work print on the screen, the filmmaker tells the sound engineer the relative volume each track must have.

6) Once the sound mix has been finished, the original film must be cut to *conform* to the edited work print. The edge numbers on the side of the work print and original help somewhat, but the job is tedious and exacting: One frame ruined and an entire film will be out of synch.

7) Complex equipment is necessary to print the sound track and the two rolls of original shots onto one *married print*.

8) Exacting chemical analysis of developing solutions is necessary for consistent results in processing.

9) The final printed copy of the film passes through the various processing solutions in a continuous strip which must never touch itself, and with time and temperature accurately controlled.

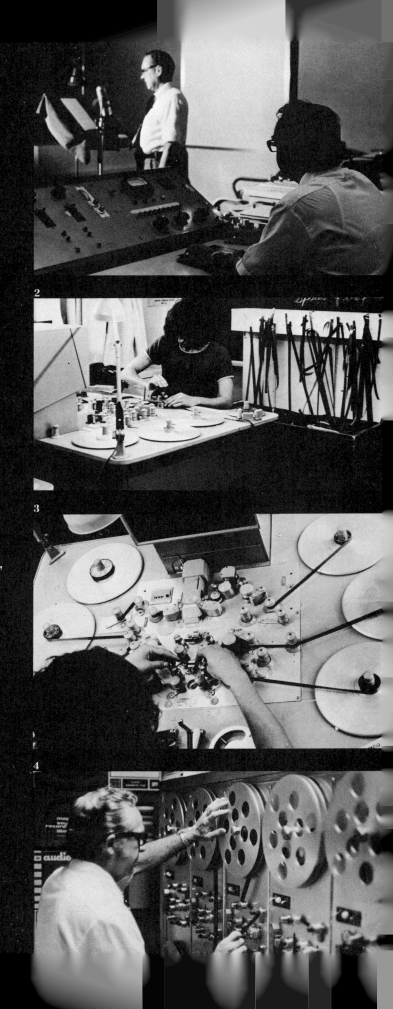

2

3

4

THE DIRECTOR

8

Motion and color, light and sound, creating shots and ordering them in a special way—these are the tools of film language, ways in which a person can communicate with film. Now we should talk about the director, the person who decides how these tools should be used.

Before we discuss the relationship of a director to his or her films, let's first look at some examples of the relationship between a person and speech. Suppose, on walking home from school some afternoon, you hear someone call to you from behind. "Hello, Jim," you might call back. Without turning around, you know who the person is. The reason for this is that you recognized the sound of his voice, that is, his *style* of speaking. At another time, suppose you are listening to a friend's account of a conversation she was in earlier. "Who were those guys?" you ask her. "I don't know," she says. "But there was this one guy who was always talking about his new girl friend." You reply, "That's Jack; that's all he ever talks about." This time you recognized the person by what he talks about, what he's *concerned with* most of the time.

In both of these examples, a person's identity was established by his speech. Everyone has personal characteristics in their speech, and by getting

Orson Welles not only directed Hollywood features in his early career but acted in them as well. He played the part of Kane in his first film **Citizen Kane** (1941).

to know somebody, by spending time with him, you come to know some of these particular characteristics of speech. You know how he talks and what he always talks about.

THE DIRECTOR'S STYLE

It has often been mentioned that film and speech are both modes of communicating. In both media, moreover, people communicate in their own personal way. And just as you can pick out one of your friends by how he uses speech or by what he's always talking about, so you can identify a director by how he uses film, what tools he uses and how he uses them, and by what he's always concerned about in his films, his content.

We have already talked about sound and how film directors can use it to communicate. As an example of how a director's techniques become recognizable as his, let's look at how one film director uses sound in his films in his own particular manner. Director Roman Polanski, before he started directing feature-length movies, made a number of short films. All of the short films are similar in at least one way: They do not use dialog sound to communicate, but rather music and some natural sounds. Polanski feels that using speech in his short films would make them too complicated, too much like full-length films. When people start talking, says Polanski, you expect to see a two-

The short films of Roman Polanski all have a similar appearance and deal with similar subjects. From **Two Men and a Wardrobe**.

hour movie. So when Polanski communicates using a short film, his *style* doesn't include words.

In *When Angels Fall*, one of Polanski's short films, the only sounds to be heard are music and certain natural sounds that Polanski amplified much louder than normal so that the audience cannot help but notice them. Water dripping, feet marching, doors creaking, toilets flushing, all are sounds that Polanski feels will tell something about the dreariness of his setting, a public restroom. Amplified loudly, with a hollow ring to them, such sounds communicate a feeling of loneliness, boredom, depression, hollowness. And for much of his film, Polanski shut off even natural sounds and used only music. The music suggests to the audience how to feel, how to react.

The short film *Two Men and a Wardrobe*, which Polanski made in 1958, one year before *When Angels Fall*, uses sounds in a similar way. Only if natural sounds are important for communication are they used. Since the film deals with two men experiencing our world for the first time, noises are heard which underline the ugliness and cruelty the two men experience. When one of the people the two men pass by is pickpocketing another person under the guise of friendship, the audience hears the phony laughter of the pickpocket. A drunk staggers up some steps, then staggers back down again; his footsteps are amplified loudly. One character is smashing a man's face with a rock; the dull thuds as the rock hits the victim and the vic-

tim's moaning are heard. These sounds, like the sounds Polanski used in *When Angels Fall*, are amplified much louder than normal. And for most of *Two Men and a Wardrobe*, as in *When Angels Fall*, music suggests the audience's reactions and marks the changes in mood during the film.

The use of music as an important communication technique continues in Polanski's two later short films, *The Fat and the Lean* and *Mammals*, both made in 1960. In these films, changes in music again indicate places where the audience should react differently.

These four short films don't just sound alike; they look alike, too. Polanski's personal style shows through in what the audience *sees* as well as in what it hears. Making subjects or situations look realistic in his short films never seems to be one of Polanski's chief concerns. In *When Angels Fall*, a young man is forcibly drafted by some soldiers. The struggling of the man and the actions of the soldiers resemble dances more than they do real fighting. In one of the scenes in *Two Men and a Wardrobe*, a watchman chases the men out of a junkyard filled with used barrels. The watchman beats them with a barrel stave, but again rather than being realistic, the action is more like a dance.

In *Mammals* and *The Fat and the Lean*,

Polanski continues this non-realistic, pantomime style of visuals. In *Mammals*, two men, now with a sled rather than a wardrobe, take turns pulling each other through the snow. Pantomime fits in with Polanski's idea of making short films less complicated than features. After watching the pantomime style of acting in some of his short films, the viewer begins to recognize Polanski by his style of filmmaking, just as we can recognize our friends by their style of speaking. And when a scene in one of Polanski's films doesn't seem real, it isn't disturbing because the viewer comes to realize that it is just Polanski's style of making short films. For example, toward the end of *When Angels Fall* a young soldier lies dead in the snow, under a fruit-laden tree. By learning Polanski's film techniques, however, we can accept this highly unrealistic shot of a tree bearing fruit in winter.

All of these examples refer to a director's style, to how he employs the tools of film communication in his own special way. Other directors, of course, have different ways of making films. Robert Enrico's style is obvious to anyone who has seen his trilogy of *Occurrence at Owl Creek Bridge, Mockingbird,* and *Chickamauga.* Enrico enjoys moving his camera as much as possible and using sounds to disclose things to his audience. In *Occurrence at Owl Creek Bridge,* Enrico used a spiritual-type song, the words of the "Living Man" theme, to signify how much the condemned man in his film wants to live. In *Chickamauga,* Enrico used a similar song to reveal that a little boy, although he looks quite innocent, bears the curse of the ancestors' sins. And in *Mockingbird,* Enrico played a melody over and over again, until it is as familiar to his audience as it is to Private Graylock, and then repeats the melody as a clue later in the film.

American director Roger Corman likes to use the hand-held camera often in his films. The reason is that most of Corman's films are action-filled, and Corman feels that the hand-held camera can best lead the audience into the movement. Whenever he is photographing a fight or chase or group of people, Corman grabs a camera and goes into the crowds.

The particular style of French director Robert Enrico is evident in films like **Chickamauga**, part of a trilogy including **Occurrence at Owl Creek Bridge** and **Mockingbird**.

Japanese director Yasujiro Ozu's films, on the other hand, show no camera movement at all. In these films, the camera sits down near the floor, totally motionless, focusing on a corridor or a doorway and characters move across the camera's line of vision. Rather than moving around with the camera, the audience at one of Ozu's films views Ozu's characters from one position: the low position of a person sitting down on the floor.

In both director's styles, there is a close relationship between how a director shows us something and what he shows us. For Corman the world is full of action, and he wants us to be a part of it. For Ozu, the world is something to be watched, to be contemplated.

As further examples, Alain Resnais' characteristic style of using a constantly moving camera has already been mentioned, as well as the way director Arthur Penn uses light as part of his style of making films.

Sometimes a director's technique becomes so famous that it dominates the styles of other people. Walt Disney established a style of animation film which was distinctly his own. So popular was Disney's realistic animation style, and so successful, that other directors tried to copy it. Today, Disney's style of animation is so prevalent in the United States that when you say the word "animation," many people immediately think of Disney's style, as if it were the only style around.

THE DIRECTOR'S MESSAGE

Perhaps even more important, however, than *how* he says it, is *what* a director says to us in his films. To go back to the examples we used at the chapter's beginning, it may be easier for you to pick out a friend by how he talks; but if you can identify him by what he's always talking about, you probably know a lot more about him. The more we know about a director and the more we get to know him or her by his films, the more we can understand what a director is trying to tell us about the way she or he sees life. Getting to know a director is a lot like getting to know a new friend; the more you talk to him, the more time you spend with him, the better you get to know him. And the better you get

to know somebody, the more you enjoy that person's company, or in this case, the more you enjoy his or her films.

In many of Roman Polanski's films, for example, it may be noticed that violence of some sort or other plays an important part. And in his short films, Polanski concentrates on the way two persons relate to each other. In *Two Men and a Wardrobe*, for example, two men who carry around a dresser see and experience a great deal of violence. One of them gets beaten up by some hoods; later on, a watchman beats them up. All around them, people are pickpocketing, staggering around drunk, or beating people's faces in with rocks. All in all, it's a lousy picture of the world.

When Angels Fall continues this picture of a cruel world with an overabundance of violence. A young boy beats a frog with a stick: Two soldiers are talking to each other, an explosion occurs, and one soldier's legs are blown off. One soldier kills an enemy soldier who was offering him a couple of cigarettes. The story itself is concerned with one old lady and her son; again we see an ugly world and how it affects two people.

Mammals also depicts the relationship between two people and how violence exists all around them in the world. Since Polanski's pantomime style acting removes them from real danger, however, the actual violence is in terms of exploitation rather than physical threats. In *Mammals*, one man pulls

another one through the snow in a sled. Soon, the man pulling decides he should be riding instead of pulling. They switch. Now the puller gets tired and fakes an injury. They switch. Whoever gets stuck pulling the sled thinks up a new excuse to be pulled rather than to pull.

Polanski continues to portray violence and exploitation in his feature length films. *Knife in the Water* (1961), Polanski's first feature-length film, shows how an outsider can bring out the very worst in people. *Repulsion* (1965) shows violence and insanity. *Cul de Sac* (1965) wallows in cruelty. Devilish forces triumph in *The Fearless Vampire Killers* (1967) and in *Rosemary's Baby* (1968). Polanski's 1971 version of *Macbeth* was even more violent than the original Shakespearian play. And Polanski's 1974 film *Chinatown* even included a scene where Polanski himself appears to slash Jack Nicholson's nose with a knife. Polanski had made a similar guest appearance in his earlier film *Two Men and a Wardrobe*. The more one watches Polanski's films, the more it seems he is showing us life as a bizarre event, filled with violence and death.

Why is violence so important in Polanski's films? Why do we see people exploited and exploiting each other? What is it Polanski wants us to understand? Can we find out anything about Polanski from his films?

One film by a director is like one fragment of his life, which is a puzzle to other people. By putting all the pieces together, all of a director's films, the director as a person can be better understood. If we put Polanski's films together, what do we end up with? *Who* do we end up with? An easy answer is Polanski, his life, and his experiences.

Unless they're film researchers or critics, however, most people don't get to see all the films a director makes, especially if that director has been a busy man. Director Howard Hawks, for example, has made films from 1926 through 1971. Watching his almost fifty features would take a great deal of time, but the more films we see by a director, the more complete a picture we get of him and of what he's trying to say.

In Polanski's case, it is not surprising that he depicts violence and exploitation. He has seen much of it himself. Polanski was three years old when his parents, both Polish, went back to Poland just before the Second World War. At eight, Polanski saw his mother sent to a concentration camp, where she later died. His father survived the camps, but Polanski spent most of his childhood wandering from one family to another. Because Polanski didn't look Jewish, he escaped some of the difficulties other Jews were experiencing. But he experienced enough violence and mistreatment as a child to last him a lifetime.

Some people who haven't experienced what Polanski went through criticize his films for having too much violence. But as a person and as a director that's the way Polanski sees things.

Other directors use their films to criticize present society and state how they feel about it. Arthur Penn sees a large amount of violence in present day American society, and describes it through his films. *The Chase* (1966) shows a world where lawlessness has gone wild. Marlon Brando, playing Sheriff Calder, has a difficult job keeping order in the small town he runs. Bubber Reeves, an escaped convict, accused of a murder he didn't commit, is coming back to the town. Sheriff Calder has to protect the convict from the townspeople, a raving bunch of trigger-happy drunks who would like nothing better than to get their hands on a man accused of a murder.

Almost everybody in *The Chase* packs a gun and uses it at the slightest provocation "The law gives you the right to carry guns," Calder says, "most of you got two, but deputies you're not." *The Chase* even includes a reenactment of Jack Ruby killing Lee Harvey Oswald. It's not a pretty film by any means, but *The Chase* is an engrossing statement about the violence in present-day society.

Penn's earlier films also deal with violence and exploitation. Billy the Kid seems to be forced into crime by the lawlessness around him in Penn's first film, *The Left-Handed Gun* (1958). *The Miracle Worker* (1962) shows much of the violence a blind girl experiences. *Mickey One* (1965), a highly experimental and somewhat difficult film, concentrates on some of the pressures on a night club entertainer and what happens to him because of them. In 1967 Penn directed what turned into one of his most controversial statements about violence in America—*Bonnie and Clyde.*

Viewers familiar with Penn's earlier films were not surprised by the violence in *Bonnie and Clyde*. But other people, unfamiliar with Penn and how he feels about violence, claimed that *Bonnie and Clyde* somehow glorified and encouraged lawlessness. A few people became so upset with the film that they tried to prove that watching a film like *Bonnie and Clyde* could actually *cause* violence.

Penn, of course, wishes to show violence in his films because he sees much of it around him. But he understands the great difference between reflecting violence in his films and causing more of it. The violence he's talking about, Penn claims, was around long before his movies.

Alice's Restaurant (1969) again depicts prejudice and violence in the present United States, this time concentrating on younger people. And *Little Big Man* (1970) covers the often violent life of the 121 year-old Indian fighter Jack Crabb. This movie is a bold statement about the white man's treatment of the Indians. *Night Moves* (1975) uses a gangster film structure to continue Penn's ideas about violence.

Violence isn't the only thing in Penn's films, of course. Many other ideas are contained in his movies. For instance, the central characters of his films live very different lives: Billy the Kid, a night club entertainer, Helen Keller, a southern sheriff, Arlo Guthrie, an Indian fighter. But no matter who the central character is, all of Penn's films have one thing in common: The hero is an American, in other words, a member of our society.

The heroes of Penn's films are also "outsiders." In *The Left-Handed Gun*, Billy the Kid is an outlaw; in *The Miracle Worker*, the blind girl is separated from everyone; Clyde is an outsider who comes into town and picks up Bonnie.

When Bonnie and Clyde start robbing banks, they both become outsiders. Clyde tells Bonnie's mother that Bonnie wants to settle down near her. "Bonnie and I were just talking the other day, Mother Parker, about how she wants to live no more than three miles from you." But not being an outsider isn't the way Penn sees things for his central characters. "She lives three miles from me, she'll be dead," Mother Parker replies. In *Little Big Man* Jack Crabb, as a 121 year-old Indian fighter, is an outsider throughout the entire film; when he's with the Indians, he's really a white man,

Violence in American life is a characteristic element in the films by Arthur Penn. His feature **The Chase** describes a lawless community.

and when he goes back to the whites, they feel he's an Indian. And Harry Moseby, the hero of Penn's 1975 film *Night Moves*, suffers the effects of a maimed childhood but is determined to remain a loner in a corporate society. The main case Moseby takes up is a troubled youngster searching for parental love.

Penn admits he can find it easy to see things as an outsider, and when he describes the feelings of an outsider in his films, it rings true. Penn himself came from a divorced family, grew up moving back and forth from one section of New York City to another every six months. And in living with people who suffered during the Depression, Penn became accustomed to suffering in life early in his childhood.

THE DIRECTOR'S FREEDOM

There's much to be said about how a director reveals what he's thinking in his films. His concerns and his personality can be learned and understood by watching his films.

Sometimes, however, it isn't the director's concerns that are communicated in a film. Other people can get in his way, take over his film, cut off his money, or simply make themselves enough of a nuisance that they keep a director from having the freedom to make his movie the way he wants to. And with the large number of people involved in the process of making movies, a director can easily lose control of his film. If this happens, the director stops being the author of his film and becomes just another technician on the assembly line of a film.

When movies became big business, this was a major difficulty for directors. During the forties and fifties, before television kept many film viewers home from the theaters, Hollywood was the sole supplier to a gigantic entertainment market. Many times, films were made by an assembly line process that was better suited to making cars than to artistic expressions. Somebody would write a script, the studio that owned the script would pick out some "stars" they owned, and a director would find the script in his mailbox: "You'll be directing this film this week" the note might read. When the

director was done, the studio would send his film to an editor they owned, and the director would be given another script to direct. You can see how, under these conditions, it would be difficult for a director to use film to communicate to an audience how he sees things.

Some directors, however, had strong personalities, good reputations, or both and could choose what scripts they wanted to direct, select actors, and work with the editors. Their films were obviously *their films*; they were the *authors* of the films that had their names on them, rather than technicians who organized them for some studio. Directors like Howard Hawks, John Ford, Alfred Hitchcock, and Jules Dassin could work in such a system and still keep artistic control of their films. Sometimes they had to be clever to do it though. Hitchcock, for example, devised a way to keep editors from changing the meaning of what he shot. He simply photographed everything one way, instead of from different angles. All the editor had to do was put the shots together. Since Hitchcock made sure that the shots could only go together one way, he kept control of his films even when somebody else edited them. John Ford used the same trick.

Today, things aren't so bad for directors. With the collapse of the big studios and the rise of smaller productions, directors sometimes can find more freedom. Modern equipment can allow the filmmaker to shoot "on location," and simpler stories, without a constellation of name "stars" cost less to make. Usually, the less a film costs to make, the less control producers will attempt to exercise over a director.

In the forties, studios tried to make films for everybody; today, directors can slice off their own segment of the American viewing public and make films for it.

Directors, of course, still have many problems which can keep them from being the authors of their films. For instance, when Italian director Michelangelo Antonioni came to the United States to make *Zabriskie Point*, he brought his own cameramen over from Italy, men he was used to working with. But American cameramen, on the set due to union restrictions, harrassed the Italians. Not only

Director Vittorio de Sica dealt with the problems of post-war Italy in his classic film **The Bicycle Thief**.

that, but wild rumors were circulated by local citizens about the filmmakers. Because they looked strange, it was concluded they must be doing something wrong! The rumors were outrageous enough that the FBI came in to investigate. More and more such problems kept piling up, until Antonioni decided to go back to Italy. *Zabriskie Point* wasn't his film anymore. *The Passenger*, Antonioni's 1975 film starring Jack Nicholson, was made on Antonioni's home ground. It continues the same type of story Antonioni had created in his earlier work. In *The Passenger*, however, Antonioni was again free to communicate his particular, personal ideas, and the film reflects the director's freedom.

Other great directors have run into similar problems trying to make films their way. Sergei Eisenstein came to the United States in 1930 to work for Paramount Pictures. He received money from Upton Sinclair to make a movie in Mexico. But trouble started, and Eisenstein never finished the film. He went back to Russia where he was accused of having Western ideals because he had been in the West.

Director Erich von Stroheim had problems making a film called *McTeague*. MGM told him to make any film he wanted to. So Von Stroheim made a film from Frank Norris's novel *McTeague*. There was one problem: The film lasted ten hours. MGM didn't want to release it. Von Stroheim suggested cutting it in half and releasing it in parts. MGM didn't like that idea so they had it edited down to two hours and released it in 1924 under the title *Greed*.

Orson Welles had so much trouble with studios cutting his budgets and interfering with him as a director that he was only honored for his films in 1971 by receiving an Oscar—almost thirty years after his time.

Roman Polanski had complete control of all his films except for the American version of *The Fearless Vampire Killers*. In this version, twenty minutes had been cut from the film, the sound re-dubbed, music moved around, and a three-minute animated prologue had been added to the original film. Polanski was so angry that he disowned the American version of the film. He didn't consider himself the author of the film as it was being shown. Interestingly enough, *The Fearless Vampire Killers* was a tremendous success all over the world where

Polanski's version is shown. In America, however, the changed version of *The Fearless Vampire Killers* was a flop.

It seems logical that directors who don't need much money to make a film will be more free to do what they want than directors who must have huge budgets for their films. *Easy Rider* and *The Graduate*, for example, were made for very little money and earned a lot of money. In them the directors were more free to do what they wanted to do. Not too many people must buy tickets for a movie which costs less than a million dollars for it to break even, but a lot more people will have to like a film that

European directors, working on smaller scale, were traditionally more free than American directors. From French director Francois Truffaut's **Jules and Jim**.

costs five million; there are a lot of tickets between the two figures. For a few years after these two pictures, studios favored the low-budget production, for obvious reasons. Directors were encouraged to make low-budget films, and many were produced.

Directors who like to make "big" movies weren't too happy about the trend to lower budget films; they claimed it deprived them of the freedom to make expansive, expensive films. Director John Frankenheimer likes to make "big" movies. That's his style, the way he sees the world. To get the scenes he wanted for his feature *The Horseman*, director Frankenheimer had to bring his crew and cast to Afghanistan. These scenes, Frankenheimer felt, would show things the way he wanted them shown. But such extravagance was difficult. In the middle 1970's, however, the trend away from high-budget films reversed. Producers found that audiences again were willing to see expensive films like *The Godfather* parts I and II. Expensive films could recoup their losses. The 1975 feature *Jaws* cost eight million dollars to film. The studio planned to spend another couple of million advertising the film. By requiring theaters that wanted to open the film to guarantee a large share of the box office draw to the studio and to deposit that money before showing the film, the studio was able to pay for *Jaws* and its advertising and earn several million dollars profit before anyone even saw the film. The future of expensive movies, then, looks better than it did in the early 1970's. Some directors, however, still prefer the freedom of a low-budget movie. Director Peter Bogdanovich, for example, once stated that, "Nothing makes me more unhappy than an expensive movie."

Many problems can stop a director from being the author of his or her films. Censorship, sponsors, producers, studio heads, all can be factors limiting the freedom of a director. With that freedom, however, a director can use films to express what he or she feels.

THE DIRECTOR'S AUDIENCE

Another problem is that a director, once she or he has made a film, must have a group of viewers who like his or her style and are willing to go to the film. Otherwise, he won't find the money to make another. If there's anything worse for a director than not being the author of his film, probably it's not getting to do a film at all. Roman Polanski was nominated for an Oscar for his first feature film *Knife in the Water* in 1961, but he didn't get to make another feature film until 1965. It took him four years to find somebody to put up the money. Producers were afraid that not enough people would go to see Polanski's film, and therefore they wouldn't get their money back.

Sometimes the way a director sees the world will limit his audience. Federico Fellini, for example, says that he sees no real boundary between reality and fantasy; he sees much that is real in the world of fantasy and doesn't feel that it's his job to draw the line between the two. Seeing a Fellini film, especially some of the more recent ones, presents a problem to some viewers. Sitting in the theater and trying to sort out which parts are supposed to be real and which parts are supposed to be fantasy takes a lot of effort. And by the time a person has begun sorting things out, the movie is over.

Watching such a film, of course, forces a viewer to go along not only with *what* the director shows you but also with *how* he or she shows it to you. In films directed by Fellini, that means seeing reality and fantasy scrambled together. Some people find this hard to do. We are used to seeing things our own way most of the time. If we are asked to see things through somebody's else's eyes and his way of seeing things is very different from ours, we may be hesitant to do it. And if a director forces an audience to see things in a way they find difficult, he or she is going to cut down the size of his audience. Every director must take his chances and hope that enough viewers are willing to look at things his way and that they will pay for his films. If not, he'll be through making films—unless he's got a very rich uncle.

In meeting a new director it should be remembered that it is like meeting a new person. We aren't going to like every director, just as we cannot like every person we meet. The more we get to know a particular director, however, the more we can decide if we like him or not. That's another way movies are fun.

THE DIRECTOR

ACTIVITIES

1) Rock groups, although they go through changes of personnel and development of different styles, carry recognizable sounds and ideas in their music. The Beatles, for example, through the many distinct periods of their music, were always recognizable. Confusing a Beatles sound with a song by the Stones, for example, would be difficult.

Pick a group or performer that has been successful enough to come out with more than one album. Create an audio tape with selections from the group or performer's different albums. Look for similarities in style and ideas. You could make your job easy by selecting a group with a long history, a large number of albums, and a star with a strong personality, such as the Stones or the Doors before the death of Jim Morrison. You might follow one person through different groups, such as Eric Clapton or one of the other members of the short-lived Blind Faith group. Or you might concentrate on one artist, Judy Collins, for example, and follow her through a segment of her career.

Analyze the similarities of style present in the music. Comment upon recurring themes and concerns. Present your project as an audio tape, with your commentary interspersed with the selections from the group or performer. Or present the project in written form.

2) Select a film director and make a list of all his feature films, together with their dates of release. Describe the ones you have seen. For the films you haven't seen, you'll have to rely on descriptions in film books or 16mm film catalogs. Try to pick out recurring styles or ideas. Then read an interview with the director, to compare his views about his films with the views of critics who write about films, and with your views.

3) For regrettable reasons, women for many years have been excluded from the job of directing Hollywood feature films but have distinguished themselves in other areas. Dede Allen, for example edited many of Arthur Penn's greatest works. In Europe, however, directing has not been as exclusive, and some women have been able to break through the barriers of a traditionally male field. Select a woman director and report on her films. By reading interviews, find out what obstacles she had to overcome to become a director. As an alternate project, report on women in American film.

4) PBS has presented a series on famous directors titled "The Men Who Made the Movies." If any of the sequences are scheduled for viewing in your area, watch them and report on what each director feels his role is and what he is trying to communicate to his audience.

5) Television directors have different problems than film directors. What problems would a director encounter in directing a live television show that he would not encounter in film? A few film directors, such as Arthur Penn, started out in television during its heyday and then moved into film. What television technique did Penn use in filming the death of Bonnie and Clyde?

6) Painters leave their "trademarks" in their work just as film directors do. Collect some paintings, etchings, or artworks by one artist and report on them. Note similarities in technique and themes among the works.

GENRE

The genre (zhäṅ re) is the Kool-Aid of the movie world. In the genre, characters and their backgrounds are prepared beforehand; to make a movie, just add a director.

Genre films include those in which the often-used characters and situations are very familiar to the audience. Many directors use a genre because this familiarity on the part of the audience allows them more freedom to say and do what they want. A **genre**, then, is a group of similar films sharing certain recognizable objects, ideas, or situations.

In the last chapter, we mentioned that one way to understand more about a director and his or her films is to watch all of the films by that director. We said that when a director is free to be the author of his films, his personality will show through.

Another way to learn about film is to pick out similar films by different directors and look for similar ideas, characters, or themes. John Ford, Howard Hawks, Oscar (Budd) Boetticher, and Sam Peckinpah are some of the many directors who have chosen to make movies within the Western genre. The similarities in the Westerns made by these directors allows us to set up a category of films called the Western genre. Studying the similarities in Western films by different directors helps us to learn about the genre itself, and just as we can

Godzilla follows in the footsteps of many another monster film, one of the most popular genre forms.

watch a director grow from one film to the next, we can watch a genre grow as different directors add new elements to it.

THE WESTERN

Of the genres familiar to movie viewers, the Western genre is one of the most popular. When a director makes a film in the Western genre, all he has to do is costume one of his characters, and instantly his audience knows a great deal about the person. Put a man, well-dressed in Eastern fashion, into a saloon. Perhaps he wears a top hat, flared at the top. We know immediately that the guy is a professional card player. He probably cheats, too. Without having to tell us anything, the director has defined his character because we recognize him from other films we've seen in the same genre. It's a kind of shorthand for audience communication.

In older Westerns, the good guys wore the white hats. They could be depended upon to be honest, upstanding people. So effective a communications device is the use of costume in the Western genre that one car manufacturer, wishing to portray its dealers as upstanding people like the early Western heroes, developed an advertising campaign picturing its dealers with white hats. This particular symbol, the use of white hats to designate the good people in a movie, can be traced

back to religious painting, in which especially good people usually had halos of light around their heads.

This shorthand is convenient for the director, who can rely on our previous experience with other films in the same genre. Situations, characters, and ideas need little elaboration since we remember them from previously seen films. We may even recognize similarities outside of a film genre. For example, a director filming in the Western genre might show us a sheriff as a good man who brings law and order to a town in chaos by fighting outlaws. The struggle of this good man fighting evil is familiar to us from other films we've seen in the Western genre. The story is also familiar to us from more ancient sources, where the sheriff's character may have been represented as a knight of the Round Table, for instance. Anthropologists and Jungian psychologists tell us that this story of the good man fighting evil to bring order out of chaos is a story common to all peoples. If an image, character, or incident is found in the stories and experiences of all peoples, we call it an "archetype." Many of the characters and situations we notice in films of certain genres, especially the Western genre, are ancient enough to be called archetypes.

In its most simple form, the Western genre portrays the struggle between good and evil. The good guy rides a white horse, wears a matching hat, is tall, straight, and a good shot. The bad guy is stooping, wears dirty clothes, a dark hat and gloves, rides a dark-colored horse and looks evil. So important was this visual presentation of the good guy that the director of *Shane* used careful camera positioning and certain tricks to make Alan Ladd, the good guy, look tall. Jack Palance, the actor portraying the bad guy, was actually taller; but you would never know it by watching the film. Again, the long television run of *Gunsmoke* may be partly attributable to the way Matt Dillon, played by James Arness, used his great physical size (well over six feet) to fit the genre conception of a lawman. And although anti-discrimination lawsuits are changing the practice, many modern-day police departments retain minimum height requirements for lawmen.

Genres change as directors add new elements to them; they also change as societies change. Director John Ford's changing use of the Western genre throughout his long career is an example of the development of one genre. In Ford's early films, like *Stagecoach*, John Wayne plays a shy hero, a man with the best of American idealism in his character. Henry Fonda's Wyatt Earp in *My Darling*

Clementine is also an idealist. But in his later films, when Ford began to question the success of traditional American idealism, in films like _Two Rode Together_ or _Cheyenne Autumn_, his heroes are tired, seedy characters played by James Stewart.

The image of the American Indian in the Western genre is an excellent example of how changing social attitudes change the ingredients in a genre. The Indian in early Westerns was portrayed as somewhat less than human, an evil savage who tortured women and children, who was fit only to be killed. Inumerable examples could be cited for this. In the late 1960's, however, spurred partially by events in Southeast Asia, people began to re-examine this part of the Western genre. In incredibly violent scenes from films like _Soldier Blue_ and _Little Big Man_, the U.S. Cavalry, not the Indians, were portrayed as the savages. Later, the _Billy Jack_ films brought this idea to the present-day setting, again reversing the good guy/bad guy labels of earlier films.

THE GANGSTER FILM

Sociologists are interested in the way genres change because they know that these changes can mark new attitudes among people. Another genre popular in American film has been the gangster genre. Basically, the gangster is an outlaw, a self-made man whose main drive is to make it "up the ladder," usually by "rubbing out" all the other people on the ladder. Typically, the gangster gets "bumped off" himself after he reaches the top. Like the Western genre, the gangster genre is more ancient than films, and many societies can provide similar story structures. Shakespeare's Macbeth, for example, was a gangster, and Ken Hughes's 1955 film _Joe Macbeth_, a gangster film, was an homage to this ancestral gangster story.

In America, the earliest "real" gangster film was Mervyn Le Roy's _Little Caesar_, (1930); it was closely followed by William Wellman's _Public Enemy_ (1931) and Howard Hawk's _Scarface_ (1932). In these films, the image of the little man fighting his way up emerges: It was an image Depression-era Americans could easily identify with. After one criminal act, the gangster's path is set in crime,

and he is not free to go back and change his ways. Unlike the Western, gangster films take place in the city, and the hero is usually short of stature: Edward G. Robinson, James Cagney, Alan Ladd, George Raft, Mickey Rooney, and Al Pacino are all short actors. A district attorney or policeman, usually a man of sterling character, is the pursuer.

Later gangster films challenged this earlier convention. By the arrival of _Bonnie and Clyde_ (1967), the gangster genre had changed enough to show the pair as rural criminals, young, anti-establishment types whose only function is anti-social: "We rob banks." Like earlier gangster-heroes, though, Bonnie and Clyde are fixed in their life of crime after one robbery. Bonnie is not recognized during the first robbery, and so Clyde urges her to quit, but she does not. Once she joins him, there's no turning back.

The development of gangster films also shows gangsters as businessmen. Films repeatedly show gangsters presiding over board meetings in their plush offices, business meetings indistinguishable, at first glance, from those conducted by legitimate businesses. The long-running television series _The Untouchables_, frequently rerun on certain stations, had many excellent examples of these meetings in swanky offices, as did Roger Corman's 1967 gangster

Genres can be combined with interesting effects. French director Jean-Luc Godard combined the gangster genre and the science fiction genre in **Alphaville**.

film *The St. Valentine's Day Massacre* and Francis Ford Coppola's *Godfather* films.

The image of crime as big business (or the realization that crime in America *is* a big business) reaches a high point in British television director John Boorman's American feature *Point Blank* (1967). Lee Marvin is trying to get some money owed him by certain gangsters. But the gangsters have become such big business, and so legitimate, that they deal only in checks and balances and legers and never actually dirty their hands with actual money. Marvin kills his way up and up in the organization to try to get his money, all to no avail. This is a business, one gangster tells Marvin, we don't have any money!

Director Costa-Gavras used an adaptation of the gangster genre to make his feature film *Z*. *Z* seems like a modern-day political story. In reality, all Costa-Gavras had to do was substitute modern parallel situations into the gangster genre, and he had his film. The gangsters in *Z* are members of a right-wing military government, but they look and act like gangsters. Their crime is the murder of a popular leader of the opposition. The prosecutor is a man of sterling character, as untouchable as Eliott Ness.

HORROR AND SCIENCE FICTION FILMS

Horror and science fiction films constitute another interesting and important genre. Many monsters, of course, had some historical basis and became the product of folk tales, told, retold, and improved upon. Dracula, for example, was known also as Vlad Tepes the Impaler and was Prince of Wallachia in the fifteenth century. A certain medical syndrome, characterized by abundant facial hair growth and extreme sensitivity of the eyes to light, could be the basis for the stories of the Wolfman howling (in pain) from the light of the full moon.

More important, however, is what the popularity of the horror film genre tells us. *Dracula* (1931), *Frankenstein* (1932), and *King Kong* (1933) were Depression-era films. Dr. Frankenstein created a monster which ultimately killed him, just as many overly-ambitious investors created a stock market that in 1929 ultimately destroyed them. When King Kong ran rampant through New York, some audiences cheered him; they blamed the big cities for their economic problems.

Monsters in horror films have many arche-

Genres can be updated and changed easily. *Z* is a modern use of the gangster genre, with gangster-type violence and a good guy of pure character who tries to defeat the gangsters.

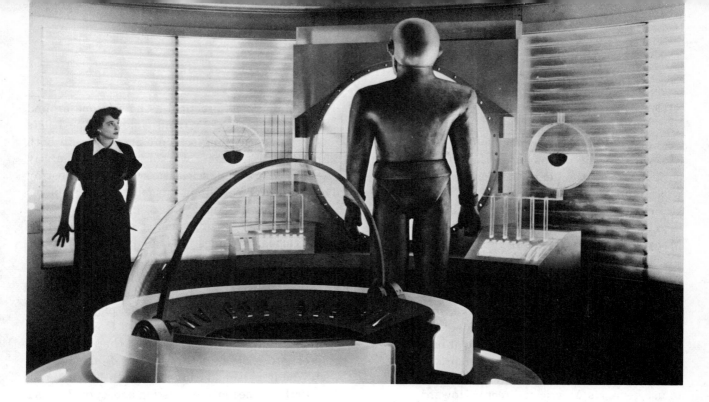

typical stories to build on: St. George and the Dragon, Beowulf and Grendel, and many others portray man's struggle against the unknown. Monsters in horror films are usually immortal creatures, and being immortal cuts the monster off from regular people. The Wolfman constantly falls in love, only to realize he's going to kill, or at least outlive, each new love. Frankenstein's monster experiences similar loneliness, as does King Kong. Dracula solves the problem by initiating his victims into immortality, so that he can have them around for good. But like most monsters, his feeding habits create a burden to the society he lives in.

Many monsters owe their existence to a scientist who gets too involved in his work. Other monsters, especially those in Japanese horror films after World War II, were released from their prehistoric graves by atomic blasts. Traditional weapons are of little use in dealing with monsters, and special methods must be devised. Sometimes, though, the hero must die to rid everyone of the horror (*The Omega Man*, *The Exorcist*). Recently, however, horror films have been set in a future time. The monster has been created by science itself, rather than by the one corrupt scientist of earlier horror films. In some of these films, the "monster" becomes a computer, for instance, in Stanley Kubrick's *2001: A Space Odyssey*. *Zardoz*, *The Omega Man*, *Planet of the Apes*, *Soylent Green*,

Robert Wise's 1951 science fiction feature **The Day the Earth Stood Still** is an example of a genre film which includes film techniques and treats issues often associated only with "art films."

Silent Running—all are examples of reputable science going awry at some future date. The 1975 film *Rollerball* (partly inspired by an earlier Italian film *The Tenth Victim*) depicts a future where people have been dehumanized, much like the hero of Kubrick's 1972 film *A Clockwork Orange*. Some horror films, like *Rollerball*, also suggest the possibility that the monster may be inside ourselves: *Dr. Jekyll and Mr. Hyde*, the classic story of this inner struggle, has been made into a film several times. Indeed, Junigan psychologists tell us that the universal archetype of monster stories derives from the fact that all people fear a monster inside of themselves (our so-called "animal nature" over which we have very little control) and that monsters in ancient stories, or on the screen, are simply external expressions of an internal struggle common to all people. Films like *Jaws*, *Towering Inferno*, *Earthquake*, *The Exorcist* (and all of the imitations they spawned) all play on this fear of a monster that cannot be controlled by natural means. Whatever the explanation for their popularity, horror films have been effective and popular cinema. Directors wouldn't continue making such films if they weren't.

THE DIRECTOR AND THE GENRE

It's important to remember that some directors with strong personalities show their personalities through the genre they choose. No matter what genre they choose, their films tell the same stories. Using a genre structure, then, allows a director to build on what has been done in the past. Many times making a genre film allows a director to get more involved in his film. With all the groundwork already done for him, the director can say what he wants to say, right away. And since the director can spend his time involved in the film itself, rather than developing incidentals, often a genre film can possess more personal involvement than a film which does not use a genre.

One of the best known filmmakers who prefers to use genres is American director Howard Hawks. Hawks has been making a feature film almost every year since he started in 1926. Most of his films fall into familiar genres; to name but a few of his films: *Scarface* (1932) is a gangster film; *Bringing Up Baby* (1938), a situation comedy; *Sergeant York* (1941), a war film; *The Thing* (1951), a science-fiction film; *Rio Bravo* (1959), a Western; *Hatari* (1962), an adventure film. In all of his films, no matter what genre he decides to use, Hawks presents a similar view of life, expresses his personality and describes things he's interested in.

Similar situations recur throughout Hawks's films. Usually they are set in remote places. A small group of men are going about their job in this remote area. A woman comes into the situation, but she is not accepted by the all-male group. Like the members of the group, she must prove herself worthy of acceptance.

Rio Bravo's small group of men exist at the jailhouse of a Western town. *Hatari*'s group of men is isolated deep in Africa. In *The Thing* (produced by Hawks and directed by his editor Christian Nyby), the group of men is isolated in the Arctic circle. Feathers comes to the Western town and sets up residence at the hotel; she has her eye on Sheriff John T. Chance, but she hasn't proved herself. Dallas comes to Africa as a photographer; she has her eye on Sean Mercer, but again, she's got to prove herself worthy. Having a woman along on a rhino hunt is as practical as having one around a jailhouse, in Hawks's mind. John Wayne reacts predictably, according to genre standards, in both films. And Nikki has a way of getting in the way of the soldiers and scientists who must destroy The Thing. Women are not usually shown as man's equals in Hawks's films.

Hawks likes using genres so much that he usually chooses names for his characters that emphasize that they are "genre people"—their names sound like nicknames. Chance, Dude, Colorado, Feathers, and Stumpy play in *Rio Bravo*; Dallas, Chips, Pockets, Brandy, and Indian play in *Hatari*.

It is the similarity among all of Hawks's films, however, that underlines the fact that the viewer is seeing the director through his films; he is a man who is personally involved with his material.

Perhaps the most interesting aspect of Hawks's approach, though, is that he makes films with people he *likes*. It shows through in his films. Just as Marcello Mastroianni fits into the way Federico Fellini makes films, so do people like John Wayne, Cary Grant, and earlier in Hawk's career, Humphrey Bogart, seem suitable for Hawks's style of filmmaking. Even when he must pick an actor to play a monster from outer space, Hawks picks his actor very carefully. Casting a hulking monster composed entirely of vegetable matter, a sort of smart carrot who doesn't like humans, might seem difficult; but James Arness, later to become famous as Marshal Matt Dillon in "Gunsmoke," was able to walk correctly to play the part of The Thing. Arness' physical size gave him the ability to lumber with enough frightening effect to add a great deal to the film. Big monsters are more frightening than little ones. Rather than choose a low camera angle to create a feeling of hugeness, Hawks chose a large actor. Unlike most science-fiction directors, Hawks did not use special trick photography or special effects; he just shot *The Thing* as he would any other picture.

One of the reasons that Hawks's films seem so natural, so un-acted, is that Hawks not only uses actors he likes as persons, but he is willing to

Henry King's 1950 film **The Gunfighter** deals with the complex question of killing using the Western genre.

change things to suit them. In *Rio Bravo*, Hawks has remarked, there is one part when Dean Martin is supposed to roll a cigarette. The alcoholic lawman's fingers aren't equal to the task, however, and John Wayne keeps passing them to him. The gesture emphasizes that the two are good friends. The action was discovered one day when Dean Martin asked Hawks how he was supposed to roll cigarettes if his fingers were shaky. Wayne said, "Here, I'll hand you one," and suddenly there was a new gesture for the movie. That's the way Hawks lets his actors be themselves.

Hawks also tries to utilize all the talents of his actors. When he cast Rick Nelson and Dean Martin in *Rio Bravo*, Hawks knew that he would have to let them do a song together somewhere in the film. The difference between the song in *Rio Bravo*, when it finally does occur, and the songs written into many films is that this song forms a natural part of the film. Three imperfect characters join in the song: Dean Martin, a reformed drunk, Rick Nelson, who has proved himself irresponsible in the film, and Walter Brennan, a cripple, who accompanies them on a harmonica. John Wayne can't join in; there's nothing wrong with him. Rather than being an exploitation of two of the stars, the song is an important symbol in the film, used to express the unity of three characters.

Hawks's use of the group in his Westerns could be compared to Sam Peckinpah's use of the same element in his film *The Wild Bunch* (1969). Peckinpah tells us something is different in his Western by allowing an automobile to appear in his film. This new element clues us in: We know that the film will be different than the usual Western, which is set in the period between 1865 and 1890. Indeed, the incredible violence of *The Wild Bunch* happens because the group of men in the film are living too late; their genre expired years before. Rather than being the elite group of men who do their job well, like the group of men in Hawk's films, the men in *The Wild Bunch* are simply that: a wild bunch of men, fit only for cannon fodder.

What is important to remember about a genre is that it is only a framework which a director uses in making a film. More important than the genre is what the director says using it.

Director Fred Zinnemann used the Western genre to make his classic film *High Noon* (1952). Standard characters people the film: The marshall, his new bride, the townspeople, the saloon crowd, the semi-intelligent deputy, all the rest of the characters seen many times before. The standard situation in the Western genre also happens: Some bad guys come in from outside to stir up trouble. In *High Noon*, they're coming in on the noon train.

What's important in *High Noon*, of course, is what director Zinnemann says during the film. By extracting some of his ideas we can observe how a director uses a genre to communicate his personal ideas. In *High Noon* Zinnemann tells us that: People really don't care about law and order; you can't run from your job; a *man* will stand and fight; politicians are too lenient with murderers; and, interestingly enough, a pacifist will renounce his religion and shoot somebody in the back—if the chips are really down.

The point is that these ideas come from what seems to be a typical Western. What the director wants to say in a genre film often hides behind the genre he uses to make his film. We have to go past the genre—what's up front—before we find the director, who is standing behind it. In genre films many times, it's what's up *back* that counts.

The advantages for a director using genres in his or her filmmaking are obvious. The advantages in changing elements in a genre are also obvious. The scene of a group of cowboys sitting around the campfire eating beans is a common element of the Western genre. By adding the sound produced by the flatulence that eating beans can generate to the sound track of his film *Blazing Saddles* allowed director Mel Brooks to create a comic effect. Moreover, because of our familiarity with the Western genre, we expect the bad guy to ride into town on a black horse. When Mel Brooks has him ride in on a steer, only to be knocked out by a little old lady, the effect is comic. *Young Frankenstein* (1975) allowed Brooks to create another comic effect by placing new elements into another genre familiar to his audience. Because of the success of Humphrey Bogart in gangster and espionage films, we expect secret agents to look somewhat like Bogart. Woody Allen included sequences of the

Although the story of the Russian feature film **Ballad of a Soldier** is unique, the film uses many situations found in other films of the war film genre.

famous 1942 Bogart film *Casablanca*, directed by Michael Curtiz (Mihaly Kertesz) in his film *Play it Again, Sam*. The contrast between Woody Allen's physical appearance and that of his genre hero provides added comedy. Paul Morrissey, Andy Warhol's director for many films, used the Dracula and Frankenstein genres for two X-rated features. Warhol's star, Joe Dallesandro, uses his matter-of-fact acting style and mumbling New York dialect to increase the comic effect of Andy Warhol's *Frankenstein*. In the horror film genre, we expect an actor to have a European accent, like Bela Lugosi's. Breaking the "rules" of a genre can be fun for a director: Peter Bogdanovich, for example, didn't want a happy ending for his musical *At Long Last Love* precisely because musicals usually have happy endings. Doing a Western in which no characters ever pull a gun would also be "exhilarating," says Bogdanovich, because it would be "breaking the rules."

GENRE AND ART

Studying genres, then, is one method of film criticism. Film criticism is the process of deepening our appreciation, understanding, and enjoyment of films. If we're aware of genres, how they change and when they are used, we can increase our understanding, appreciation, and enjoyment of films that use genre structures, just as we increase our understanding, appreciation, and enjoyment of films by a particular director when we see all of his or her films and compare them.

Some people, however, feel uncomfortable when they study genre films. These people are not uncomfortable when they study editing, sound, or any of the other techniques all directors use. But the use of genre presents a particular problem for them because many genre films are extremely popular with large groups of people. If these films are so popular, they ask, can they really deserve study? For example, one genre director, Roger Corman, prefers to make low-budget genre films because it gives him the freedom to do what he wants to do, to say what he wants to say. It's easier, quicker, and many of Corman's films have a refreshing naturalness that high-budget films sometimes lack. A good example of how fast Corman can work is the film *Bucket of Blood*. One day in 1959, Corman got an idea for a new feature. Five days later, he completed *Bucket of Blood*.

The next year, Corman made *The Fall of the House of Usher*, beginning a long series of films based upon the writings of Edgar Allen Poe, which is usually considered among the best examples of Corman's work. But he hasn't limited himself only to the horror film genre. Corman's filmography, starting in 1954, includes 60 films he has directed and 110 films he has produced, including films from many genres. We see the horror film genre represented in films like *Tales of Terror* (1962) and *The Pit and the Pendulum* (1961); the motorcycle genre, as in *The Wild Angels* (1966); the drug genre, *The Trip* (1967); the gangster genre, *The St. Valentine's Day Massacre* (1967) and *Machine Gun Kelly* (1958).

Films such as these sound like popular entertainment, and some people feel strange about studying a popular art form. Mistakenly, they associate "art" only with something "esoteric," "difficult," or "old."

Other people feel guilty about liking something entertaining. Maybe it dates back to a grade school experience when they went to an art museum and some teacher told them not to enjoy themselves because it was supposed to be educational. Film critic Pauline Kael pinpoints this confusion between "art" and entertainment when she says that after watching an "art film" she feels like going out to a movie.

Genre films often suffer because of this false distinction some people have set up between "art films" and "entertainment films." *The Day the Earth Stood Still* surely doesn't sound like an art film; maybe it is *only* entertainment. But don't judge a film by its genre, any more than you would judge a book by its cover.

Some people feel more comfortable studying films that look esoteric, difficult, or "artsy," and prefer films of the European art cinema. Ingmar Bergman's *The Seventh Seal* is a good example of the type of film we mean when we talk about the European art cinema. *The Seventh Seal*, which has been mentioned earlier for its excellent use of lighting

and motion techniques, can be a more difficult film to watch than Corman's *The St. Valentine's Day Massacre* or Robert Wise's 1951 science fiction feature *The Day the Earth Stood Still. The Seventh Seal*, for example, is in Swedish; viewers have to read subtitles. Also, its plot treats philosophical subjects. A knight, Antonius Block, is returning from a useless crusade and is trying to do one significant action in his wasted life. He attempts to buy time from Death, who appears as a black-robed character. The acting style of *The Seventh Seal* is deliberately unrealistic and resembles a medieval morality play. For people who like their films to look like "art," *The Seventh Seal* is topnotch. Does that mean that because *The Seventh Seal* is a film from the European art cinema, it is necessarily more important or more worthy of study than any genre film? Hardly.

In *The Day the Earth Stood Still*, Klaatu, visiting earth from outer space, lands in Washington, D.C., along with his faithful robot companion Gort. Klaatu's spaceship is immediately surrounded by the Army. Rather than being welcomed, Klaatu is injured by a barrage of bullets fired at him, even though he has made no threatening gesture. Klaatu prevents Gort from fighting back. Klaatu escapes and hides out with a young widow and her son, who do not know his true identity. The peace of the widow and her son, so much in contrast to Klaatu's hostile welcome, compares with a similar peaceful episode in *The Seventh Seal* in which the Knight meets Jof, Mia, and their son Michael. Klaatu, after revealing his secret identity to the widow, leaves to tell his message to the world. Leave the H-bomb and other devices alone, Klaatu warns, "you are irresponsible children whose powers exceed your wisdom. Grow up or put aside your evil toys." To demonstrate his powers, Klaatu short-circuits all the electric power on earth. But Klaatu is killed, his warning unheeded. The widow begs Gort to bring Klaatu back to life so that the world will have one last chance to save itself.

Other interesting similarities exist between *The Day the Earth Stood Still* and *The Seventh Seal*. Both films use somber, low-key photography. Everything is gray in *The Day the Earth Stood*

Still except Klaatu, his gleaming silver robot, and his white spaceship. The characters in *The Seventh Seal* spend their time fleeing the Black Death, and its terror distorts their personalities into grotesque forms. In *The Day the Earth Stood Still*, Cold War Americans have the H-bomb as their Black Death, and it provokes the same fear and mindless fury.

At first glance, some people might dismiss *The Day the Earth Stood Still* as a "cheap entertainment film" (as if there were something wrong with entertainment!) Closer analysis, however, reveals that it deals with issues similar to those treated in *The Seventh Seal*, a film which looks very little like "cheap entertainment."

Choosing a genre, then, doesn't prevent a director from dealing with complicated or mature ideas. And it is surely wrong to dismiss genre films as "just popular art" (as if there was something wrong with art being popular!). *The Seventh Seal*, one example of the European art cinema, and *The Day the Earth Stood Still*, one example of the American genre film, can both be appreciated and enjoyed as two different film approaches to similar themes. Neither film, however, deserves critical acceptance or rejection just because of the approach its director selects.

Becoming familiar with genres and how directors usually employ them helps us when we see a director changing around genre elements. *The Gunfighter*, Henry King's 1950 Western, treats the character of Jimmy Ringo, played by Gregory Peck. All the genre elements we recognize from all other Westerns are present in *The Gunfighter*, but only as backgrounds. What director Henry King is interested in is the psychological problems of Jimmy Ringo. What's it really like to be a gunfighter, anyhow? Everywhere you go somebody wants to blow your head off to make a name for himself. What does that do to your psychological status? The genre elements in *The Gunfighter* are set-ups for a more complicated story. The saloon, the gunfights, repeated so similarly that they become ritual, all are props for the real story of *The Gunfighter*. Familiarity with these genre elements helps us see how director Henry King uses them to deal with a complex story.

GENRE STEREOTYPES

Genre, then, has advantages when followed and when used as a group of conventions to be unconventional with. Genres, however, have one serious problem. Because structures and characters can be used over and over again by directors, *stereotypes* can develop. It's an advantage for a director to use a character from among the group of stock characters in a genre. The director can spend his time communicating his ideas and feelings without wasting time developing minor characters. But stock characters, like the well-dressed card shark in a Western saloon, can turn into *stereotypes* if overused. Then a director who wants his gambler to be shabbily dressed has a problem, since his audience expects saloon gamblers to be well dressed.

The danger of stereotyping in film extends much wider than film itself. Because film influences us so much, stereotypes developed by film during its history have a tendency to remain after viewing. How much of our image of the American Indian, for example, comes from stereotyped Hollywood Western filmmaking and how much from other sources? For too many years, Hollywood perpetuated stereotypes of Indians, of blacks, of women, and of other groups, stereotypes that may have been handy for storytelling but which are unflattering and inaccurate. Sometimes, deliberate stereotypes were created, especially during the Second World War. *Know Your Enemy—Japan*, made in 1944 to be viewed by American draftees and written largely by Carl Foreman, depicted the Japanese as believing they have "been commanded by heaven to conquer all other races and peoples." To underline the idea that soldiers were killing stereotypes, and not people, the commentary added "he and his brother soldiers are as much alike as photographic prints off the same negative." *The Negro Soldier*, made about the same time, was designed to cut down agitation over the segregation practiced by the Armed Forces. Instead, the film simply perpetuated old Hollywood stereotypes of blacks.

Hopefully, the era of stereotypes of minorities and of women is now over and can be studied as part of the history of film.

GENRE

ACTIVITIES

1) Pick a director who has made genre films. List each film he or she has made with a short description of each film. Use film books or film catalogs for information.

2) Choose a genre and describe the elements you usually find included in it. Would a film really fit into the genre if it didn't have at least some of these elements? Why or why not?

3) Write a description for a film you might make that would combine two genres. For example, you might describe a Western film where the bad guy is really a vampire. How would the sheriff have to kill him? At what time of day? Would a silver bullet work?

4) Write a script for a scene in a film that you might make which would change or reverse a genre element to create a comic effect. What if the hero, for instance, rode into town on a pony while his sidekick rode a stallion?

5) One important genre in American filmmaking is the musical genre. Pick a "classic" musical, such as the 1952 *Singin' in the Rain* or the 1945 *Meet Me in St. Louis* compare it to a more contemporary member of the same genre.

6) Movie producers design *logos*, or symbols, for their films to be used in newspaper and billboard advertising. Collect the movie section from the Sunday section of a major newspaper for four Sundays. Cut out the advertisements for several newly-opening films. How does the "logo" tell you what type of genre the film belongs to? Do the words of the ad clue you in? Alternatively, you might collect your ads from movie "press books" which distributors send out to theatres. Press books are

collections of ads and descriptive articles on the movie being promoted.

7) Role-play a genre movie, perhaps a Western, a gangster movie, or a science-fiction. Each person should choose a role and think up characteristic responses and gestures. You might wish to costume yourselves. Then reverse some of the genre dialog, actions, and roles to see what effects can be produced.

8) Some comic books follow many genre conventions. Select a genre comic book, possibly a war, Western, or horror comic book. Compare the structures and characters in the comic book to the movie versions. What similarities and differences do you find?

9) Was the Wild West really that way? Do some research. Select a common Western character, such as Billy the Kid, and compare his movie portrayal to his real life existence. Buffalo Bill, Wild Bill Hickok, and Calamity Jane are also interesting characters. Perhaps you would rather select a real event, such as the famous gunfight between the Clantons and Wyatt Earp and his cohorts at the O.K. Corral. Maybe you'll want to be more general in your treatment of the West. Perhaps Al Capone interests you more; do some research on his movie portrayal and his real-life character. You may want to present your research in the form of a paper, or a slide show, or an audio tape.

DOCUMENTARY

We have seen what a director can do with movement, light, color, and sound—with the ability of the camera to create shots from just these elements. It seems as though a director has almost complete control over what he wants to show to his audience. He can decide what his audience sees, how long they see it, what they hear, and how loud they hear it.

Directors have used this complete control to make film a powerful communications tool. And they enjoy this control over their audience; Orson Welles liked film tools so much that he once claimed they were the best set of electric trains any boy would ever want.

How many little kids do you know who are ready to give up their favorite toys, especially if they're the best anyone would ever want? Not too many.

Do you think any director would give up the complete control he has over what he shows his audience? You wouldn't think so. But some directors do. They choose to make **documentaries**.

There are as many definitions for the word "documentary" as there are people who make them. Maybe more. Definitions set limits on things; they include some things and eliminate others. Some definitions of "documentary" would eliminate films which use actors; other definitions would leave out films which don't show some sort of social concern.

By recording current events, documentary filmmakers are preserving history for viewers, present and future.

A few definitions would exclude films which interpret or change reality; and still others would eliminate films which don't interpret reality.

Enough definitions for "documentary" already exist, so we won't add to the confusion by making up another. Let's just describe one characteristic that most documentaries usually have. In films that people call "documentary films," the filmmaker gives up some of the control he could have over his film in order to make it seem to be more *real*. Documentary filmmakers would rather *record* an event than *create* one. Once the event is over, the filmmaker can control our perception of the event with editing devices and the like; but the idea of recording, rather than creating, is usually present.

Where did it all start, this documentary movement? Right from the beginning of film. When motion pictures were first invented, filmmakers didn't know what to do with the motion picture camera. They used it like a still camera, to take pictures, pictures that moved. Louis and Auguste Lumiere, back in 1895, made films like *Workers Leaving the Lumiere Factory* and *Train Coming into the Station*, which were simply moving snapshots, or documents of actual events. Once the novelty of motion wore off, however, movies started to tell stories. Some of the stories were fantastic, unreal adventures. George Méliès, an ex-magician, combined magic with movies and created stories such as *A Trip to the Moon* (1902). Hardly documentary, *A Trip to the*

Moon was entertaining, and audiences began to enjoy the fact that movies could tell stories, rather than simply record events. After all, audiences felt, once you've seen one train coming into Paris, you've seen them all. Documentaries soon lost ground to narrative films. But no one ever forgot the fact that the motion picture camera is particularly suited to capture reality.

Imagine two neighbors bickering because one of them has painted his house. The other neighbor is angry; how ugly the color is compared to his own house. But then he notices how faded his house really is. He paints his own house in a color much like his neighbor's. Flattered, the neighbor starts a friendship that lasts, until the other guy puts new shingles on his roof. Then they're at it again.

You've just read a description of the relationship between the documentary film and the fiction film. All through the history of film, documentary filmmakers and feature filmmakers have argued against the excesses of each other, have overreacted, and then have settled down for the next wave of events, sometimes borrowing ideas from each other. The intertwining development of the two modes of filmmaking helps us to understand the confusion of documentary and fiction films, and why one definition really isn't possible for "documentary." Such films have been called documentaries, semi-

documentaries, pseudo-documentaries, features with documentary techniques, feature documentaries, neo-realist fiction films, *cinema verité*, social documentaries, feature films posing as documentaries, documentaries posing as feature films, and many more kind-of-a-lot-like-but-really-not-documentaries. All of these types of films have grown from the relationship between the documentary films of the Lumiere brothers and the story films of George Méliès.

One of Thomas Edison's earliest Kinetoscope subjects was *The Execution of Mary, Queen of Scots* (1893), which looked like a documentary of the actual event which had occurred three hundred years earlier. Obviously fiction, the film was made in documentary style. Even this early narrative, or story, film shared techniques with documentary films.

EARLY DOCUMENTARIES

One of the earliest filmmakers to start a group of people thinking about documentary filmmaking was an early director working in Russia, Denis Kaufman, who liked to call himself Dziga-Vertov.

Although film history began with documentaries like **Arrival of a Train at the Station** (1895), fiction films like **A Trip to the Moon** (1902) soon became popular.

Dziga-Vertov got the idea that everybody up until his time was one hundred percent wrong about film and that a new way of looking at film and its purposes was needed. Letting go of the control he could have had, Dziga-Vertov made his films outside a studio, without actors, sets, or scripts. His films were therefore "purer" than anyone else's, he claimed, because they were written by the camera and not by a person. Films like his *Kino-Pravda* ("film-truth") series in 1922 and his *Kino-Eye* series in 1924 demonstrate Dziga-Vertov's ideas. Using real people and real situations, the camera goes into a situation and reacts like a person, noticing things, being distracted, going back to look at something again.

Immediately, of course, Dziga-Vertov's neighbors in theater reacted. If he was going to make films like that, they were going to go in the opposite direction, away from reality and toward art based upon the tradition of circus acting, where the body movements of an actor would be extremely important and carefully controlled. They started a movement to counter Dziga-Vertov called "The Factory of the Eccentric Actor" or FEX.

Dziga-Vertov's ideas caught on with more people than did the ideas of the FEX people, and

The affection filmmaker Robert Flaherty had for his subject shows through in **Nanook of the North**.

documentary filmmakers still follow many of the basic concepts that he formulated. His films closely resemble in technique the television news films we see today.

About the same time, another man, Robert Flaherty, was making a name for himself as a documentary filmmaker. Robert Flaherty had started out as a miner and explorer. His first film *Nanook of the North* came out in 1922. *Nanook of the North* remains an interesting film to watch even today and is a good example of one type of documentary film, the **personal documentary**. This type of documentary introduces its audience to an interesting person, somebody viewers would not get a chance to meet otherwise.

Nanook was an Eskimo whom Flaherty had met and had grown to like. If other people would see Nanook and get to know him, Flaherty reasoned, they would like him too. But rather than bringing Nanook to a studio, rather than writing a script based on Nanook's life, Flaherty brought his cameras to Nanook, lived with him and his family, and recorded the events that happened to Nanook during that time. Rather than control his subject, he watched and photographed. As a result Flaherty is able to engross his audience in the struggle Nanook must put up to provide his family with food.

Nanook of the North became immediately

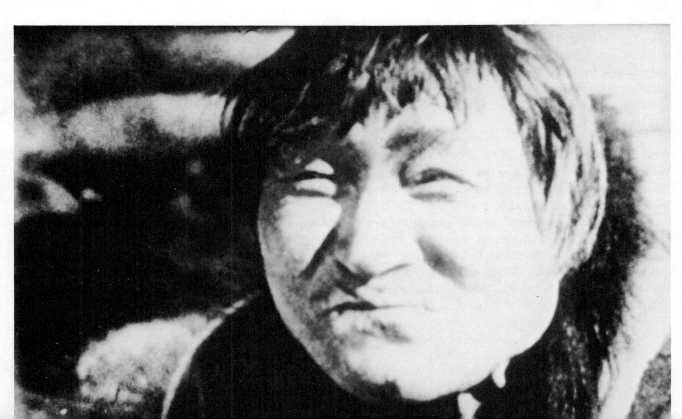

popular. The affection and respect that Flaherty had for Nanook shows through in the film and is one of the reasons the film still fascinates audiences. Some versions of *Nanook of the North* shown today have a sound track and music added to Flaherty's original silent film; viewers who see these versions of the film rarely suspect that the original was a silent film created in 1922.

One particular scene in the film shows how Flaherty's respect for Nanook and sympathy for his struggles are communicated using the documentary technique. Nanook is shown hunting, trying to kill a seal for his family to eat. In the fiction film, the process of killing a seal would be dramatized. We would see the action in a series of shots, perhaps cutting back and forth from the seal to Nanook, using close-ups as well as long shots to create variety and motion. Close-ups of Nanook could show his determination to kill the seal. Close-ups of the seal could show his determination to get away.

That isn't how Flaherty filmed the scene, however. Instead, the entire process of Nanook hunting the seal is shown in long shots. We see the entire area of action and the entire action with few cuts. Rather than use the control of time and interest that editing would offer him, Flaherty used the entire action; rather than dramatize the event, Flaherty recorded it. The triumph of Nanook when he does catch the seal is greater because Flaherty has not intruded into the reality of the event by editing. Had Flaherty polished up the sequence, we might have asked, "Is that how it really happened?" But after seeing the entire sequence, uncut and unpolished, we say, "So that's how it happened," and our respect for Nanook increases.

Flaherty took a risk: The sequence might have bored his audience. He could have used controls to avoid this risk, but he chose not to. Viewing the film now, we can see that his risk succeeded. There are no rules in film, only risks.

Seeking to capitalize on the popularity of *Nanook of the North*, producers sent Flaherty to make a "Nanook of the South," complete with South Sea island girls. They thought Flaherty could eliminate the story of struggles in the wilderness and instead depict the idyllic life of natives sipping coconut milk all day. How could such a film fail at the box office?

When Flaherty got to Samoa, however, the idyllic life the producers had in mind wasn't all there was. Instead, the documentary Flaherty filmed, *Moana*, described the same struggle for life that *Nanook of the North* had shown. Rather than make up a luscious South Seas island story to please the producers, Flaherty recorded all the pain and struggling that he saw. Life down there wasn't a bowl of tropical fruit, and Flaherty showed it like it was. The dancing girls the producers expected to see weren't there, but as a documentary *Moana* was a success.

Flaherty's films had the charm of allowing audiences to see far-off places and brave people struggling against nature to survive. Today, with television carrying us from continent to continent with every newscast and with networks competing for the most exotic "special," the excitement of trudging through the wild with Flaherty seems commonplace. But Flaherty's ability to communicate his respect and affection for his subjects makes his work exceptional. And his style of using documentary film to introduce the audience to an interesting person remains an important concept in film.

SOCIAL DOCUMENTARIES

The word **documentary** was coined by an Englishman named John Grierson in a review of *Moana* that Grierson wrote for the New York *Sun*. When Grierson returned to England, he joined a group of other filmmakers and began plans for a new type of documentary, quite different from Flaherty's. Grierson and his friends rebelled against the fact that entertainment films had a monopoly on theaters. Grierson wanted to photograph living stories against real backgrounds, with real people whose stories would be more interesting than fictional stories.

This sounds very similar to what Flaherty was doing. But there were certain aspects of Flaherty's films that were unacceptable to Grierson. Though it was a noble thing to fight for food in the wilderness, Grierson said, we should be more concerned about people at home who are fighting for food in the midst of plenty. Flaherty's films, although they were an interesting trip into the wilderness, could be a form of escapism. Grierson felt the social impact of documentaries about local people would be enormous.

The more people know about their country, Grierson thought, the more they will love it, and the better citizens they will be. Also, the more they know about events, the more willing they will be to support new programs for social change. Many of the films Grierson produced and directed, therefore, dealt with people in Britain and parts of the British Empire. A typical film, *Granton Trawler* (1939), describes how fishermen off of Scotland caught the fish Britishers enjoyed.

Perhaps one of the best examples of the type of **social documentary** Grierson produced is the film Basil Wright and Harry Watt co-directed in 1936, entitled *Night Mail*. Today, *Night Mail* seems even more dated than *Nanook of the North* because it deals with a super-speed mail train, the Postal Special, that delivered letters from England to Scotland. Although many Eskimos today still live like Nanook did in 1922, a picture of a 1936 steam engine dates a film precisely.

Watching *Night Mail*, however, can give a good idea of the type of documentary film Grierson and his crew turned out. The story of the film is a true story: How the Postal Service rushed letters from England to Scotland. The characters are the employees of the Postal Service who sort letters as the train speeds along, pick up mail sacks from the ingeniously constructed standards, drop newspapers and mail along the way. Watching *Night Mail* today, we can still feel the rhythm and speed with which the Postal Special rushed the mail to its destinations.

In the Year of the Pig is a political propaganda documentary by filmmaker Emile de Antonio dealing with the war in Vietnam. Also covered in the film are the political events in the 1968 Presidential election in which Richard Nixon campaigned against Hubert Humphrey.

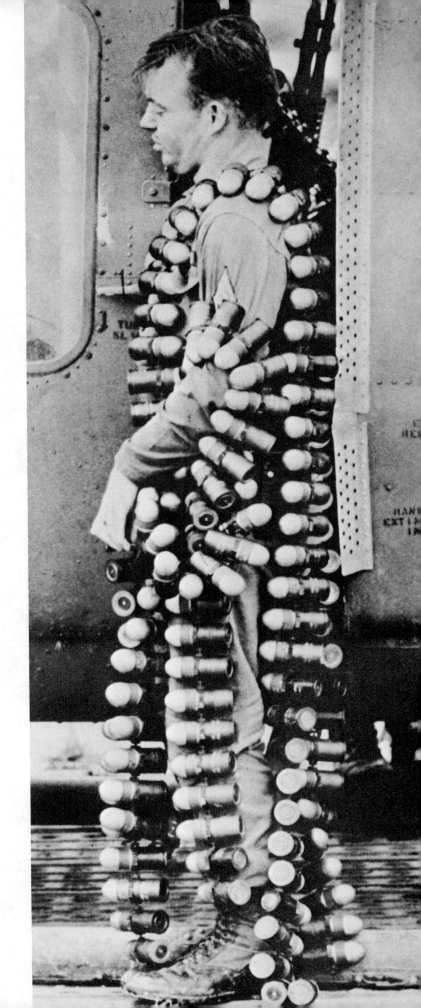

PROPAGANDA DOCUMENTARIES

In the United States, films similar to Grierson's introduced Americans to other parts of their own country and filled a similar social purpose. *The River* (1937), made by former film critic Pare Lorentz, tells the story of the Mississippi River. As expansive as its subject, *The River* combines geography, history, and commerce into one film and goes still further. A poetic commentary tries to reflect the surging of the river, much as the commentary in *Night Mail* tries to reflect the rhythm of a steam engine.

But *The River* goes beyond simply describing the Mississippi River. After showing how the vast industrial and agricultural use of the river has created ecological problems, the film tells how a government program, the Tennessee Valley Authority, helps to control the problems of the Mississippi.

Produced by agencies of the United States government, these **propaganda documentaries** were extremely important in America. Unlike strictly informational films, propaganda documentaries push specific programs or ideas. They are similar to social documentaries, the films Grierson made, but most of them have a particular problem-solution structure. First the films present a specific social problem, then they present a government program as a solution.

Willard Van Dyke, who had worked on *The River* as a photographer, made *The City* in 1939. First, we see old fashioned cities, poorly planned, overcrowded, dirty, with too many cars and plenty of pollution. We agree, as an audience, that things are lousy in the city. We have a problem.

Now we are in an airplane, flying over a different city. The solution to the problems of the city will be new cities, planned by the government, with parks and schools situated close to homes, with industry segregated outside the living area of the city.

Another problem-solution film shows how awful life is on the farm. Homes in the city have all the electricity they want, but many farm homes do not. Farmers need electricity to make their chores easier, but most power companies don't have the money to run power lines out to the farm homes. After the audience agrees that the problem is a big one, the film gives its solution. Since nobody will help, or things are so bad that no one else can, it's time for a new government program. The farmers will be helped to receive the electricity they need through the Rural Electrification Administration, a new federal program. Jorris Ivens made *Power and the Land* (1940), the film we've been talking about. And there were many more films like it: If some new program needed public acceptance, out came another problem-solution documentary.

Remember that television didn't exist yet. Today the viewpoints in most of the documentaries we see are those of the television networks who produce them rather than of the government. But seeing a few of these old government documentaries makes watching today's television documentaries a bit more interesting, especially when the government and the television networks lock horns, as they did over CBS's documentary *The Selling of the Pentagon* (1971) which we will discuss later in this chapter.

At the beginning of the Second World War, the purpose of the documentary film became immediately clear. World War II was a "total war": It required full cooperation of the civilian populations. Propaganda documentary films became the means governments used to create and maintain the total effort necessary among civilians. One German general remarked at the beginning of the war that the side which had the best cameras and films would win the war and not the side with the best weapons. The result of the war proved that he was more correct than he knew.

In Britain, documentaries praised the courage of the British people in films like *London Can Take It* (1940), *Listen to Britain* (1941). Other films encouraged farmers to produce more food and to make sacrifices for the war effort. Even the titles of films let us know how they united the civilian population and made them feel like they were involved in the war effort in an important way. *They Also Serve* (1943) praises women who work in defense industries and still have time to help their neighbors with their problems. Even people who performed

in the arts were honored for their efforts to help British culture survive the war.

Regular documentaries told people about the progress of the war effort. Military people, of course, were the heroes of many films, like *Target for Tonight* (1941) which tells the story of a dangerous night-bombing mission.

In Germany, propaganda filmmaking reached great heights. Three hundred German cameramen were in action for the conquest of Norway. The attack on the Polish city of Gdynia was delayed so that German cameramen could get ahead of the assault troops, to get better camera angles. *Baptism of Fire* and *Campaign in Poland* picture Nazi destruction as a sword of retribution. *The Eternal Jew*, also a 1941 film, was an anti-Semitic documentary, the work of Fritz Hippler. *The Eternal Jew* showed the tragic shots of misery caused by the Nazis when they starved out the Warsaw ghetto. Hippler used the footage to show Jews in "their natural state"! Starving people to near death and then using the footage to portray the suffering people as living in their natural state must rank as one of the most inhumane events in film history.

In Russia, documentary filmmaking shifted into high gear. Dziga-Vertov's follower Roman Gregoriev was in charge of assembling newsreels and combat documentaries. Some four hundred cameramen sent footage to Moscow for editing; more than one hundred Soviet cameramen died in action. Their ranks were filled with graduates from the state film school, which had added a combat photography course. Diplomas from the school were earned in part through front-line filmmaking. Leonid Varlamov's 1942 film *Defeat of the German Armies near Moscow* was edited into an American version entitled *Moscow Strikes Back* and won an Academy Award in 1943. Soviet documentaries helped lower anti-Soviet sentiment in the United States during the war.

In the United States, documentaries were equally important. Hollywood's best directors were commissioned into the service to produce propaganda films for soldiers and for the home viewers. To underline the importance of a united civilian population, the war was said to be fought on the "home front," and films were the main weapon used on the home front. Minnie Mouse, for example, showed housewives how to save bacon grease, which had become an important commodity during the war. People on the home front could watch the progress of the war in the newspapers and by viewing government films. And the films were everywhere: at movie theaters, in schools, at factories during the lunch hour.

One of the most famous series of American films were the *Why We Fight* films. General George C. Marshall called in Hollywood filmmaker Frank Capra, newly-made Major Frank Capra, and explained the problem. Many American soldiers were unaware of the reasons they had been drafted. A series of documentary films, General Marshall said, would help spur soldiers to fight. Capra objected. He'd never made a documentary film. "Capra, I have never been chief of staff before," replied Marshall, and the plans for the *Why We Fight* series began. The films were immensely successful and became a required part of military training. Opinion studies on draftees showed the films worked. Anti-British sentiment declined significantly after one viewing of *The Battle of Britain.* American allies used the films to tell their citizens about the progress of the war. *The Battle of Russia* was shown widely in Russia, by order of Stalin himself. And *The Battle of Britain* received similar exposure in England, under Churchill's order.

Director John Huston also made a number of films for the Army after being made Major John Huston. One of his most famous was *The Battle of San Pietro.* In one respect, the film resembled the earlier problem-solution documentaries. This time the problem was that people on the home front had expected the Allies to reach Rome much quicker than they were able to. A film was needed to show civilians why the Allies were having such a problem.

The power of *The Battle of San Pietro,* however, is in its reality. Director Huston gave up much of his control over his material in order to capture the reality of war. Before Huston made *The Battle of San Pietro,* cameramen preferred to control the risks of battle by faking combat footage. Canvas tanks were photographed in California, air battles were filmed over Orlando, Florida, and

ground forces fought in front of cameras in California. Faking war footage made things easier for directors; if a battle didn't look right, it could be filmed over. And faking a battle gave the cameraman a much larger choice of camera positions. Pictures from behind "enemy" lines could be taken of Americans advancing toward the battle, a difficult shot to get under combat conditions.

Huston decided to give up these crutches and simply to record the military action from wherever he could get his camera. It meant risks both artistically and otherwise. Following an intelligence report that there were no Germans in a particular village, Huston moved in to prepare some shots. The intelligence report proved incorrect, however, and shots of a different kind started flying at Huston; he escaped.

Huston wrote the commentary for his film and narrated it himself. In it a series of long shots of a peaceful looking valley are shown. But Huston states ominously that it was a bad year for grapes and olives in the Liri valley. Throughout the film, Huston's commentary adds new dimensions to what is shown. Pictures show a volunteer patrol going out on a mission. Huston comments that not one member of these patrols ever returned alive.

The progress of the battle is shown on a large map, classroom style, during the beginning of the film, so that the film could be used as a training film as well as an informational film.

The Battle of San Pietro was the first time real infantry combat conditions involving Americans had ever been filmed. When Huston finished editing the documentary late in the summer of 1944, he presented it to the War Department. It was a powerful film; too powerful, it seemed. One general in the Pentagon claimed it was pacifistic, an anti-war film. Huston objected. Although the film was extremely realistic, Huston claimed, he had made the film not as an anti-war effort but rather out of profound admiration for the courage of the men involved.

That didn't help. The War Department at first didn't want to release *The Battle of San Pietro* at all. Finally in April 1945, however, it did release a version of the film. The version was shortened from the original sixty minutes to thirty-six minutes with many of the more realistic scenes of American casualties cut out. The War Department also added its own introduction. General Mark Clark explains the necessity of the campaign and adds that it was a successful battle, although some viewers, watching the film that follows, might feel otherwise. The original version of *The Battle of San Pietro* was "discarded," in the words of the War Department. Even today, although television news has accustomed us to the realities of war, we can still feel much of the power of Huston's film in the available censored version. After seeing the film, we don't ask, "Is that how it really happened?" but on the contrary we can say, "So that's how it happened."

THE DOCUMENTARY AND TELEVISION

When the television set became as common a piece of furniture in American homes as the sofa, documentary film got a new boost. The events which people experience watching television not only seem real, they also seem to happen *now*. This increased reality suits the purposes of documentary film very well. One other characteristic of television also seems to increase the effect of documentary film. The television picture is not as clear and sharp as the motion picture image. Viewers watching a documentary on television must therefore complete the indistinct image using their imaginations. Because of the additional effort television viewers must expend filling in the indistinct mosaic picture television provides, they participate more fully in creating the television picture and thus become more involved in the actions they are watching.

Soon after its introduction, television gave documentary films a huge new audience. Earlier, directors had to bring documentaries to small audiences of people. But with television, an entire nation can see a documentary at exactly the same time. This ability lends films a special power. Many people remember the funeral of President Kennedy as one of the ways television can unite the sympathies of an entire nation. And the lunar landing in 1969 and the American-Soviet handshake in space in 1975 also demonstrate how television can document an event and allow people in all parts of the world to participate in a single event, even if it happens thousands of miles from them.

Much of the power of John Huston's **The Battle of San Pietro** came from its use of actual combat footage.

This simultaneous participation of the entire world in a single event, with all peoples viewing the event the same way, has important effects on us, as communication theorists like Marshall McLuhan note. After Gutenberg's discovery of the printing press, Western culture, which had been united like a single tribe in thought, religion, and empire, became fragmented. Individuals, each reading his own book in isolation, could come to a different conclusion. Television, because it allows all the world's peoples to simultaneously participate in events, helps break down these individual barriers and restores some of the tribal unity of pre-Gutenberg Europe.

One famous television documentary which used the ability of television to show an entire nation a film at an opportune time was the CBS-TV produced film *Harvest of Shame* (1960). The film deals with the plight of the migrant workers who pick much of the food that Americans eat. The conditions under which the workers have to slave are miserable, according to the film.

Harvest of Shame doesn't pull any punches. CBS knew it would have a powerful effect on its audience. But to increase its effect CBS used the new control that television transmission offers film: You can control *when* your audience sees a film.

When would be a good time to show a film on the depressing conditions of workers who provide food for Americans? On November 25, 1960, millions of Americans, stuffed with Thanksgiving turkey, sat down to relax after dinner, turned on their television sets, and heard Edward R. Murrow tell them that much of the food they had just consumed along with their turkey was brought to them by the sufferings of mistreated migrant workers. That was hard to take, especially on a full stomach. And viewers got the message about who was supposed to feel ashamed for the *Harvest of Shame*.

Harvest of Shame is a powerful film which brings its message across much more clearly than a staged drama could have done. Of course, there are two sides to any story, and the growers who

Documentaries allow viewers to be present at important events, such as presidential inaugurations.

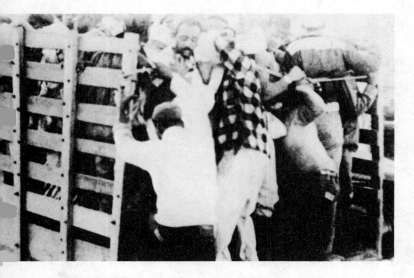

employed the migrant workers shown in the film didn't think their side was fairly presented in the film. Many of the growers complained to CBS that *Harvest of Shame* was one-sided, slanted news that CBS should be ashamed of putting on the air.

Naturally any film is slanted. Films are made by people, and people have points of view. When they make a film, directors select what they want to include and what they want to leave out. Many times films transmitted by television look so much like reality that people sometimes forget about the directors, the people between the real and the reel. Many of the growers that saw *Harvest of Shame* protested, however, that CBS shouldn't give its own opinion on things but only present events as they happened.

CBS defended its right to show *Harvest of Shame*, claiming that television networks have the right to editorialize as long as they don't distort facts unfairly. That was in 1960. The problem of just how much freedom television networks should have over documentary film is still unsolved.

CINEMA VERITÉ

Two new inventions in the early 1960's changed the whole documentary scene. Engineers created a silent, portable, battery-powered camera that could always be depended upon to run at exactly the same speed. Other inventors came up with a small battery-powered tape recorder capable of extremely high fidelity recording, which could be hooked up to the new silent camera.

Before these two inventions, directors had to make extensive preparation if they wanted to take films of people and hear them at the same time. Lights had to be set up, recorders wheeled in, huge cameras had to be set up and covered with quilted covers to muffle their noise. By the time all of the equipment was set, the event was usually over. Some cameras could record sound on the side of the film, but the fidelity was so low that working with these cameras was almost impossible.

CBS's documentary **Harvest of Shame** was a controversial program dealing with migrant workers.

With the new camera and tape recorders, a filmmaker could walk into almost any room and film events as they happened, with actual sounds and dialog recorded on the spot. A whole new style of documentary opened up. People called the new style **cinema verité**, or direct cinema. The name *cinema verité*, a translation of "Kino-Pravda," caught on.

Cinema verité caused a new trend in the style of documentaries. Before *cinema verité* equipment was invented, most documentaries used a narrator to tell the audience what was going on; but with the new equipment, the audience can listen to the characters for themselves and figure out what's going on. Again, the audience participates more in the event, adding to the feeling of reality. Documentaries made before *cinema verité* looked real; now they could *sound* real, too.

Of course, *cinema verité* filmmakers lose the control they could have over sound. Recording live dialog on film can include background noises, such as passing trains, barking dogs, exploding shells, and even the natural boominess of a large room. Getting a microphone near the person speaking isn't always easy. But all the work seems to pay off in the feeling of reality, and *cinema verité* offers directors an exciting method of filmmaking.

Early *cinema verité* documentary filmmakers put to good use the feeling of "actually being there." They attached themselves to important persons and recorded what happened to them. An early effort, *Adventures on the New Frontier*, gives audiences the feeling of being behind the scenes with John F. Kennedy and his staff. The reality of "being there" adds interest; it was an exciting place to be. And such films combined the personalist type of documentary in the Flaherty tradition with the social documentary that Grierson made popular.

The big problem for such films is finding places where the audiences would "like to be" or finding characters interesting enough to watch. Jane Fonda opens in a new play in an early *cinema verité* film, *Jane*; Eddie Sachs races to win in *Indianapolis 500*; Paul Crump, condemned to the electric chair, tries to obtain pardon from the then-governor of Illinois, Otto Kerner, in *The Chair*.

In *The Chair*, Don Moore, a young lawyer, had decided to take Crump's case and try to save him from the death penalty. The camera films Moore in his office. Things haven't been going too well. Tension is building up. Moore needs public support for his plea that Crump has reformed and that he should therefore not be executed. The phone rings, and a teacher from Ohio is calling. Her grade school children have been saving pennies to help Moore in his struggle to save Paul Crump's life. Moore begins to choke up with emotion; the phone call was totally unexpected, coming at a time when he was feeling quite alone in his struggle.

Moore hangs up the phone and begins to cry. Watching the scene, the audience knows it is real. A real man, crying real tears. The power of such a shot is in its reality. Such a scene could never have been captured without portable *cinema verité* equipment that allowed the lawyer to forget about the presence of a camera.

A similar incident happens in *Antonia*, Judy Collins's 1974 documentary. When the subject of the film relates her disappointment about the fact that she can conduct a symphony orchestra only a few times a year, she almost begins to cry. In this instant, we know that we have been privileged to "see into" the deepest reality of how another person feels.

Many times *cinema verité* allows filmmakers to introduce us to stories and people we would not usually think interesting. David and Albert Mayseles, two brothers who make *cinema verité* documentaries, followed five Bible salesmen and recorded their efforts to sell $49.95 Bibles door-to-door. During the filming of *Salesman*, one of the five loses confidence in himself, and his sales of Bibles fall off. What started out as a story of five men changed unexpectedly; now it becomes a story of one man being destroyed, his life coming apart.

A similar film, *I.F. Stone's Weekly*, follows the career of an independent journalist whose newspaper, during its existence, was a watchdog on government duplicity. Watching a man write a newspaper doesn't sound like an interesting subject; but careful filming and editing makes *I.F. Stone's Weekly* an exciting feature-length documentary.

Documentary filmmakers have so little control

over what is going to happen in their films that they have to shoot many times more film than directors who have control over their subjects. *Cinema verité* filmmakers try to be around as much as possible, hoping that important events will happen when they have their cameras available. Many times the story that such films finally tell will not be found until *after* the filmmakers finish shooting, look at the shots they have, and see what they can do with the film. Many documentary filmmakers *discover* their subjects, rather than *direct* them.

This kind of discovery was made by the Mayseles brothers during the filming of *Gimmie Shelter*, the *cinema verité* documentary they made about the rock group the Rolling Stones. During the rock festival at Altamont field, a young man was killed — and the filmmakers happened to get the actual killing on film. The tragedy of this event became a focal point for their film and set a new tone for the story, one of tragedy. The filmmakers underline the importance of this event by repeating it, frame by frame, and by showing Mick Jagger of the Stones watching the murder on the editing machine in the filmmakers' studios. When they started, the filmmakers had no idea of what kind of story they would find by following the Stones; it turned out to be a tragic one.

Sometimes *cinema verité* techniques and equipment can be used to go beyond reality, beyond giving us the feeling that we are "actually there." Films like *Woodstock* or *Ladies and Gentlemen, The Rolling Stones* can cover one event with a few cameras set in different places. Editing these various shots of the same event into one film allows us to feel more like "being there" as three different people at the same time. It's the logical extension of *cinema verité* beyond reality.

CHANGES FROM THE REAL TO THE REEL

Give somebody enough rope and he'll hang himself, so the saying goes. Film someone with film and tape, and he'll say something that a filmmaker can use to hang him. A documentary filmmaker, armed with unobtrusive *cinema verité* equipment, can usually turn his cameras on an event and wait for somebody to make a fool of himself. Sooner or later, a subject will say something that can be taken out of context and used for a filmmaker's purposes. With the added reality that *cinema verité* gives, the person making a fool of himself seems like a *real* fool!

Flowers on a One Way Street contains an interesting example of this particular use of *cinema*

Cinema verite techniques allowed the Mayseles brothers to film a tragic murder at a Rolling Stones concert. Mick Jagger watches the sequence on the editing machine.

verité. A group of young people want to close a street to car traffic. The Toronto authorities don't think it's as good an idea as the kids do, and various confrontations increase the tension. Finally the young people decide to go down to city hall and present their case to the controllers. What emerges is a huge childish squabble—among the aldermen. Although the young people provoke the aldermen at times—by taking over the seats of the aldermen when they're out to lunch, for example—most of the really dumb things seem to be done by the aldermen themselves. At least that's what the film shows. Parliamentary procedures are invoked to keep the young people from being heard. The aldermen fight among themselves in a scene totally out of control. The city council scene in *Flowers on a One Way Street* is composed of real aldermen really making fools of themselves. As it has been said, give anybody enough film, and they'll hang themselves.

Frederick Wiseman gets permission to enter institutions and record what happens. From hours and hours of film, Wiseman edits segments which tell the story, as he sees it, of the workings of the institution. No narration is used. The titles of the films give their locations: *Titicut Follies* (1967—about a Massachusetts institution for the insane), *Law and Order* (1969—the police), *Hospital* (1970), *Basic Training* (1971), *Essene* (1972—a monastery), *Juvenile Court* (1973), *Primate* (1974), *Welfare* (1975), and others. Wiseman feels his experience in law school in going through lengthy cases to pick out the core fact in each case helps him in editing down the over thirty hours usually shot for each film. In Wiseman's films, sound is usually more important than pictures. A cameraman shoots the film, with Wiseman holding the microphone. *High School* looks to be as bad a place to go to school as the school Christopher Wood attends in the fiction film *No Reason to Stay*. But *High School* is real.

Richard Leacock took his *cinema verité* equipment to a police chiefs' convention in Hawaii. Leacock obtained permission to make a documentary. He got that permission in writing, which was smart because when the people who let him in saw *Chiefs*, they weren't happy. *Chiefs* was never made to win friends and influence police chiefs. Leacock seized on the shots he wanted: Fat police chiefs in gaudy pineapple shirts smile devilishly at new weapons demonstrated for them by a sinister looking man with a black patch over his eye. Skinny police chiefs without pineapple shirts who attended the convention were probably offended at this less than complimentary picture. Leacock showed only what really happened at that convention; but a filmmaker can edit a film to obtain those parts he wants to use. The audience is given the impression that what they see is *all* that happened.

CBS-TV stirred up a discussion about this kind of editing when they aired their film *The Selling of the Pentagon* in 1971. The film deals with the way the Pentagon publicizes its activities, and it shows excerpts from some of the films the Pentagon distributes as "information" and which CBS claims are propaganda.

Certain parts of *The Selling of the Pentagon* caused a national controversy. In it, Roger Mudd, the narrator, states that colonels sent around the country by the Pentagon are not supposed to discuss politics; next, we see a colonel discussing politics. The Pentagon objected: The colonel was quoting Laotian Premier Souvanna Phouma in the excerpts CBS showed, not giving his own views. CBS countered that the colonel's words and the premier's were so closely intertwined that no separation was really possible.

In another sequence of *The Selling of the Pentagon*, Army soldiers demonstrate karate killing techniques "to a thousand kids," says the narrator. Immediately after watching the demonstration, we see some children fighting, using the killing techniques they have just seen. Did the cameraman "set up" the scene of the children fighting, asking them to "Try out some of that stuff for the camera, kids?" Or did the event really happen, with the children actually trying the killing techniques?

One thing that angered the Pentagon was the way CBS edited one speech a colonel gave in Peoria, Illinois. In the film, we see what looks like a connected speech. Actually, the Pentagon protested, the colonel's opening statement came from page 55

of his prepared text, the second statement from page 36, the third and fourth from page 48, the fifth from page 73, the last from page 88. This rearrangement, the Pentagon claimed, changed what the colonel actually said.

Film editors can cover up such rearrangements in a person's speech by inserting *cut-away shots*. We see a person making a speech. While he's talking, the editor cuts away to a shot of the audience, the interviewer, or a picture on the wall. Now we come back to the speaker. While we were looking at the cut-away shot, the editor could have cut to a different portion of the speaker's talk. By carefully joining the sound tracks, so that we cannot hear the difference and by using the cut-away to cover up any change in the picture, an editor can easily rearrange a speaker's words.

Newspapers, of course, edit news, too, and rarely print all of what a person says. But people tend to *believe* documentaries because they look like something that really happened. The film which won the Academy Award in 1975 for Best Documentary Film, *Hearts and Minds*, shows a long sequence of Vietnamese weeping at a funeral. One woman, hysterical, even tries to crawl into the grave of one of the dead. A little child, holding a soldier's picture, weeps uncontrollably. Immediately after this long sequence, we see an interview with General William Westmoreland, American commander in Vietnam for part of the war. Westmoreland begins with a statement that in Vietnam, life is cheap, and people don't care as much about death as they do in the U.S. Westmoreland's comment appears ridiculous after the long, tearful sequence preceding it.

Cinema verité equipment, while making it easy to probe into people's lives and show them to us, creates its own questions for that same reason. How much privacy should a person have against the prying eye of a camera? Has the possibility of snooping into people's lives eliminated the possibility and value of privacy, or has it made it more important?

Filmmaker Mike Tabor uses a stick to improvise a boom for his microphone while filming a documentary for the Canadian Bureau of Fisheries.

The problem of professional interest overriding human sensitivity is described in its extreme at the beginning of the feature film *Medium Cool*, where a television cameraman and his sound man are riding in their station wagon. They come upon a serious automobile accident. Quickly they grab their equipment and record the scene on film. After they finish, they call an ambulance for the victim. In the personal thinking of these two film-makers recording the event was more important than quickly radioing for help.

Today, fiction filmmakers copy documentary film techniques to give their films some of this feeling of reality. We see hand-held cameras during fight sequences to simulate the feeling we associate with newsreel records of the same events. In his feature film *Nobody Waved Goodbye*, director Don Owen didn't use a script. Rather, he told his actors Peter and Julie what was happening and let them make up their own lines as they went along. Owen even let them use their own names in the film so that they would sound more realistic.

Director Pier Paolo Pasolini used the hand-held camera technique of documentary filmmaking to make it appear as though *The Gospel According to St. Matthew* was "filmed as it happened," though the script was two thousand years old. Gillo Pontecorvo's film *The Battle of Algiers* looks so real that Pontecorvo had to include an explanation at the beginning of his film stating that none of the shots were newsreel shots. Improvised dialog, poor quality sound, harsh lighting, shaky camera, all these techniques can be used by a fiction film-maker to give the feeling of reality to his film.

With the downfall of the Hollywood studios, we will probably see more independently produced films, probably employing more of the techniques of the documentary filmmaker. Although in the past documentary and theater fiction films have usually been at odds, the success of theater documentaries like *Woodstock*, *Gimmie Shelter*, *Salesman*, and *Ladies and Gentlemen, The Rolling Stones* will probably encourage more of this kind of film. And fiction films, made outside the studios on location, will often prefer the real-life feeling of the documentaries to the polished feeling of the feature film.

DOCUMENTARY

ACTIVITIES

1) Watch a network evening news program and notice the headline news story (the first one the anchorperson reads). Then get a newspaper and read an account of the same story. Compare the video and print versions of the same story. Which version was more effective for you? Which was more complete? Which was more up-to-date? Which was more believable? Why?

2) Media critic Marshall McLuhan called the Vietnam war "the first television war" and explained that the dissent to the United States' involvement in that war stemmed from the fact that the war came into everyone's home on the suppertime news. Is McLuhan correct in his observation? Were there other factors in the amount of dissent to the war? Would these have explained entirely the amount of dissent?

3) Although a great deal of the Watergate affair was televised, much of the "leg work" in uncovering the facts of the case was done by two print journalists and not by television or film documentarians. Hollywood's response to the situation was simply to honor the two journalists by making them the subjects of a feature film. Why was the investigation reporting done by print journalists? Should television do more or less than print in exposing political corruption? Which medium is more effective in this regard? What about local political corruption?

4) The *Chicago Tribune* prints the following on its editorial page daily: "The newspaper is an institution developed by modern civilization to present the news of the day, to foster commerce and industry, to inform and lead public opinion, and to furnish that check upon government which no constitution has ever been able to provide." *The New York Times* is famous for its slogan,

"All the news that's fit to print." Write a slogan for a television show that presents weekly documentary films. Should television news broadcasting include the ideas behind the slogans of these two newspapers? Should TV news do more to "provide a check on government?" Does the fact that TV network news allows a few people to communicate their views on political events to an entire nation give those people too much power over voters? Should the people who create network news remain free to write as they please, or should they periodically have to "render an account for their stewardship?" If so, to whom?

5) Discuss whether the federal government should have its own TV network.

6) What is the "fairness doctrine" on television? What is the purpose of it and what problems have developed from using it?

ANIMATION

In film, few generalizations exist, but one general rule which seems to hold true in film is: "You can't usually photograph a generalization." This rule seems to make a lot of sense. Generalizations exist in people's minds. Movies can only be made about specific things that reflect light. So it would seem difficult to make a film that was about an *idea*, about a general truth, rather than about a specific thing.

Making a film about "the problems of young people today" for instance, would be difficult. You could make a film about the problems of one particular young person, his problem parents and their plastic friends. But, in the end, the film wouldn't be a generalization; it would be about one specific person.

The Graduate portrays Benjamin Braddock and his problems. People like to say that most college students are like Benjamin Braddock, and many of them have parents who are just as bad, and so *The Graduate* makes a point about them. Maybe that's true. But when you get right down to it, *The Graduate* is still about one college student. When one thinks about *The Graduate*, he thinks about Benjamin Braddock, not about "young people." And when one imagines Benjamin Braddock, he doesn't look like "young people in general"; he

Animation sections in the short film **Why Man Creates** present general truths about creativity.

looks like a young Dustin Hoffman. It's difficult to photograph a generalization, says the general rule. It's difficult; but it's not impossible. And when a director wishes to photograph a generalization, he will probably consider making an **animation film.**

When a director makes a film that creates motion in something that didn't move before, or *creates* a new way of moving for something that already moves, he's creating an animation film. Not all animation films are used to photograph generalizations, of course; that would be an incorrect generalization. Some directors make animation films just because they enjoy motion and like to create it. But if a director wants to portray a generalization, he will seriously consider doing an animation film to make his point.

For example, the Kaiser Aluminum Company wanted filmmaker Saul Bass to do a film on *creativity*. That is a complex subject to make a film on. He might have made a film on a couple of creative people or something like that. But how does a director approach the problem of making a film on such a general topic?

Director Saul Bass decided to make an eight-part film and to utilize animation in three parts of his film *Why Man Creates*. The first section, entitled "The Edifice," shows a building created by piling one idea on top of another, from the time of the cave men to the present. Animation allowed

Bass to photograph this generalization: "One idea builds upon all the ideas before it, but adds something new of its own." Since ideas don't reflect light, such a generalization would have been hard to communicate without animation. And animation also offers a quick way of conveying ideas. Bass wanted to cover all the ages of man and make generalizations about them in his film.

The entire Greek period of history in *Why Man Creates* runs for twenty seconds. In these twenty seconds, Bass wanted to communicate, with pictures and sound, the following statement: "The contribution of Greek society and Greek culture to our history was generally a result of its discursive and investigatory character. In spite of all the talk its thinkers engaged in about freedom, about the expansion of the mind, however, Greece was a state built upon slavery. Greek society never perceived this essential contradiction. In fact, it was one of the reasons that Greece crumbled."

Anyone with a speed reading course behind him probably got through the last paragraph in less than twenty seconds. All of the general facts contained in that paragraph also occur in *Why Man Creates*, and in a much more interesting way. Saul Bass used animated drawings to present these generalizations in twenty seconds, about the same time it takes to read them. If someone wanted to photograph the same generalizations in a movie, he might find it difficult to think of a way to do it without using animation's ability to photograph generalizations. Try to imagine doing it, and restrict yourself to the twenty seconds that Bass used.

Filmmakers John and Faith Hubley wanted to make a film that expressed the following generalization: "Governments are the real cause of many wars because they divide people artificially; left to themselves, people can usually get along with each other pretty well." The Hubleys decided to make their short film *The Hat* using the animation mode. *The Hat* shows two soldiers walking back and forth guarding a boundary line. One soldier drops his hat over the boundary line and wants to cross over to get it. But crossing over the line is against the rules of war, and so even though the two soldiers seem to get along pretty well as people, they have to follow the rules of war and act like enemies. While they are arguing about the hat, however, animals are freely walking across the line.

An earlier animation done by the Hubleys, entitled *The Hole*, also dealt with a general idea. *The Hole* concerns itself with the idea that "Nations which have offensive weapons will probably use them; disarmament would therefore be one step toward world peace." *The Hole* won an Academy Award for the Hubleys. Again it demonstrates how a general idea can be communicated easily and enjoyably by animation film.

Consider how much easier it is for an animated film like *The Hat* to make a general statement than it would be for a film using real people to make the same statement. *The Hat* shows two men in different uniforms. The filmmakers didn't worry about putting particular uniforms on their characters or telling what war they are in, where they are, or anything like that. They're just two men somewhere, guarding a boundary line somewhere. Instead of showing particular people, *The Hat* shows two men who could be anybodies.

How would you show a boundary line on film if you were photographing the story of *The Hat* with real characters? It would be difficult. Boundary lines, unless they are formed by a river or a coast, are imaginary lines, which just don't show up on film. To make a film like *The Hat* without using animation, you'd have to build a barbed wire fence or a wall or something to indicate the boundary line. What do the Hubleys do to create a boundary line in *The Hat*? Draw it on the ground. It is easily done in animation film.

It is evident that by making *The Hat* in the animation mode, the Hubleys gained several advantages. Using animation lets them express a general idea which could apply to anybody, rather than a particular statement which would have seemed to apply only to the people shown in the film. If they had used real actors, for example, *The Hat* would have been about these two men in one particular war, just like the film *The Graduate* was about Benjamin Braddock and only secondarily about the problems all kids have.

Terry and Denis Sanders also wanted to make a film that dealt with boundary lines and persons involved in following the rules of war. The Sanders brothers, however, decided to use real people, rather than animated people. Their short film, *A Time Out of War*, made as a master's thesis project, conveys much the same idea as *The Hat*. *A Time Out of War* shows two soldiers on one side of a boundary and one soldier on the other side. Because they were using real actors, the boundary had to be real; it is a stream. After shooting at each other for a while, the men agree to call a truce for a few hours so that they can rest and fish. During the truce, the soldiers relate to each other as friends, with mutual respect for each other. They trade supplies with each other. Although their governments are at war, these men decide to quit shooting at each other and act like friends. As in *The Hat*, however, the soldiers don't disobey the rules of war. They don't cross the boundary between them, the stream. The supplies traded are thrown across the stream. And at the end of both films, it is assumed that the men of *The Hat* and the men of *A Time Out of War* go back to fighting each other, although the audience never actually sees it happen in either film. Both films end just at nightfall.

Although both films present the same idea,

the advantage of using the animated mode to present generalized ideas can be seen easily. *The Hat* is about *some* war, but *A Time Out of War* is about the Civil War. *The Hat* shows two men in different uniforms; *A Time Out of War* shows two men in the blue uniforms of the North and a man in the gray of the South. The men in the animated film aren't real. The men in *A Time Out of War* are real; they have names, for one thing. To prove that the men in *A Time Out of War* are remembered as particular men, watch both films and then find somebody who hasn't seen either of them. Try to describe the two men in *The Hat* to him; then try to describe the three men in *A Time Out of War*. You will remember much more about the men in *A Time Out of War* as particular men than about the men in *The Hat*. But if you attempted to tell somebody what each film said, what general idea each tried to communicate, you would find it easier to pick out the general idea in *The Hat*. When a director wishes to say something which he wants to apply

John Hubley's **The Adventures of *** comments on the way in which many children grow up.

to everybody, the animation mode of expression comes in handy.

Jiri Trnka wanted to make a film that would express a general idea that he thought people should think about: "Totalitarian governments which don't work for their people but rather expect their people to work for them, have to have all of their citizens thinking alike. If somebody disagrees with them, he's got to be won over, by bribery, by force, or by whatever method will work. If he conforms, fine. Otherwise, he's got to be rubbed out."

Because there are many different kinds of governments like that, running organizations and countries, Trnka did not want to make a film which would describe just one such government. So Trnka chose the animation mode. His short film *The Hand* uses a puppet for animation rather than a drawing. In it a young man is shown making clay pots. The hand (a real hand), wants the young man to sculpt hands like itself, rather than clay pots. Trouble starts. Using bribery, propaganda, force, the hand resorts to anything it thinks will make this person conform. Finally, the young man rebels and dies. Trnka is trying to make a general statement about all such governments. Animation allows him to do that, without worrying about people confusing his film with one particular government.

Director Costa-Gavras wanted to make a film which would make a similar point about governments which demand absolute conformity. His feature Z, which won an Academy Award for best foreign film in 1970, shows how one government, run by extreme right wing military rulers, tries to maintain the same conformity as does The Hand in Trnka's film.

Costa-Gavras didn't want to particularize his film, and so he did not set it in any particular country. However, since all the events Costa-Gavras shows in Z happened in Greece not long ago, viewers tended to particularize his film. "It's all about Greece," people would say, "It really cuts them down." Rather than realize that Z was about *all* governments which try to keep everybody think-

Jiri Trnka's animation film **The Hand** uses a puppet and a real hand to present a general idea about totalitarian governments.

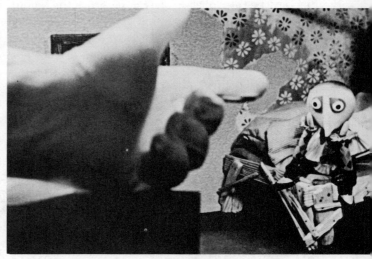

ing alike, viewers *particularized* the film saying it "cut down" one particular government or one particular type of conformist government.

Costa-Gavras had to make another film, *The Confession* (1970) about the same topic as *Z*, before many people realized that he was talking about the dangers of *all* kinds of conformist governments, rather than about just one in particular. *The Confession* takes Yves Montand, the star of *Z*, and puts him in Hungary during a time when conformism was being strictly enforced. *The Confession* ends with the 1968 entry of Warsaw Pact troops into Prague to insure conformism. It took two feature-length films for Costa-Gavras to make sure that people didn't misunderstand what he was talking about. People naturally tried to particularize his meaning to one specific government, rather than see a general statement in the film. Animation film can evade this difficulty.

Like Costa-Gavras, George Orwell did not want to describe one particular society when he wrote his book *Animal Farm*. So Orwell chose to write about a farm where the animals take over from their human master and proceed to establish a farm where all animals would be equal. Soon, however, some animals get to be "more equal" than others. Orwell's book was much like an animation film; and when the film *Animal Farm* was made, it was made as a full feature-length animation film, preserving the feeling of generality that Orwell put into his original.

HOW ANIMATION DEVELOPED

Animation is an old movie technique. It actually was around *before* movies. Many of the early devices inventors experimented with to create the illusion of movement actually work like today's film viewers. Early in film history, experimentors tried various techniques of animation. In America, Winsor McKay created *Gertie the Dinosaur* between 1910 and 1918. Other animators followed popular cartoon strips like *Mutt and Jeff* and *The Katzenjammer Kids* but their animation films tended to be static efforts, tied as they were to comic strips. Uninhibited by a comic strip, Pat Sullivan created the vigorous and fluid *Felix the*

The Halas and Batchelor production of **Animal Farm** is a feature-length cartoon dealing with problems described by author George Orwell.

Cat films. Max and David Fleisher created *Popeye* and *Betty Boop*, a character so lively she was condemned by the Legion of Decency. The increased expense of sound brought pre-eminence to the "big" animators with great financial resources. Walt Disney, with his human-like animals *Mickey Mouse*, *Donald Duck*, *Pluto*, and *Goofy*, came out on top. In the thirties, Disney's optimistic cartoon *The Three Little Pigs* rallied Americans with its message against the Depression, "Who's Afraid of the Big Bad Wolf?"

In success came failure. The freedom and vitality of Disney's original work soured as the Disney studios in Burbank became a factory committed to the assembly-line production of one feature film and forty-eight shorts per year. The original characters became stereotypes, and the vitality faded. *Fantasia* (1941) was Disney's attempt at linking animation to popular musical classics. Although visually exciting in its use of objects seeming to jump in and out of the screen, *Fantasia* was a failure at that time. When it was re-released in the mid-1970's and billed as "The Ultimate Trip," however, *Fantasia* attracted great numbers of patrons.

In Europe, animators were unaffected by Disney's success and continued to experiment. Alexandre Alexeieff produced his frightening *Night on Bald Mountain* in 1933 by animating shadows

created by bouncing light off the heads of thousands of pins stuck in designs in a board. The sequence resembles a dream and is much more effective than the similar sequence in Disney's later film *Fantasia*, which followed a realistic style. In Germany, Oscar Fischinger used animation to create abstract cartoons.

During the Second World War, Disney studios helped the war effort by creating animated films for the government. After the war, the Disney empire broke. Reacting against the saccharine immaturity of content in Disney's films, animators (many of them former Disney artists) created new cartoons. Bugs Bunny, Woody Woodpecker, Sylvester, Droopy, and others followed the Disney pictorial style of realistic animation, but they added unreal, violent, and sadistic humor. Reacting against the visual style of Disney animation, Disney former employee Steve Bosustow founded the animation company UPA Films. UPA cartoons showed simple, unrealistic, and vigorous drawings in characters such as Gerald McBoing Boing and the nearsighted Mr. Magoo.

Although these animators and many other artists working in the United States and Europe treated adult subjects in their animation films, the Disney success identified animation with *children's films*. Possibly because of this association of animation and children, directors in America usually shy away from using animation films to communicate with adult audiences. "Adult animations," like *Animal Farm*, are few and far between. *Yellow Submarine*, another adult animation, has achieved lasting success, especially with high school and college age audiences. But nobody really knows whether *Yellow Submarine*'s success was due to its extremely original and successful use of the animation technique, or to the popularity of the Beatles. In any case, directors haven't been rushing to bring out feature-length animations for the over-twelve crowd. And today, much of the creative

A filmmaker can animate anything. **The Wall**, an animation film from Zagreb, Yugoslavia, uses animated drawings. Elliot Noyes's film **Clay** shows clay creatures in evolution. And in **A Chairy Tale**, Norman McLaren makes a chair seem to have a mind of its own.

work in short animation films still comes, not from the United States, but from Canada, France, Poland, and Yugoslavia, countries unaffected by the Disney success.

ANIMATION POSSIBILITIES

A filmmaker can animate *anything*. Drawings, of course, can be made to move, but also dots, lines, loops, as well as chairs, tables, ping pong balls, even people—all can be animated.

The short animation *Renaissance* shows us a room that's been destroyed by a bomb. Everything has been wrecked, the walls are burned, nothing moves. Suddenly, though, motion starts; things slowly begin to move, putting themselves back together, piece by piece. A stuffed owl puts its feathers on again; a trumpet reassembles itself; a bowl of grapes bunches up again, coming together grape by grape. Finally, after a long process, the room is back together again, the burned walls are repaired, everything is in its place—including a hand grenade connected to an alarm clock. The grenade explodes, and the room is back to where it started in the first place.

Although *Renaissance* is enjoyable to watch simply because of its fascinating movement and clever sound track, its director has shown us a generalized idea: "Everything repeats itself. Things pass away, only to come again. To everything there is a season, turn, turn, turn." Animation makes it easy for a director to present such complex general ideas. Although it's fun to watch, *Renaissance* also communicates; it has something to say.

One man whose name usually comes up when animation is mentioned is Canadian filmmaker Norman McLaren. *Opening Speech* shows McLaren trying to talk to a group of people. However, McLaren's microphone has a mind of its own and begins its own Microphone's Liberation Movement. Although microphones traditionally were built to serve man, animation shows McLaren's microphone refusing.

A Chairy Tale also shows McLaren's use of animation to question man's relationship with things. McLaren wants to sit down on a chair. But the chair he wants to sit on doesn't want to be sat upon. It's another revolt. Coaxing, violence, trickery, all fail for McLaren. Finally, however, love succeeds. Like *Opening Speech*, *A Chairy Tale* is fascinating to watch simply because of its movement. But the idea communicated by the film is a generalized, complex one about man's relation to things.

The problem of man's relationship to things like machines and electronic brains is a problem that bothers many thinkers today. Filmmakers can explore the problem by using animation techniques, because animation can make machines or things move around and act like quite advanced organisms. Again, without animation, filmmakers would not be able to talk to us about such topics.

One of Norman McLaren's most famous animations is his film *Neighbors*. Although it's an old film and looks like it from the clothes the characters wear, *Neighbors* still remains an exciting film to watch. Two men live next to each other. A flower blooms on the boundary line between their yards. They fight over the flower, each claiming that the flower is on his side of the boundary line. The fight continues to their deaths. Much of their movement, however, is animated rather than real. Instead of walking over their lawn, they slide, fly, float, and move in many strange animated ways. McLaren made up the word **pixillation** to describe this process of creating a new kind of movement for objects that would move on their own. Pixillation comes from the abbreviation *pix*, the word newspaper people use to refer to pictures. Pixillation makes real people into pictures, and then makes them move.

At the end of *Neighbors*, as in many of his other films, McLaren underlines the fact that animation films are a good means for a director to use in presenting general, universal ideas. After showing these two neighbors killing each other off over the boundary line between their property, McLaren warns his viewers, in a motto expressed in many languages, "Love your neighbor."

Sometimes filmmakers have to use many different methods of animation to get the effect they want. Saul Bass wanted to animate a ping pong ball in the fifth section of his film *Why Man Creates*. A ping pong ball is rejected by the ping pong ball factory because he bounces too high. Thrown outside into the garbage, the ping pong ball realizes he might as well be himself and bounces over to a park, where he intrigues other balls. To make the ball seem to move, Bass rolled it, blew it around with air, and bounced it around. Again, Bass was trying to communicate a general idea; he entitled this section of his film "A Parable" to underline the fact that he was presenting a general idea.

Orange and Blue also uses animated balls, two volleyballs which bounce around a forest and a junkyard, enjoying each other's company. The balls are animated simply by throwing them around and bouncing them. Sometimes the director shows sequences in reverse, to make the volleyballs seem to bounce upwards rather than fall downwards.

Elliot Noyes, Jr. discovered that clay is a fantastic substance to animate. His short film *Clay, or the Origin of Species* shows clay objects eating each other up, growing larger and larger, evolving into various different species. *Clay* never stops moving; its constant change puts the word motion back into "motion pictures." So popular is Noyes' film that numerous imitations crop up as more and more students see it. Noyes also tried his hand at animating sand, with interesting results.

Norman McLaren pioneered animation films made without using cameras. It's possible to draw directly on film and create motion. Drawing lines along the length of a film creates vertical lines which move back and forth across the screen. McLaren's film *Lines Vertical* shows a good example of this technique. Through a process of re-copying these lines with a device called an **optical printer**, a filmmaker can twist these lines over on their side so that they run across the screen and move up and down. McLaren's *Lines Horizontal* shows how this can be done. It's even possible to paint dots on clear film or loops, or any other patterns you want. McLaren's films *Dots* and *Loops* show two examples of this technique. And *Pen Point Percussion* shows how McLaren draws his animated films and creates sound tracks for them by drawing the sound tracks with pen and ink alone.

WHAT ANIMATION CAN SAY

Many directors are beginning to use the animation mode of filmmaking to allow themselves to explore new areas of filmmaking in new ways. *Les Escargots*, a short science fiction thriller, shows giant snails invading a civilization. First, they start by eating up a farmer's crops and then proceed to terrorize the nearby town. Finally, the plague of snails leaves. Things look peaceful. Are the town's problems over? They seem to be—until giant rabbits appear on the horizon. *Les Escargots* allows its filmmaker to create a world where nothing is real; hence he does not have to worry about the problem most science fiction films have—the monster looks less real than the background. Animation gives a filmmaker the freedom to create a world where nothing seems real, nothing makes any sense at all. Thus, he's not tied to reality anymore; he can say and do whatever he wants.

Polish filmmaker Jan Lenica shows us a town governed by a strange scientist in his film *Labyrinth*. Strange monsters crawl or fly through the town; walruses with butterfly wings, strange birds, people's heads with no bodies attached to them—all these creatures populate a world where nothing makes any sense at all. There are days when everybody gets the feeling that nothing makes any sense; that's the way things are everyday in the world created by Jan Lenica. Again, animation allows a filmmaker to create any sort of world he wants. More and more filmmakers today are using animation films to tell us what they think about life and living. For Jan Lenica in *Labyrinth*, life doesn't seem to make much sense at all.

There's not much that a filmmaker can't animate. *Les Astraunautes* uses collage-type paste-ups to show us a man who decides to start his own space program. Rather than using a realistic drawing of a spaceship, the filmmaker creates a spaceship by pasting newspaper cut-outs and various other objects on top of each other. Again, animation filmmaking doesn't require a director to stick with realism.

Albert Lamorisse used various methods of animation in his short film *The Red Balloon* to allow a balloon to react like a person. Animation can allow a filmmaker to breathe life and motion into a large variety of objects and actually make them into characters in his film.

Sometimes a filmmaker can use repetition of the same image to create an animated effect. Perhaps the best example of this technique is Norman McLaren's film *Pas de Deux*. McLaren started with a ballet dance and carefully lit his two dancers so that they would be outlined in light. Then he photographed them performing a dance. When he got his film back, he used an optical printer to re-photograph past frames onto later frames, over and over again. Whenever one of his dancers moves, they are followed by rapidly fading ghost images of themselves. By repeating the same pictures again and again, McLaren has animated the dancers and completely altered their movements.

Perhaps the most interesting work now being done in animation comes from a school of animation filmmakers in Zagreb, Yugoslavia.

Most Zagreb films raise mature questions about life, usually in a cynical manner. In *Elegy*, for example, a man is imprisoned and lonely. A flower grows outside his cell, keeping him company from season to season. The flower is his only friend.

Finally, we hear the cell door open, and the man's face leaves the window. He goes outside the cell, suitcase in hand. As he walks away free, he steps on the flower and crushes it to death.

Drawn in an extremely abstract style, sometimes mixing live action with animation, the Zagreb films are the complete opposite of the stereotyped Disney style of animation in technique, content, and intended audience.

Using the animation mode of filmmaking allows a filmmaker to create movement and life where there was none before. When the filmmaker restricts himself to the documentary mode of filmmaking, he loses some of the control over his subject which he might have had, but he gains a feeling of reality. When a filmmaker chooses to restrict himself to the animation mode of filmmaking, he loses reality, but he gains a new way of looking at motion, a new type of motion picture. By restricting himself or herself to animation filmmaking, the director *creates* the motion in his or her motion picture.

Ersatz, a Zagreb animation, depicts a horrifying world of plastic inflatable substitutes for everything.

ANIMATION

ACTIVITIES

1) Make a flip book. Draw a sequence of pictures or stick figures on a note pad. Make each figure similar to the figure on the previous page but with some little change in movement. For example, a stick figure could wave or walk across the page. Then flip through the book as you would through a deck of cards.

2) Many devices preceded the invention of the movie camera. The phenakistiscope was a disc with various sequential drawings on it, each separated by a slit. You viewed the drawings by spinning the disc in front of a mirror and looking through the slits. More convenient to view was the zoetrope, which had a slotted revolving drum with pictures drawn on the inside of the drum. Again viewing was done through slits. The praxinoscope substituted a polygonal drum of mirrors at the center of the drum. The viewing slit was not necessary since the moving image could be seen in the mirrors as the drum rotated.

Find pictures of these and other early animation devices. Then, construct your own device. Paper plates, glued together for stiffness, are handy for making the phenakistoscope. Draw lines dividing the plate into eight or more equal sections. Cut a slit at the same place on each line. Draw a series of pictures, stick figures, or whatever, in the same area of each section. Or mount representative segments of your flip book in the spaces. Mount the paper plate so that it can be spun easily and view through the slits into a mirror.

3) Obtain some clear movie film—16mm film is easiest to use. Draw on the emulsion side with felt tip pens. Permanent felt tips stick better than washable ones. To identify the emulsion side, put a dot on both sides of the film and try to wipe each off. The emulsion side is the side that the color sticks to better. Experiment with drawing vertical lines down the film. Then try drawing simple

pictures on successive frames. Remember to draw enough pictures and to pace your action well. Some 16mm projectors operate only at sound speed, so it will take you twenty-four frames to cover one second. Many 16mm projectors, however, can be slowed down to 16 frames per second silent speed.

Alternatively, you might scratch lines by scraping the emulsion off of black opaque 16mm film. The point of a drawing compass is a handy tool. Color the lines if you wish. This is obviously a more tedious method than simply drawing on clear film but it gives an entirely different effect. You should really try both methods.

You can make clear film stock for drawing by removing the pictures on some waste film. Just wash the film in straight chlorine bleach (Dangerous stuff! Wear rubber gloves and protect your eyes). Rinse well in clear water after the pictures have come off and hang the film up to dry. Colors don't stick as well to film prepared in this manner, so be careful not to smear your drawings.

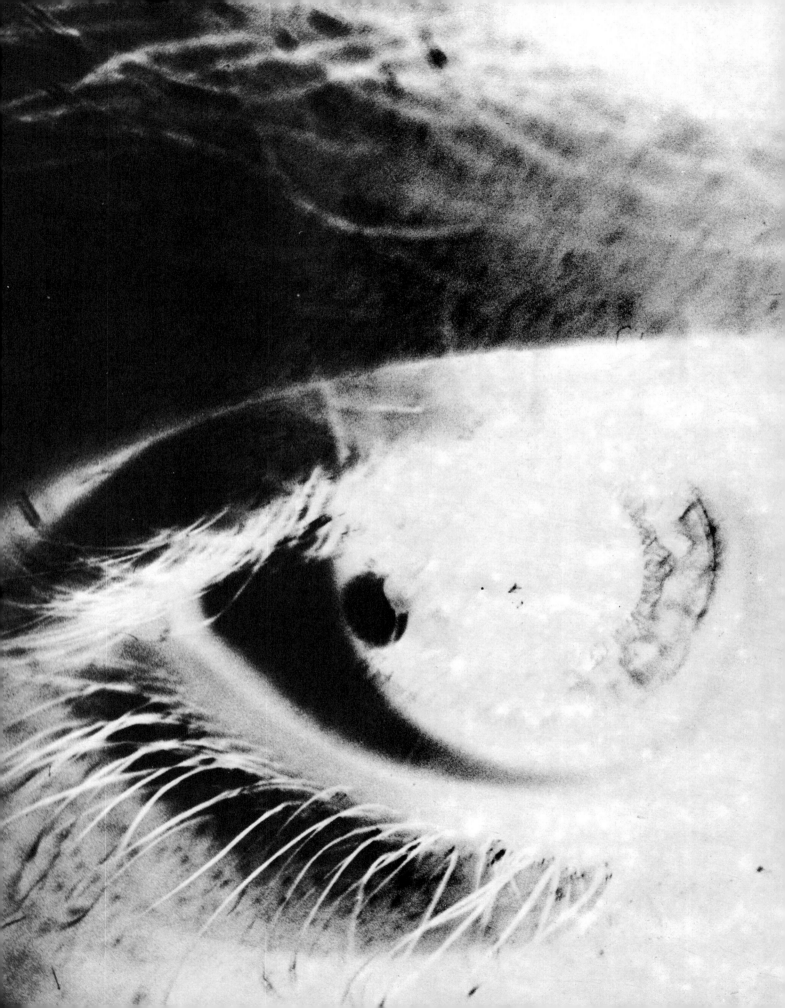

NOW - FILM

12

There's an old story about a group of blind men trying to describe an elephant. One of them had his hand on the elephant's tail; he declared that an elephant is like a piece of rope. Another got hold of the elephant's leg, and said no, that an elephant is like a tree. And other blind men, depending on what they were touching, had different impressions of what an elephant is. Because **now-film** is such a large and complicated creature, like an elephant, it is just as difficult to get a complete picture of just what **now-film** is. Deciding on a definition for now-film would be more difficult for us than discovering what an elephant was for the group of blind men in the story.

Let's begin talking about some now-films anyway and about some of the elephants usually found in what are called now-films. We may never discover exactly what a now-film is, but our investigation will give us a better understanding of the general area.

There are many different terms which people use to refer to what we will call now-films. Some idea can be gained of how large an area is included by knowing that people have labeled them experimental films, independent films, The New American Cinema, underground films, personalist films,

Now-filmmakers experiment with ways of showing us things in a different way than we are used to seeing them, including extreme close-ups.

expanded cinema, free films, synaesthetic cinema, synergistic cinema, psychedelic movies, and non-linear films; and many more names exist. Some of these names are more precise than the word **now-film**, but our name has three advantages: first, it gives the idea that now-films refer to films being made today in large numbers; second, the name is shorter than the others; and third, there isn't much worry about spelling it incorrectly.

EXPERIMENTING WITH FILM

The list of names in the last paragraph will also give a good idea of some of the characteristics of now-films. The first name on the list is "experimental film." That name says a lot about now-films and what they're like. By understanding what an "experiment" is, one characteristic of almost all now-films can be discovered.

Don't confuse the word *experiment* with the word *demonstration*. Most of the experiments that we're familiar with are experiments we've seen in school, perhaps in science classes. But most chemistry teachers, for example, wouldn't dare perform an *experiment* in front of a class; that is, they would not mix together chemicals without knowing for sure the outcome. The wrong chemical reaction might wipe out an entire room. So teachers wisely stick to *demonstrations*, of which they know the outcome, rather than attempt real *experiments*.

Now-filmmakers, on the other hand, are willing to try new things, to experiment without knowing exactly what's going to come of their efforts. If the experiment fails, they've lost some time and a few rolls of film. If the experiment succeeds, however, they have something new; they've succeeded in showing something in a way no one has ever seen it before; they've broadened the spectrum of film expression.

For example, when Dan McLaughlin was head of the animation department of UCLA's film school, he tried an experiment. He wanted to see how much a person could remember of images flashed upon a screen very rapidly. So, using a sixteen millimeter Bolex camera he had set up in his garage, he took pictures of photographs showing some of the world's great paintings. McLaughlin shot two frames of each painting. Since we know that a 16mm projector shows us twenty-four frames each second, we know that we'd see twelve different paintings each second. McLaughlin shot one one-hundred foot roll of film, giving him three minutes of screen time. Multiplying three minutes times sixty seconds per minute times twelve pictures per second, the film records a total of 2160 paintings in three minutes! It took McLaughlin two weeks to shoot all of the paintings. The only exception McLaughlin made in allowing two frames of film per painting occurred when he filmed the Mona Lisa. Since that was supposed to be the world's greatest painting, McLaughlin gave it twelve frames, or one-half of a second.

McLaughlin liked the film, but didn't bother to show it to anybody. Three years later, he mentioned the experiment to one of his students at UCLA. Since the student seemed interested, McLaughlin went back into his garage, dug up the film, and showed it to some of his students. They liked it. So McLaughlin decided to show his film publicly. The original title for the film was *God Is Dog Spelled Backwards*, but he decided to simplify the title into *Art*.

You can see why "experimental film" is a good name for this type of film. If you don't know what's going to happen when you finish with a film, you're doing an experiment. When McLaughlin decided to make *Art*, he used a technique that was totally new.

It was so new a technique that nobody had ever made up a name for it; McLaughlin decided on the name **iconic graphic** to describe his new style.

There's a limitation to the name *experimental*, however; it easily becomes difficult to decide what's really "experimental" and what's not. What happens if somebody else wants to duplicate the effect of a film? Is that new film still an experiment?

Filmmaker Charles Braverman had seen *Art*. He decided to make a similar film which would trace the development of America from the Revolutionary War to the present time, in the space of three minutes. He called his film *American Time Capsule*. Although he used still pictues in his film, as McLaughlin had done in *Art*, Braverman experimented with additional techniques. He added camera movements and zooms to McLaughlin's technique, so that the objects in the still pictures seem to move. Horses seem to pull wagons, cowboys ride across the screen, soldiers march, and airplanes take off. Braverman then added another technique to McLaughlin's **iconic graphic** technique. He synchronized the pictures in *American Time Capsule* to a drum solo by Sandy Nelson. Every time there is a beat in the music of *American Time Capsule*, the shot on the screen changes to a new shot. This meant that Braverman had to choose his music carefully, time each beat of the music, calculate how many frames that beat would take, and decide how to move the camera, if at all.

Braverman shot *American Time Capsule* in his garage; he spent five nights, working eight hours a night, all night, shooting the film. Later, the film was shown on the *Smothers Brothers Comedy Hour*. Again, we can see why this film represented an experiment, doing something in a new way. Braverman experimented with camera motion and varying the lengths of shots during his film, something that McLaughlin had not done in his earlier film.

Later, Braverman experimented further. In *World of 68*, he experimented with the technique of including actual moving pictures along with still pictures and pictures that seem to move. *World of 68* was totally pre-planned; Braverman spent ten days writing a script, frame by frame, for the entire film. And *World of 68* was longer than *American*

Time Capsule and *Art. World of 68* ran four and a half minutes; it was also shown on the *Smothers Brothers Comedy Hour*, and on the *CBS News*.

McLaughlin's experimentation opened up a whole new way of making films. Other filmmakers have experimented using this new technique. Braverman invented the name **kinestasis**: to make still pictures seem to move. The high school student film that won first place in the 1971 Columbia College High School Student Film Festival, held at the Museum of Contemporary Art in Chicago, was a kinestasis film called *The Iliad*. Like Braverman's film, *The Iliad* synchronizes its pictures to music. But *The Iliad* experiments with new additions to the technique of kinestasis; parts of the film are shot through colored filters, and black frames are inserted into the film, so that portions of *The Iliad* flicker on the screen like a stroboscope. Like other kinestasis films, *The Iliad* covers a great deal of actual time in a few minutes of screen time; it traces the entire history of America's race to the moon.

Another high school student film, *Nine Years in Nine Minutes*, covers the history of the Beatles, from the beginning of their career to their death as a group. Again, a new technique is added to kinestasis. Shots of four green apples are inserted into

The kinestasis film **Televisionland** includes shots like the one below.

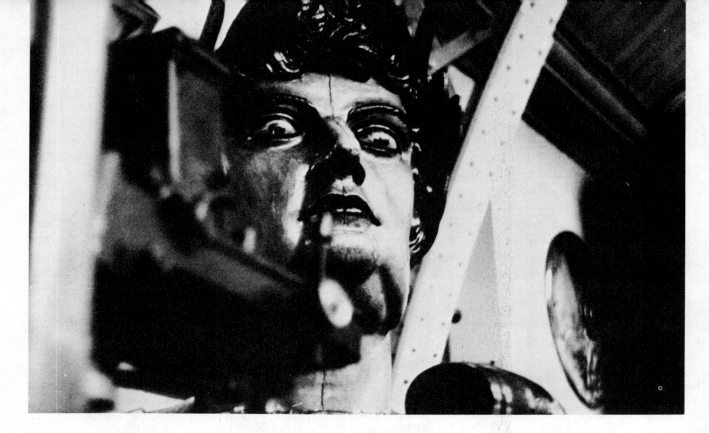

the film; by the end of the film, the apples have been eaten, and only one core is left. Animation has also been included in kinestasis as an experiment; again, it's a new technique.

One high school student, Michael Tabor, decided to experiment further. Like McLaughlin, Tabor was interested in seeing how many pictures a person could perceive in a short amount of time. Instead of showing his pictures one at a time, however, Tabor arranged his pictures on a black background so that at various times in his film, four or more pictures are visible at one time. And the pictures change at various intervals, measured down to a small fraction of a second. As an added experiment, he included cut-out headlines with the still pictures in his film, to see if his audience would rather look at his pictures or read the words he flashed at them. Tabor's film *Yourself* was a new experiment in kinestasis because it used more than one picture at a time and added printed words to the technique. Although the technique of kinestasis has been used before, it's still possible to experiment with new ways to use the technique, as many filmmakers have proved.

You can get some idea of the problem that the term *experimental* film gives us. If somebody makes a kinestasis film and doesn't try something new,

Arthur Lipsett's compilation film **Free Fall** was made by collecting scraps of films that other filmmakers had left over and putting them together into a film.

is it really an experiment? That's why we've used the name **now-film**. The word **now-film** gives us the idea of experimentation when we use it; when we see a now-film, we usually get the feeling that we're watching something for the first time, something now. We feel some of the same excitement that the filmmaker felt when his experiment "worked." Even if it's really not a true experiment, a now-film usually retains the same feeling of freedom, the same feeling of excitement of a first-time film.

PERSONALIST CINEMA

Other words that people use for now-films are **independent films**, or **personal films**. These names also offer ideas as to the characteristics of now-films. Tom Palazzolo, a Chicago filmmaker, makes films because he likes to, not because he has been assigned a film by somebody else. Palazzolo is an independent filmmaker; that means that Palazzolo, like most now-filmmakers, does what he wants to do and pays the bills himself.

One St. Patrick's Day, Palazzolo filmed a big parade that Chicago holds to celebrate that day.

It gave Palazzolo an idea for a new film. *America's In Real Trouble* shows various scenes of Chicago—the shots taken at the St. Patrick's Day parade, shots of slums, soldiers in uniform, beauty queens in a parade. For a sound track, Palazzolo collected a few patriotic songs that he felt expressed what he wanted to say about the parade. The final song in *America's In Real Trouble* gives a rather shallow definition of patriotism ("It's a new car, prettier girls") and proposes a strictly emotional test for patriotism. While the audience hears these superficial definitions of patriotism, however, the film shows shots from the slums of Chicago, shots of garbage cans, shots of dirty elevated train stations. The shallowness of the entire parade comes through effectively.

Nobody asked Palazzolo to make *America's In Real Trouble*. He made it because he wanted to. Some viewers might be offended by the way that Palazzolo feels about certain kinds of patriotism; but Palazzolo is free to say what he wants in his film, without interference, because *America's In Real Trouble* is his film. He paid for it. It can say what he wants it to say.

A few years after he completed *America's In Real Trouble*, Palazzolo decided to change the film. He had some new parade shots and some shots of plastic pink flamingo yard ornaments that he wanted to insert. So he did. Older copies of *America's In Real Trouble* don't have these shots; newer copies do. Because Palazzolo is an independent filmmaker, he didn't have to ask anybody's permission to make changes in his film. He just changed it. Most now-filmmakers work this way. They pay for their own films, and they use them to say just what they want. This freedom shows through in now-films. They usually communicate an extremely personal idea.

COMPILATION FILMS

Arthur Lipsett isn't an independent filmmaker; he works for the National Film Board of Canada. Yet his films have the same personal feeling that independent filmmakers achieve in their films. Lipsett's films are **compilation films**. To make a compilation film, you sweep the floor of an edit-

ing room and get a lot of scraps. Then you pick out the scraps that you like and splice them together in an order that says what you want to say. You can make a sound track in the same way; you go into a sound studio and sweep up around there.

Lipsett's most familiar compilation film is probably *Very Nice, Very Nice*. But Lipsett's other compilation films are similar in what they say as well as how they say it. Ugly people seem to predominate in Lipsett's films. Life seems to be a big waste of time for the people in Lipsett's films. The world Lipsett shows us is a circus, and most of the acts are performed by the clowns. Even though it's clowns who are performing, however, watching one of Lipsett's films isn't usually a happy experience. *Very Nice, Very Nice, 21-87, Free Fall*, or any other example of Lipsett's work all seem to have a common feeling of depression running through them. Even though he uses scraps of film, taken by other filmmakers, Lipsett is able to communicate the way he feels about things through the scraps he selects and the order he shows them to us. Although Lipsett really isn't an independent filmmaker, he does make personal films. Are they *experimental*? Maybe.

By now you can see some of the difficulty in giving certain names to now-films. All experimental films really aren't experiments, and all filmmakers making independent films really aren't independent.

NOW-FILMS

Why have we decided to call these films "now-films?" What's so *now* about them? First of all, most now-films are concerned with the present time. Rather than dealing with the problems of yesterday, now-films talk about today and what's happening now. Politics, prejudice, space travel, all seem to interest the now-filmmaker. And the now-film movement only started recently; earlier films were always "big" films controlled by other people, film was expensive, and cameras were hard to manage. But now, 16mm and Super 8 cameras make it easy for anybody to be a filmmaker and make film cheap enough to be a practical method of self-expression.

The main reason for calling now-films by that name, however, is that most now-films are not as *linear* as other films. In other words, big films *progress* as we watch them; they have a beginning, a middle, and an end, and it is important to see them in that developing order. These films are interesting to watch because they set up a conflict of some sort and then resolve it. In a big film, what's happening at any moment in the movie is based upon what happened before. For example, in the middle of Howard Hawks's film *Rio Bravo*, Dean Martin pours a shot of whiskey into a whiskey bottle. "Didn't spill a drop," he remarks. If a person had walked into the theater when he did that, he would probably be thinking, "So what? What's so good about being able to pour a shot of whiskey back into a bottle?" If, on the other hand, someone had been in the theater from the beginning of the film, he would recognize that this particular moment was important in *Rio Bravo*. He would know that Dean Martin was playing the part of an alcoholic lawman who was trying to reform. Martin had been on the wagon since the beginning of the film. That decision to pour back the shot of whiskey was an important moment in *Rio Bravo*, but a viewer had to be around from the beginning of the film to know that.

Big films like *Rio Bravo* and almost all other story films usually have *plots*, or *story lines*. Because they follow these story lines, they are called **linear films** — they go along a line in one direction.

Events usually occur differently in a now-film. Although they have an order of sorts, what is going on *now* is interesting enough by itself; it doesn't depend upon what happened before. The second half of Stanley Kubrick's feature *2001: A Space Odyssey* is a now-film. In this part of *2001*, it's enjoyable enough to watch what's going on *now*; knowing what went on before really doesn't make that much difference in enjoying what's happening *now*. In all now-films, any moment in the film is exciting by itself. That's the real difference between a now-film and other types of film. This is why some people use words like **non-linear** films and **experiential films** to talk about now-films. Non-linear films don't follow a story line; like the second half

of *2001*, they just happen. And the job of the audience is to *experience* them.

Of course, most now-films do have an order to them, and it wouldn't be fair to a now-filmmaker to watch them out of order. But a now-film is directed at you *now*; the filmmaker wants you to enjoy what's happening *now*. Rather than show you something now because it will be important to understand the rest of the story later on, a now-filmmaker shows you something now because it is enjoyable now.

At the end of Dan McLaughlin's film *Art*, after we've seen 2160 pictures in three minutes, a title comes on the screen saying, "You have just had all of the great art in the world indelibly etched on your brain. You are now cultured." The humor of that title depends upon the order of the film. Show the film backwards, with that title *first*, and it isn't funny. That title depends upon what's been in the film before. But *Art* is a now-film because every second we watch the film, we enjoy that second *now*, because of the quick movement of the pictures and not because of what has gone before. Many other short films are now-films as well. Norman McLaren's line animations which we have talked about already are now-films. The National Film Board of Canada's film *Sky*, for example, also would be a now-film because we watch the film's movement for enjoyment *now*. Story line films like *Occurrence at Owl Creek Bridge* are not now-films. There's much of the now-film kind of enjoyment in films like *Occurrence at Owl Creek Bridge*, of course. Camera work and editing can give us now-film enjoyment. But the real reason Robert Enrico made *Occurrence at Owl Creek Bridge* was to tell us a story with a plot, a beginning, a middle, and an end. The reason behind most of Arthur Lipsett's films, behind *America's in Real Trouble* and other of Tom Palazzolo's films, behind all now-films, is to entertain us now, at each successive instant.

This is why some viewers find it difficult to watch now-films. If a viewer is used to watching films with a story line, he keeps waiting for something that he can *understand*. When that doesn't happen, he feels he has missed something. Rather than enjoy every moment of the now-film, he has been waiting for something to understand, as if

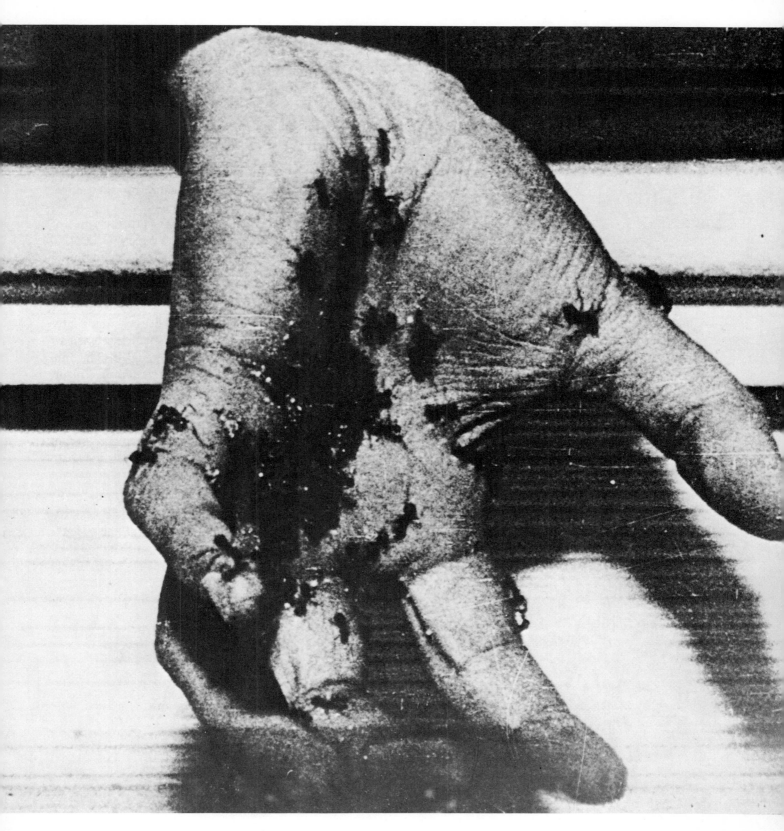

The surrealist film **Un Chien Andalou** by Luis Bunuel and
Salvador Dali contains nothing like the story lines found
in linear films.

he were watching a linear film. He should have been busy enjoying rather than waiting.

Perhaps the best way to understand the difference between how now-films and linear films affect viewers is to compare them with popular sports. Baseball is a good example of a linear, logical sport. In baseball, events happen more or less one at a time, with one event causing another. Soccer, on the other hand, represents a non-linear, simultaneous grouping of events. Experiencing the all-at-once, electronic nature of soccer compares to the now-film experience, while the mechanical experience of baseball resembles the linear film experience.

Some now-filmmakers, for example, deliberately prevent audiences from understanding a story line. When Luis Bunuel and Salvador Dali made *Un Chien Andalou* in 1929, it is said they went over the script to make sure that nothing made any linear sense. If one sequence by chance seemed to logically follow another, they changed it. The film begins with a young man (Bunuel) stropping a razor, stepping out on a balcony and in extreme close-up slicing a girl's eyeball just as a cloud passes over the moon. *Un Chien Andalou* also includes many wild grotesque images: A woman walking an amputated hand, an attempted rape, and a swarm of ants crawling out a hole in a man's hand are some of the images. *Un Chien Andalou* is a sur-

Quick cutting and the absence of a logical story line characterize the now-film **Help! My Snowman's Burning Down**.

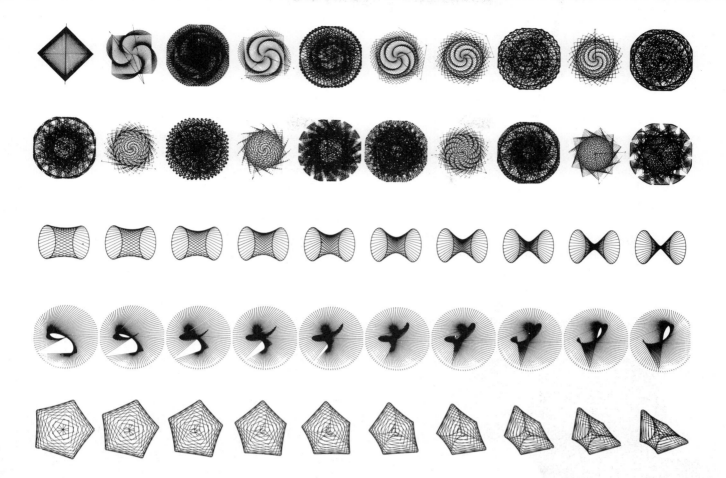

Constantly moving forms are the content of the now-films made on analog and digital computers by filmmaker John Whitney.

realist film. It puts real objects in strange and unexpected places to create a dream-like now-film effect that surrealists say is "more than real."

Although now-films existed early on in European film history because of critical and intellectual support, American now-filmmaking really developed much later. Although some now-film work was being done on off-time by Hollywood filmmakers, there was really little audience support. Such audience support needed to be created.

In the United States, the now-film "boom" began with the Second World War. We've already noted how brilliant wartime documentaries helped to indoctrinate troops and citizens. They also created a new type of audience. No longer did people associate "movies" with "theaters." They had gotten into the habit of viewing different types of films on small, portable 16mm projectors. The great now-filmmaker Maya Deren travelled around the country showing her three short film-poems *Meshes of the Afternoon* (1943), *At Land* (1944) and *Choreography for Camera* (1945). Lyrical, at times shocking, always extremely personal in content, her films were ex-

cellent examples of what now-cinema could do. And they were warmly received across the country. An audience had been created for this type of out-of-the-mainstream filmmaking, and many now-filmmakers, excited by the films and by the audience created by Maya Deren, utilized the abundant war surplus projectors, film, and equipment to make now-films.

COMPUTER FILMMAKING

Much more recently, war surplus equipment allowed one now-filmmaker to create a new way of seeing. Filmmaker John Whitney started his film work making films for other people. Working with Saul Bass, Whitney created the title sequence for Alfred Hitchcock's feature *Vertigo*, and other such film work. But Whitney wanted to attempt something new, to experiment with ways of making now-films. An M-5 antiaircraft gun director, left over from the Second World War, became the basis for Whitney's new way of creating films. He took the machine apart, rewired it completely, and added various parts. Whitney ended up with a twelve-foot high machine, an amazingly complex mechanical analog computer connected to a camera, able to create movies. Every part of Whitney's invention can be programmed to move up, down, sideways, in any combination he wants to create films showing strange patterns moving with mathematical precision, strangely looking like plants growing. Again Whitney's films were experimental, "Starting afresh every time," as he puts it. Finally, IBM became interested in Whitney's film work and made available an IBM 360 computer and an IBM 2250 Graphic Display Console.

After programming his IBM computer, Whitney controls his movies with punch cards. Various cards change the shape of the patterns which move around on the readout screen. Other signals which Whitney programs into the computer activate a camera pointed at the 21-inch television picture tube of the readout screen. The camera takes one frame at a time. When he is done, Whitney combines the images his computer has generated and adds color to them.

Interesting patterns of light and dark are part of Michael Whitney's film **Binary Bit Patterns**.

Permutations, probably Whitney's most famous computer film, creates a new language according to Whitney. The film contains various types of dot patterns which Whitney compares to the alphabet. The patterns of dots he constructs into "words," each "word" lasting eight seconds. And the words are fitted into "sentences."

Permutations is a now-film. Circles, crescents, quadrants, all kinds of geometric forms float around, interact, move in and out, and draw a viewer into the images. Again it's a now-film because Whitney wants to entertain his audience *now*, by what they see, rather than tell them a developing story.

PSYCHEDELIC FILMS

Some people call *Permutations* and other films like it **psychedelic films** because they draw the viewer into a realm of expanded consciousness. Such films, instead of *telling* an audience something, *take* them somewhere. Other computer films give the same "expanded consciousness" psychedelic feeling. John Whitney's brother James made the computer film *Lapis*, for example. It is described by James as a "Mandala that revolves eternally like the heavens." And John Whitney's sons, Michael and John, Jr., also make similar psychedelic computer films. Michael's film *Binary Bit Patterns*, made in 1969, is a film where "squadrons of polyhedral modules come pulsating out of a black void." Michael composed a guitar tape for his sound track in *Binary Bit Patterns*. As with most psychedelic films, it's hard to distinguish whether you're seeing, hearing, or feeling *Binary Bit Patterns*. But one thing is sure—however you experience the film, you experience it as a now-film.

Naturally, watching now-films is a quite different job for a viewer than watching films with plots. It requires a whole new way of watching. Viewers who watch now-films with linear-film eyes are usually disappointed. They are looking for a climax, a plot, a story line, something to enjoy by understanding; they're not used to enjoying every moment of the film as it happens. When the movie ends, some viewers still haven't found the plot or the story line, because, of course, there isn't any.

Now-filmmakers who prefer to make psychedelic, or sense-expanding films, feel that expanding the consciousness of their audiences is the most natural thing for film to do. For them, film is a whole new way of seeing. The French evolutionary philosopher Pierre Teilhard de Chardin claimed that man's whole history can be summarized as man achieving better and better eyes in a world where there's always something more to be seen. Psychedelic now-films give their audiences more and more to see and a better way to see it; instead of trying to communicate with us, psychedelic filmmakers try to take us somewhere through what we see, to create a new world for their viewers to see.

Many psychedelic filmmakers feel that using the communication devices of film that we've talked about in this book—editing, camera angles, sound, light—allows a filmmaker to *manipulate* viewers and their reactions. Rather than manipulate people, psychedelic filmmakers would rather create films which a viewer can watch and use to create his own reactions.

Jordan Belson's films are typical consciousness-expanding experiences. *Allures* (1961) is a good example of how psychedelic filmmakers try to use film to let audiences create their own worlds of experience by film. At the beginning of *Allures*, we hear bells pealing. A starburst of pink, yellow, and blue sparks comes whirling at us from the blackness. The points of the starburst cluster and it fades out. The bells become chimes, and we seem to sink into the screen. Pink web patterns spin away. A coil, looking strangely like a caterpillar, looms out at us ominously. Pink and yellow sparks start to crawl up the frame. Snakelike coils appear and then fade. Dots bounce across the screen, and a yellow-white globe of fire evolves, only to vanish. More and more happens. Finally, a pulsating sun spitting out bright particles, reveals within itself another galaxy. At the end of *Allures*, you may not be able to distinguish if you've heard or seen the film, but you know you *felt* it, you know you've been somewhere. You seem to have developed new eyes to see new things. That's what psychedelic film is all about.

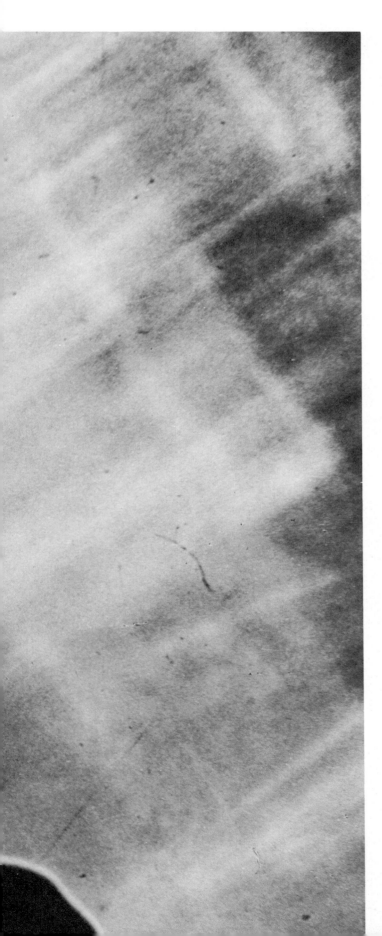

Some psychedelic films start with real objects, rather than working with abstract geometric patterns. Donald Fox's film *Omega* is a good example of this technique. Machines on earth send a huge burst of power into space, harnessing the energy of the sun. Three silhouetted figures sit, motionless, until they are hit by the blast of the power. One of the figures struggles and breaks a bond tied to his wrist. Colors explode everywhere. Trees are purple against a red sky; waves, yellow but cresting blue against purple mountains. Fox is able to use color to expand our consciousness into a new dimension. At the end of viewing *Omega*, we feel we've *been somewhere*; our consciousness has been expanded.

Filmmakers are always experimenting with devices to help them expand the possibilities of creating psychedelic films. To expand our awareness, filmmakers want to show us things in a new way; you can't expand your experience by seeing something the way you always do. Filmmaker Scott Bartlett discovered a new tool for altering reality and showing his viewers things in new ways. By combining color television equipment with film techniques, Bartlett was able to use the combination to create films that depict things never seen before.

Bartlett's film *Off-On* (1967) is the first film whose existence is due equally to film techniques and television techniques. *Off-On* started out as twenty repeating film loops that Bartlett had left over from a light show. The black and white film loops were fed into television monitors so that they caused a cross-circuited feedback, causing colors to appear. More and more electronic processes followed, until the signal finally appeared on a television monitor, where a camera filmed it.

With the electronic images down on film, Bartlett could add more color to his film and continually change the images. He separated the film into two rolls and dyed each strip with a different food color. Bartlett built a trough, filled it full of

Omega, an exciting psychedelic film by filmmaker Donald Fox, is one of the most beautiful and professional films of its type ever done. It was filmed in a basement.

dye, and rolled the film through it. The process took all night to do.

Off-On starts with a close up of a huge blue and red eyeball, pulsating in synchronization with the sound of a heartbeat. Other strange images occur. A dancer throwing her arms out in a mirror image looks like a flower blooming. It gives us a new way of seeing the dancer; thus the filmmaker has expanded our consciousness by causing new connections between things. A dancer and a flower may seem to have no connection with each other. In *Off-On*, they do.

Bartlett used another interesting technique for expanding our viewing experience in *Off-On*. Like many now-filmmakers, Bartlett stretches every property of film to its absolute limits. When he films in color, he uses color in a new way, extremely bright and rapidly changing. When he uses sound, he uses it in new ways. And Bartlett actually uses film itself to change the way we perceive his film. Movies, as it has been mentioned, seem to move because we see twenty-four still pictures per second, flickering on and off too quickly for us to see the flicker. Slow the process down, however, and we *can* notice the flicker. Bartlett created a flickering stroboscopic effect in *Off-On* by quickly alternating between black and white images of the same object; the white images, covering most of the screen, flicker on quickly, causing the screen to turn into one big stroboscope, flickering hypnotically.

The ultimate use of the flicker effect is probably Tony Conrad's film *The Flicker*, which consists of nothing more than a series of alternating lengths of clear film and pure black film. *The Flicker* flickers for forty-five minutes. After ten minutes or so of the film, viewers usually begin to see circles of color moving around and around and other colorful optical illusions. *The Flicker* and films like it use a property of motion pictures, one that most films try to cover up, to expand an audience's visual experience. Rather than manipulate their viewers by film techniques, filmmakers using such techniques allow their audiences to create visual experiences in their own minds. But let's leave psychedelic films for a little while, and come back to earth for now.

GETTING THE AUDIENCE'S ATTENTION

Filmmaker Bruce Conner wanted to make a film about the assassination of President John Kennedy. Conner wanted his audience to feel the horror of the moment when President Kennedy was shot. The sound track of Conner's film *Report* is straight news; the audience hears the actual report of the events in Dallas. The pictures, however, drill the event into the audience's minds. The viewers see movies of President Kennedy riding in the automobile moments before the gunshot. Over and over, the same few seconds of film are repeated, as if time were standing still. The audience knows, however, that when the film stops repeating itself, that the next event will be the bullet reaching the President. The film repeats itself over and over, seemingly unwilling to continue.

Conner includes other techniques in *Report*. The Academy leader of the film is shown frequently (the numbers 10, 9, 8, 7, etc., that are seen at the beginning of a movie). The numbers of the leader become a continual countdown, and the numbers seem to be viewed through a rifle sight. Such repetition allows Conner to drive home the full horror of the event.

Many times a now-filmmaker will want to com-

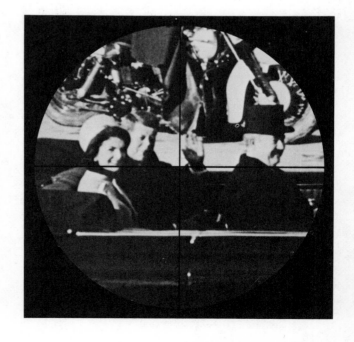

ment on how he sees a current event. Photographs from various picture magazines, shown to an audience in kinestasis fashion, can allow a now-filmmaker to use pictures of current events. Other filmmakers film directly off of their television screens and reedit what they see to describe their reactions to what is happening.

Sometimes, now-filmmakers will try to shock their audiences into paying attention to what the filmmaker wants to say in his film. Gross or ugly things are sometimes used as shock devices, as are scenes of nudity, in some now-films. Filmmaker Robert Nelson wanted to make a film showing what he thought of the way black people have been and are treated in America. Nelson uses watermelons to represent black people in his short film *Oh Dem Watermelons*. The watermelons are attacked everywhere they go, sliced up by people wearing ice skates, thrown from high places to splatter on the sidewalk, hit with baseball bats, blown up with dynamite, crushed with giant earth-moving machines, and destroyed in many sickening, splattering ways. In one unforgettable scene, a butcher even saws open a watermelon and proceeds to pull out a large quantity of intestines. Nelson includes such scenes, including a short one showing some nudity, to make sure he's got his audience's attention while he's painting his picture of how he feels blacks have been treated. Nobody would attempt to argue that there's anything subtle about *Oh Dem Watermelons*. It's a now-film that's got something to say *now*, and it screams its message in a way that's hard to forget.

Some people have used the term **underground films** to describe *Oh Dem Watermelons* and other hard-hitting films like it. The term "underground film" was actually made up first by critic Manny Farber to describe a series of low-budget films made by Howard Hawks. Later, however, the name "underground film" came to include films that were a little stronger in the way they communicated than the average film. But most films people now call "underground films" resemble now-films a great deal. And many of them are surfacing today.

Now-filmmakers combine many different techniques to create the effect they want to achieve.

High school senior Robert Schiappacasse wanted to communicate the loneliness that a young person can feel when he's really down. Schiappacasse's film *El-Trip*, which won the highest award in its class at the Fifth Chicago International Film Festival, experiments with color, editing repetition, and camera techniques, to create a new way of feeling loneliness. To emphasize the loneliness of his subject, Schiappacasse shows only one character during his film. By shooting parts of his film in black and white and then tinting them, he was able to control the color of various sections of his film to control his audience's reactions. He edited sections of *El-Trip* so that each shot established a conflicting direction to the shot before it, to underline the conflict his subject feels.

Finally, in order to make the lonely train ride appear strange, filmmaker Schiappacasse removed the pressure plate from his camera. Instead of twenty-four frames of film stopping and starting in the camera every second, twenty-four frames slide through the camera without stopping. Every streetlight becomes a strange repeating pattern of light, a long dashed line rather than a dot. The strange feeling of loneliness the boy in the film feels is well communicated to viewers by this experimental technique.

Other filmmakers do various strange things with their film to communicate with their audiences or to create effects of expanded consciousness. They heat their film in the oven until the image starts to melt; they combine various shots, one after the other, to create new effects; they experiment with new ways of creating sound tracks for us, with new ways of combining film and other arts.

We have to put on new eyes to watch many now-films. If we do, sometimes we find a person— the director—talking to us in a new language. Other times, we find ourselves creating a new world of illusion, seeing deeper than we've ever seen before. Like new telescopes for astronomers, many now-films can open new worlds for us to see and experience.

If we are open and ready to accept them for what they are, now-films can take us to places we've never been before and show us things we're used to in ways we've never seen before.

NOW · FILM

ACTIVITIES

1) Some film critics compare the film viewing experience to the way our minds work when we dream. We watch films in a dark room, with the screen hypnotically fixing our attention. Sometimes, when we get really involved in a film, we can lose track of time.

How can filmmakers utilize this hypnotic effect in their movies? Does the viewing situation change the effect of a film, that is, what is the effect of the size of the screen, the darkness of the room, the noise of the classroom projector?

2) Select a simple sequence that you might film, such as a person eating breakfast. Write a treatment for four different versions of the same action. First, show it in standard Hollywood style. Then, show it as a documentary, an animation, and finally as a now-film.

3) Make a compilation film from scraps of Super, or regular 8mm film, or from old 16mm films. Create a sound track to accompany your compilation film. Do not hesitate to scratch, dye, bleach, scrape, or experiment with your film.

4) Create a now-film experience by making a film that is to be shown on two projectors, either side-by-side or overlapping.

5) The credit sequences of Hollywood feature films and of some television shows are sometimes really now-films in miniature. Describe some credit sequences you have seen recently that resemble now-film experiences.

6) Select a now-filmmaker. Try to see as many of his or her films as you can. If you cannot see any of them, read descriptions of them in film books or film catalogs. Prepare a list of the films, with a description of each.

Compare the way now-filmmakers work to the way other filmmakers work. Do their films contain recognizable traits, or is each a new experiment?

7) Do some research on the relationship between now-films and modern art.

8) Minimalist cinema is a form of now-filmmaking. As the name suggest, minimalist films present you with little more than basic scenes. The audience is forced to create its own feelings toward the movie. One minimalist film shows you nothing more than a series of postcards, while a narrator reads the messages in a monotone voice. Describe a minimalist film you might make. Why might a filmmaker choose such an approach?

9) Now-films appeal to a smaller sized audience than other types of cinema. Evidence exists, however, that filmmakers are now able to select smaller groups of people to comprise their audiences. For example, instead of the huge theaters of the old days, exhibitors today are now building one theater equipped to show two, three, or more different films to smaller groups. Will this practice of fragmenting a mass audience add to the existence of more now-films? Can you think of any other signs that may encourage now-filmmakers to make more films?

10) What effect has video tape had on now-films? What effect will it have in the future? What about Super 8?

FILMMAKING

13

If you have seen enough films lately and have begun to experience the tremendous communication ability film offers, by now you probably want to try your hand at making a film of your own. Good. It seems that there are more good ideas for films than there are good films, simply because people never get around to translating their ideas into film.

The best way to learn how to make a film is to make one. Many people are frightened away from making a film because they have heard photographers talking in numbers. To listen to some photographers talk, you would think that learning how to shoot a film is more difficult than learning trigonometry. But numbers and measurements are not a major part of photography. In fact, this chapter should give you all of the basic information you need to shoot your first film without making expensive mistakes. After shooting your first film, you can start learning from the mistakes which do occur. You should make enough mistakes in your first film to learn a lot of things. This will help when you make your second film. And so on.

YOUR FILM IDEA

The first thing you will need to make a film

Doing-it-yourself is easy and exciting in film. Modern, automated cameras let you concentrate on getting the right picture.

is an idea. Just any old idea won't work, however. You will need a *film* idea, not a play idea or a short story idea or a television idea or anything else. A film idea.

What's a film idea? It's an idea which you can express on film, with the resources you have at hand. This probably will mean that your idea won't require you to use dialog: If your idea requires pictures of somebody talking and the audience must hear the person talking at the same time, then probably you had better scrap that idea right now, and come up with another. A little later, we will discuss why it's such a problem to film dialog scenes. It is *not* impossible, but it is such a big problem that it is not worth the trouble.

If your film idea doesn't require dialog, you're one step ahead. Is it something which you can tell with pictures? Does it move? Does it do things which film can capture? If so, it's probably a good film idea.

Next, is your idea a film idea you can manage? If it requires you to have five thousand Roman gladiators, you might seriously consider a new idea. And if your idea will require thirty minutes to show, you might consider saving it for your third film. A good film idea for a beginner is one which you will be able to film with the equipment and the time and the money and the actors available to you.

Many times you can find a good film idea from looking at other films, both professional and student or by watching television, especially commercials. You may find your film idea by listening to songs, both oldies and songs currently on the charts, or by carefully reading magazine advertisements, or by daydreaming. Whatever you choose as your subject, make sure that you try to film something you really want to film. Let's make one thing perfectly clear: Making a film will be a lot of work. Fun work, but still a lot of work. Finding out in the middle of the process that you're really not interested in what you're doing can make the work of finishing your film a real task. So choose your idea carefully.

When professional filmmakers get an idea for a movie, they develop the idea as much as they can. Then they work out a **treatment** for their idea: They decide *how* they're going to approach their subject. If you've decided to make a film on your school, for example, you will have to decide how you are going to *treat* the idea. Will the film be a documentary about the school? If so, will it be objective or will it give particular viewpoints on the school? Maybe the film will be a comedy. Maybe the film will compare the school with something it resembles, possibly with another school.

If you've chosen an idea which nobody has ever made a film on before, fine. If you have chosen an idea that *has* been filmed before—like an anti-pollution film—then be sure that you don't copy somebody else's film. Instead, put yourself into the idea. Plan to show things as *you* see them, and your film will succeed.

YOUR PLANNING

Once you've gotten an idea, you must do some *planning*. This important area seems to get slighted in most student films. When are you going to shoot your film? Will you want to shoot it in order, or will you want to shoot it out of order and edit it later? Will everybody be able to come when you've planned? If you must re-shoot certain sections, when will you do that?

Other kinds of planning also help. Some filmmakers write a complete script for their films; they plan every shot out on paper. And some filmmakers even sketch out each shot on index cards, and check off the card when they complete the shot. How much planning you have to do depends upon the type of film you're going to make, and on how you plan to treat your idea. Maybe you want to make a film which shows how a person sees a big city for the first time; planning your film too precisely might ruin the effect you're trying to achieve. Many professional directors don't believe in overplanning and re-doing shots because they feel that "first-time-through" shots have a lot more feeling than well-rehearsed shots. French filmmaker Jean-Luc Godard, for example, many times prefers to shoot his films in such a spontaneous manner. Naturally, of course, Godard does enough planning to have his actors around when he wants to shoot and the right film in the camera at the right time.

If you're planning an animation film, you probably will do a great deal of pre-planning. One high school senior, planning to do a three-minute kinestasis film containing 528 still pictures, wrote a complete script for his film, entitled *Odyssey*, numbering each still picture he had collected and marking down what effect he planned to achieve with each picture. The typed script for the film was seventeen pages long, single-spaced.

Again, the type of film and the way in which you plan to treat your idea will determine how much planning you will have to do and how much of your planning you will want to put on paper. But you should do some planning, even if you're going to do a documentary. If you don't plan your film at all, you may find yourself simply *recording* what's happening in front of your camera, rather than communicating with camera angles, changes in lens focal length, and camera effects. You should at least *think over* what you want to do before you start shooting. If you do, it will show up in your finished film. There is no single way to write a script, as there is for making an outline for an essay. Whatever helps you remember your thoughts is usually the best way to work. Professional filmmakers, for example, will usually script their shots carefully. Alfred Hitchcock meticulously scripts his films and then memorizes each shot. In the famous bathtub murder sequence of his classic feature *Psycho*, seventy-eight shots pass in forty-

Animation films are usually interesting because they move and don't require dialog.

five seconds. Hitchcock scripted each shot carefully and had it shot exactly as he had scripted it. Your film may not be as complex, and so you may not need to do more than jot down a few notes for each shot. No matter how much or how little you write, however, you should certainly think through every sequence you construct. That way, you'll be prepared for any new possibilities that arise while shooting. And you won't forget any shots, an event which can be tragic when you later begin to edit.

YOUR CAMERA

Once you have an idea in mind, you should start looking around for a camera. If you already own one, fine. If you must borrow one from your school or local camera store or friendly relative, you may have a choice among several cameras, using different film sizes. The film size you choose will make a lot of difference in the amount of money you end up spending on your film, in the ease of shooting and editing your film, and the final quality of your film.

Different cameras use different sizes of film; they're not interchangeable. Most feature filmmakers use cameras that take 35mm size film, although lavish productions are usually filmed with cameras using 70mm film. Amateurs, however, don't use film or cameras this large. The first size of film designed for amateur moviemakers was 16mm film. Some theater films like *The Endless Summer* and *Woodstock* were originally shot on 16mm size film and then enlarged onto 35mm film so that they could be shown in theaters. And almost all of the films used in classrooms are 16mm copies of films, many of which were originally photographed on 35mm film.

Some students use 16mm film for their movies. Because each frame of 16mm film is large, in comparison with the 8mm widths, 16mm student films can be as clear, sharp, and bright on the screen as any other films shown on a school projector. But 16mm is also a very expensive size of film to shoot. This becomes important for student film projects, because usually the director of a student film is also the producer. Unlimited resources are not common *anywhere* in the film industry; learning how to produce your film economically is part of the job of making a film.

One roll of film for almost any amateur camera, no matter what size, will give you about three minutes of screen time. For extremely short films, and especially for animation films, where there is very little waste, it is a good idea to use 16mm film, if a camera is available. For long films, 16mm film can get expensive.

Sixteen millimeter cameras can get expensive, too. Many documentary films, most experimental films, and virtually all television news film is 16mm. This means that 16mm is the halfway point between amateur and Hollywood work. Camera prices in 16mm, and camera features, are usually geared more for the professional than for the amateur, and few automatic 16mm cameras exist. The Japanese Canon *Scoopic M*, originally designed as a versatile hand-held camera for the Tokyo Olympics, is fully automatic and easy to use for amateurs. It sells for about $1,700. If you live in a large city, it's quite easy to *rent* cameras, and a camera like the Canon *Scoopic M* would rent for about $25.00 or $35.00 a day or a weekend—cheaper rental prices prevail on the coasts, with higher prices inland.

Many schools own the 16mm Bolex *H-16* camera, a Swiss camera that seems to be widely used for filming high school and college football games. With the Vario-Switar lens, it can be made into an automatic exposure camera; with regular lenses, the exposure must be set manually. Although this is not a problem for animation films, where the light is usually constant, setting the exposure manually requires a light meter and a knowledge of how to use it. If you can get your hands on a Bolex for your film, however, it will prove to be an efficient camera.

From the Bolex camera, prices go up rapidly. The French *Beaulieu* 16mm camera is an excellent, totally automatic camera that is much easier to hold and use than the Bolex; the *Beaulieu* usually rents for about $40.00 a weekend. And if you're really interested in your first film, you might consider the German *Arriflex* or the French *Eclair*. The "Eclair" costs over $15,000 but offers many features—if you really wish to feel like a pro on your first film.

Cheaper 16mm cameras exist, of course, some selling for as little as $25.00 at a pawn shop. Such cameras, however, usually require more photographic know-how to run; if they are "point and shoot" cameras, they may limit you to pointing them and shooting objects at least seven feet away in bright sunlight.

Usually it's better to use a camera designed for smaller size film. The amateur film widths today are the 8mm sizes. Regular 8mm cameras were the first to be developed; later on, Super 8mm replaced 8mm. Eight mm film can lower the cost of black and white filming tremendously.

Regular 8mm equipment isn't being made any more, and so most of the modern improvements are found on Super 8mm cameras. The difference between the films starts with the perforations. Super 8mm film is the same width as regular 8mm film, but the perforations are much smaller. Since you're interested in getting a bigger picture, with brighter light and sharper focus, you'd rather have small perforations and bigger picture area. Super 8mm film comes packaged in drop-in cartridges which automatically set the camera's exposure system for the type of film you're using. Other conveniences make Super 8mm film probably the best choice for your first film. Even if you can afford the luxury of shooting in 16mm, the convenience of using Super 8mm equipment many times outweighs the extra sharpness of 16mm film.

Super 8mm movies also have a different "look" than 16mm movies. It seems that many students consider 16mm a professional size—which a quick glance at the equipment and the prices would also seem to suggest. As a result, many times 16mm student films look more "set up" than Super 8mm films. A Super 8mm camera can easily become an extension of your eye; most 16mm cameras require a great deal of practice before they can be manipulated easily enough to be an extension of anything. There is a danger, of course, that the "point and shoot" convenience of Super 8mm tempts some filmmakers into pointing and shooting without *thinking* about what they are shooting. The convenience of "pointing and shooting," however, can also give a director the time to think about what he is shooting, instead of thinking about a bunch of numbers

which must be transferred from an exposure meter to the lens of the camera before he can even start shooting.

The price of Super 8mm movies is usually within the range of student filmmakers. Both black and white and color films, processing included, cost only a few dollars per minute of shooting time. Prices vary from area to area, of course. In small towns, prices are usually high; in big cities, competition tends to lower film prices a great deal. And inflation will surely change the prices. The idea is to make a budget before you start.

YOUR FILM

Once you have an idea and have decided on a film size, it's time to decide what kind of film to buy to make your movie. Perhaps you want part of your film to be in color and part in black and white; then you will need at least two kinds of film. Maybe you want to shoot your film entirely in black and white, but you want to shoot part of it inside a bowling alley and part outside. Again, you will need two different kinds of film.

Cameras have **iris diaphragms**, like your eyes do, to adjust to different amounts of light. Your eye has a much greater range than your camera, however. Because cameras are limited in the amount of adjusting they can do, film manufacturers make two basic kinds of film—film for places with much light and film for places with very little light. Choose the right film, and your camera will be able to do the rest. Film manufacturers call films designed for taking pictures where there is plenty of light "slow" films; "fast" films are designed for places where there is not much light.

Film manufacturers use **ASA numbers** to rate the speed of their films. Camera manufacturers use **f-numbers** to indicate how much light a lens can transmit when its diaphragm is wide open. All those numbers can get confusing. Here's a little example to help you wade through the confusion.

The 16mm Bolex H16 Reflex is a popular camera that can be outfitted with many accessories. Heavier cameras, like the Eclair, can be hand-held but require sturdy tripods if they are to be mounted on a tripod.

Imagine a pipe filling a bucket with water. Let's say it takes one second to fill the bucket completely. Now, imagine a bucket twice as big. It'll take two seconds for that pipe to completely fill the bigger bucket. In one second, the bigger bucket can be only half-filled, while the smaller bucket can be completely filled in that time. The only way to fill the larger bucket in one second would be to find a larger pipe to fill it with. A pipe with twice the diameter of the original pipe ought to work just fine.

Now imagine a bucket only half as big as the original bucket. This new bucket will need a pipe only half as big as the original pipe for it to fill completely in one second. Put the smaller bucket under one of the bigger pipes, and what will happen in one second? It'll overflow. But put the biggest bucket under the smallest pipe and it wouldn't be anywhere near full in one second. But each bucket, placed under the correct pipe, will be completely filled in the same time, although each size bucket requires a different size pipe.

Got that? Now the film in your camera is like a bucket; the pipe is the lens; the light is the water. We call overfilling "overexposure" and underfilling "underexposure." The iris diaphragm on your camera is like a faucet: Open it all the way, and the pipe delivers light through full blast. **Slow films** are like big buckets. Each frame requires lots of light to be fully filled. Let's say that one film, Plus-X, has an *ASA speed* of 50 and another film has an ASA speed of 25. Plus-X film can get completely filled in twice the speed that the ASA 25 film requires, so its ASA speed of 50 is twice as fast as the ASA speed of 25. Tri-X film, ASA 200, has four times as much speed as the ASA 50 film, and eight times as much speed as the ASA 25 film. Compared to the barrelfull of light the ASA 25 film needs, Tri-X is a thimble! Anything over ASA 100 rates as **fast film**.

Camera manufacturers tell you how big the pipe (lens) is by means of f-numbers. Because these numbers are the bottom part of fractions, the smaller f-numbers refer to bigger pipes. As an arbitrary example, ½-inch pipe, for example, might be called a #2 pipe, while a ¼-inch pipe might be called a #4 pipe. As a filmmaker, you're interested in how big the pipe is when the faucet (iris diaphragm)

is open full blast, so you talk about an f/2 lens as one which can open as far as f/2 when its all the way open. The smaller the f/stop, the bigger the lens. A big lens can let more light in than a small lens. Therefore, the camera with the lens whose f/stop has the smallest number will be more effective in extremely low light situations than a camera with a lens with a bigger f-number and therefore a smaller lens. Therefore, the camera with the lens whose f/stop is the smallest will be more effective in extremely low light situations than a camera with a lens with a bigger f-number and therefore a smaller lens. Cameras made specially for low light situations, like the XL cameras made by Kodak, will have big lenses to let in all the light possible in low light situations. Some of these cameras even have slower shutter speeds to let in light *longer* than regular cameras.

How can you tell when to use which kind of film? If you are taking pictures outside, anytime from a little after sunrise to a little after sunset, no matter how cloudy it may seem, there is plenty of light; you need a slow film. If you are taking pictures inside, no matter how bright it seems, even if you're on what seems like an amazingly bright stage, you really have comparatively little light; you need a fast film. It's as simple as that.

If you want to shoot outdoors during the day

Neutral density filters allow fast films like Tri-X or Ektachrome 160 to be used outdoors without overexposure. The filters act like sunglasses.

and want to have your movies come out in black and white, you will want a slow black and white film. Kodak's *Plus-X* film (ASA 50) is a good choice and is available in all film sizes (although in regular 8mm, it's hard to find *any* black and white film except by mail order.) If you want to take black and white shots indoors, you will need a fast black and white film: Kodak's *Tri-X* (ASA 200) is a good choice. If the light's very dim, you can buy Kodak's *Four-X* (ASA 400) film; and if you're really in trouble, GAF's *Supreme* (ASA 500) is faster yet.

How dark can it be and still allow you to take movies? With most cameras, an average basketball floor is usually bright enough to film; the stands are usually too dim. At a mixer, the band is usually bright enough to film, the dancing floor is usually too dark, although certain Super 8mm cameras like the "XL" series cameras, when teamed with fast films, can sometimes film in these locations. Bright objects, like street lights or neon signs, of course, will always show up.

If you are shooting outside during the daytime and want your movies to turn out in color, you need a slow color film. There are many brands on the market; Kodak's *Kodachrome 40* is probably the most widely used; *Ektachrome 40* is an alternate choice.

If you are shooting indoors and want color movies, you will want to buy Kodak's *Ektachrome 160* or *Ektachrome G*, both of which are fast color films. Expect to pay a bit more for *Ektachrome* and expect it to take more time to be developed.

It's possible, of course, to use slow films indoors, by flooding the subject that you are going to shoot with enough light so that it is as bright indoors as it is outdoors. But such bright light is discomforting to your subject and unless carefully controlled can be very distracting, ugly, flat, and uninteresting. Unless you're doing an animation, where it's possible to flood the work area with plenty of light, it's better to use fast films and make use of the natural light of the room you're shooting in. Filming outdoors on bright days with fast film in your camera is a bit easier; you just buy a gray **neutral density filter** and put it on your camera's lens. It's like a pair of sunglasses for your camera and allows you to cut out a great deal of the light coming into the camera, permitting the camera's iris to squint down enough for you to use fast film outdoors. If you don't have a neutral density filter, you can shoot fast film outdoors on a bright day: Just move into the shade, or shoot early in the morning or in the evening. On a dull day, you'll usually be able to shoot fast film outdoors without a neutral density filter.

Color films have one special problem black and white films don't have. Lighting color varies all over the place. Indoors, light bulbs produce a reddish light. Sunlight is bluish in comparison. Our brains make the necessary correction when we look at different objects. Film, however, cannot make this correction, so color Super 8mm films are balanced for indoor light color. Outdoors, you must switch in the orangish filter built into the camera. Some Super 8mm cameras have a switch for this filter, others have a removable key or pin to adjust the filter. Check your instruction book. One Super 8mm color film, Kodak's Ektachrome G, (ASA 160) (slow or fast?) is balanced to compromise for all colors of light and give acceptable, but not perfect, color balance in a wide range of lighting conditions. Always shoot Ektachrome G *without* the filter in place. Ektachrome G is handy for subjects in low-lighting situations, especially if lit by fluorescent lights, mercury vapor lights, or combinations of different lighting sources. Because Ektachrome G is a compromise film, however, choose the regular Ektachrome 160 film when possible, to get more perfect color balance.

YOUR TECHNIQUE

Learning how to hold your camera steadily is important. One way to make sure a camera doesn't jiggle is to screw it to a tripod. Tripod shooting is steady, but confining and time consuming. While a tripod keeps a camera from moving when you don't want it to move, it can make moving the camera when you *do* want it to move a big pain. If you are planning to hand-hold the camera, you might want to shoot in wide-angle rather than telephoto position, because the more your camera is zoomed out to the telephoto position, the more your hand's natural shaking is magnified. Always hold

your camera with *both* hands, resting the camera against your face and your elbows against your body. Lean against a wall, sit on the ground, brace yourself any way you can. Unless you're trying for a special effect remember that you're holding a camera, not a flag.

If you're taking a picture of a moving subject, you can move the camera to follow along with the subject. Otherwise, you'll probably be better off not moving the camera very much. It's usually better to pick a subject which moves and let it do the moving for you.

Some cameras you will use have only one lens, a **normal lens**, attached to them. Other cameras may have a turret that allows you to choose from two or three different lenses to create your shots with. And most Super 8mm cameras will have a **zoom lens**, to allow you to create wide-angle shots, normal shots, telephoto shots, and zoom shots. Since we talked about all these different shots in our first chapter, let's not repeat ourselves. We will just mention how to focus the lenses that you'll find on the camera.

Some cameras will have pre-focused lenses, set by the factory so that pictures taken at least five feet or so away from the camera will come out sharp and clear. But most cameras require you to focus the camera before you shoot. Some cameras allow you to look through the lens and focus with some sort of focusing aid; other cameras require you to guess how far away you are from your subject and adjust the focus that way. If you have to guess, you should practice guessing distances— most people are bad guesstimators. If you have a zoom lens on your camera, and you must focus the lens, always zoom the lens out to telephoto as far as it will go, then focus, and then zoom back to wherever you want to before you push the button. This way, your pictures will be in sharp focus throughout all your shooting.

All cameras will accept close-up lenses; they allow you to get closer to your subject than usual,

Extending the elevator of a tripod (top) only magnifies the jiggle of the tripod. Even though the elevator is convenient, it should be extended as little as possible for steady shots (bottom).

up to even a few inches away. Getting that close opens up new worlds for the filmmaker, and close-up lenses are a good investment. Some cameras have **macro lenses**, allowing you to shoot in extreme close-up without added lenses.

One problem which many student filmmakers seem to have is knowing how long to let each shot last. Naturally, there is no general answer to that question, but as a guideline, it's a good idea to take too much footage rather than too little. You can always shorten a shot, but it's impossible to make it last longer. Close-ups usually don't have to last as long as long shots, because people are able to recognize them quicker.

YOUR EDITING

Students who think that they are going to "go out and shoot a movie" usually come back disappointed. The best way seems to be looking at the shooting process as a way to *collect* a number of shots, which you will later edit into a film. The biggest surprise in making a film is usually the length of time it takes to edit the film you've shot. Editing is probably the slowest, most time-consuming process of filmmaking; but since it's also one of the most important parts of filmmaking, it deserves a big outlay of time.

Once you have all your shots collected and are ready to edit, you should watch the shots over and over again on a projector so that you get to know

what they look like on a screen at the speed they'll end up in your movie. Then you can start cutting them apart. Most students start by cutting out the obviously bad shots and putting them out of the way somewhere. Then they assemble the shots in roughly the order they intend to use them. After this **rough cut** is done, they start trimming it down, intercutting back and forth between shots, shortening shots as much as possible. It seems difficult for many students to cut out and throw away film that they've bought, shot, and processed. But in film, the less you need to make a point or the more you can cut out, the better what is left usually looks.

You will have to make decisions on how you want to splice together your shots. Some people prefer **tape splicers**, which join shots together by cutting them so that they butt together and then holding them together with perforated tape. Although these are the easiest splices to make, they usually are the worst in the long run. If not properly made, they catch in many projectors, especially Super 8mm projectors. They pick up dust and dirt. And they're rather expensive. The very worst type of tape splices are made with splicers that make an "S" shaped cut in the film; every splice shows

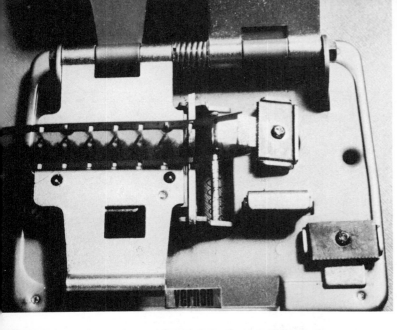
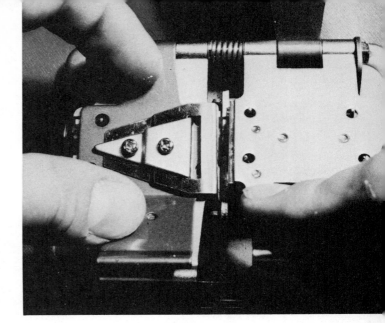
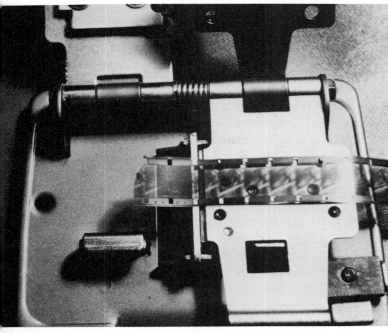
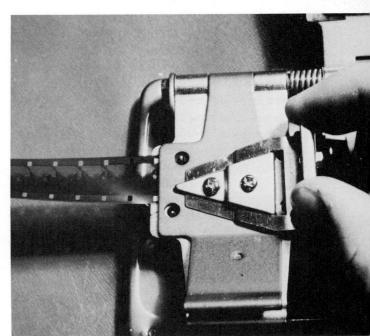
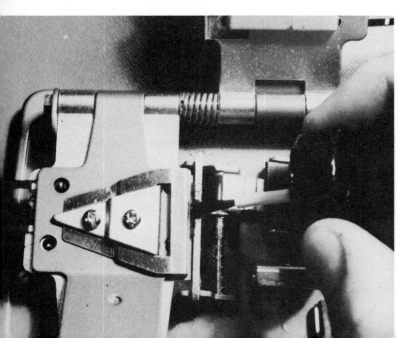
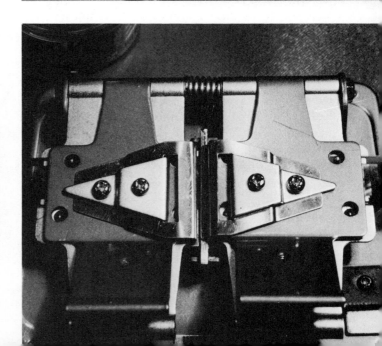

what looks like a flash of lightning running through the frame at the splice.

Much better, and in the long run much easier to use, are **wet** or **cement splicers.** In a cement splice, two shots are joined together by overlapping a portion of two frames and welding them together with cement. Such splices are the best in the long run because they don't clog up projectors or attract lint and are cheap and fast to make. In Super 8mm, most students who have used both methods prefer to work with cement splices. Kodak Professional Film Cement or Jefrona Film Cement are two good brands of film cement.

After you start cutting up your film into individual shots, you will discover that one of the biggest problems is what to do with the perhaps fifty to two hundred strips of film you end up with. You should develop your own cataloging method. Some students like to save egg cartons, roll their shots up, and put them into the egg cartons. Other students prefer to hang their shots on the wall with pins, or stick them on with a piece of tape. Still other students, working with short shots, use wax paper sandwich bags and place their shots in them. What ever method you end up using, you will probably find it easiest if you edit one sequence at a time.

YOUR SOUND TRACK

Once you have edited your film, you will probably want to devise some sort of sound track for it. Music is the easiest to use and the most readily available source of sound, but narration, noises, or mixtures of these sounds are all possible. Trying to make an exact sound track for a film usually ends in failure; tape recorders and projectors have

Making a cement splice is easy. The film is placed in the splicer with the dull (emulsion) side up (top left). Then it is cut to length with the other blade of the splicer (top right). The other piece of film is put into the right side of the splicer and cut to length (middle left). Then the emulsion is scraped off of the exposed piece of film on the right side until the film is clear (middle right). Splicing cement is applied quickly (bottom left) and the splicer is closed quickly for 10-15 seconds to weld the two pieces of film together (bottom right).

one thing in common with lightning: they rarely strike the same place twice. If you think your film will be distracting if a door closes and you don't hear the sound of the door, imagine how much *more* distracting it will be if you see the door close and hear it close two seconds later! Without a sound stripped onto the side of your film, you run that risk.

Although simple music usually is the easiest type of sound track, many students will want to experiment with more complex sound tracks. Quarter-inch tape is easier to edit than film, and a tape sound track, if well made, can enhance a film. Mixing sounds is easy on a stereo tape recorder; music can be recorded on one track, and narration or noises can be recorded on the other channel. With a monaural tape recorder, it is necessary to put a small piece of masking tape over the erase head if you intend to record narration or other noises *over* music. The masking tape keeps the tape from being erased, and allows you to mix as many tracks onto one as you want. (The erase head is the *first* head the tape passes over.)

Lip-synchronized sound is possible to film with some Super 8mm systems. Editing is technically difficult with some sync sound setups and aesthetically difficult even for experienced Hollywood filmmakers. If you need dialog for your first few films, you probably didn't choose *film* ideas. Try something you can communicate visually, and save the problems of dialog for later. There are enough problems in communicating visually.

Experimentation offers exciting possibilities for you to communicate with your audience. Scratching your film, baking it in the oven until the pictures start to run a little bit, painting your film with magic markers, using chemical tints and toners to give color to black and white film, all offer you many possibilities for showing your audiences something as nobody has ever seen it before.

Perhaps the best source of information for filmmaking is your local camera store, or a professional filmmaker in your area. And any good amateur photographer with lots of experience in still photography will be able to answer almost all of your technical questions.

Hopefully, your first film will become the *first* of many films.

FILMMAKING

ACTIVITIES

1) Come up with ten film ideas. Have a brainstorm session if necessary. The films shouldn't be more than three minutes long and need only sound effects or music to communicate. Write a complete script for one of the ideas.

2) Check with your local camera store and make a list of prices for slow and fast black and white and color films and the processing charges (and times!) for each of the films. Make a budget for your film in money and days.

3) Make a commercial. You could satirize a current TV commercial. Or you could do an original idea. Restrict yourself to one minute of screen time. Shoot only one and a half minutes (a half roll) of film for your commercial. Thus two people can shoot different commercials on the same roll of film.

4) Select a popular song and create a film to fit it.

5) Make an experimental film.

6) Make a documentary.

7) Select something that moves: a car, a person, a movie projector, a tricycle, a bicycle, a unicycle. Make a short (under 1½ minutes) film re-interpreting the movement. Be fluid with your camera and editing.

8) Learn to animate! You'll need a camera that has single-frame capabilities. Cut out a 4-inch square piece of cardboard. Obtain a 2-by-2 foot piece of contrasting color cardboard as a background. Don't use extremely light or dark colors for the background, or you'll have

exposure problems. Tape a ruler to the long edge of a piece of cardboard 6 by 12 inches and tape the other long edge of the cardboard to the center of the bottom edge of the background so that you can flip the piece of cardboard with attached ruler on and off of the background.

Light the board evenly, mount the camera on a tripod, and point the camera directly down at the board so that its field includes almost all the background. Now flip the ruler scale up onto the field and lay the right edge of the 4-inch square of cardboard on the 1-inch mark of the ruler. Flip the scale out of the picture, being careful not to move the smaller square. Turn on the camera and take a couple of seconds of film. Since a Super 8 projector will show your film at 18 frames per second, you'll need 36 frames for two seconds.

Flip the scale back and move the cardboard square's right edge to the 2-inch line. Flip the scale out, carefully, and take four frames. Flip the scale back in and move the square to the 3-inch mark, take four frames, and continue this process until you move the square off the ruler.

Next, repeat the whole process. This time, however, move the square only ½ inch each time, and take only two frames each time.

Next, do it all over again, but this time move the square only ¼ inch each time and take only one frame each time.

Now, learn about acceleration and deceleration. Move the square in one inch increments up to the 4 inch mark, taking two frames, each time. Then, move the square to the 4 3/4-inch mark and take two frames. Next, move it to 5¼, take two frames; then to 5½, two frames; then 5 5/8, two frames; then 5 11/16 and take two *seconds*. Then reverse the process of deceleration to accelerate the square back up to 2 frames per move. Project your film and study it. When you do, you'll have learned most of what you need to know about animation.

INDEX

A number shown in boldface (**76**) indicates the page on which a term is defined. A number in italics (*29*) refers to a picture and its caption.

Adventures of *, The, *171*
Adventures on the New Frontier, 161
Alexeieff, Alexandre, 173
Alice's Restaurant, 126
Allen, Dede, *53*, 133
Allen, Woody, 142-43
Allures, 191
Alphaville, 80, *83*, 137
American Graffiti, 65
American Time Capsule, 182-83
America's in Real Trouble, 185, 186
Anderson, Lindsay, 32, 97-98, 106-7
Animal Farm, *173*, 174
Animation, 124, **169**-79; activities, 178-79, 210-11; history of, 173-75
Antonia, 161
Antonio, Emile de, *153*
Antonioni, Michelangelo, 128-29
Arriflex BL camera, 41, 202
Arrival of a Train at the Station, 1, *2, 150*
Art, 182, 183, 186
"Art" films, 143-45
ASA numbers, 203-5
At Land, 189
At Long Last Love, 143
Auden, W.H., 109
Audience movement, **33**-34; activity, 36

Background motion, 26-27; activity, 37
Back lighting, 84
Baille, Bruce, 58
Balazs, Bela, 10
Ballad of Love, 115
Ballad of a Soldier, 75-76, *143*
Baptism of Fire, 155
Barn doors, *38*
Barney, *88*
Bartlett, Scott, 193-94
Basic Training, 163
Bass, Saul, 169-70, 175-76, 189
Battle of Algiers, The, *83*, 111, 165
Battle of Britain, The, 156
Battle of Russia, The, 156
Battle of San Pietro, The, 156-57
Battleship Potemkin, The, 51, *52*, 92
Bazin, Andre, 83
Beaulieu 16mm camera, 202
Becky Sharp, 91
Belson, Jordan, 191
Bergman, Ingmar, *8, 26, 58*, 76-77, 94, *97, 106, 125*, 144

Betty Boop, 173
Bicycle Thief, The, 83, *129*
Big Shave, The, 93
Billy Budd, 94
Billy Jack, 46, 137
Binary Bit Patterns, *190*, 191
Birth of a Nation, The, 5, 92
Black and white film: speeds of, 205; *vs.* color, 94-101, 205
Black Girl, *80*
Black Pirate, The, 91
Blazing Saddles, 142
Blinkity Blank, 115
Boenish, Carl, 34
Boetticher, Oscar (Budd), 135
Bogdanovich, Peter, 96, 131, 143
Bolex 16mm camera, 182, 202, *203*
Bonnie and Clyde, 31-32, 58, 79, 126, 133, 137
Boogie-Doodle, 115
Boom shot. *See* Crane shot
Boorman, John, 138
Bosustow, Steve, 174
Braverman, Charles, 182-83
Bringing Up Baby, 140
Broken Blossoms, 5
Brook, Peter, 18-19
Brooks, Mel, 142
Brown, Roger, *32*
Bucket of Blood, 144
Bunuel, Luis, *187*, 188
Butch Cassidy and the Sundance Kid, 65

Camera angles, effects of, **15**-18, 26, 46, 51, 86. *See also* High-angle shots; Low-angle shots; Normal-angle shots
Camera movement, 18-19, 27-28, 34, 124; activities, 36-37
Camera noise, 41, 86, 160-61
Camera speed, 29-32
Cameras, 201-3; battery-powered, 160; cost of, 185, 201-3; 8mm, 201, 202; noise of, 41, 86, 160-61; 16mm, 43, 72, 86, 182, 201, 202; sound, 160-161; Super 8, 14, 185, 202-3, 205, 206, 207, 209. *See also* Lenses; Filters; *specific brand names*
Campaign in Poland, 155
Canon *Scoopic M* camera, 202
Capra, Frank, 156
Cartoons. *See* Animation films
Casabianca, Denise de, 45

Casablanca, 143
Castro Street, 58
Catch the Joy—Dune Buggies, 15, *24*
Cattle Ranch, 50-51, 109
Cement splicers, **209**
Chair, The, 161
Chairy Tale, A, *174*, 175
Chaplin, Charlie, 58, 105
Chase, The, 79, *126*
Cheyenne Autumn, 137
Chickamauga, 26, *49*, 64, *65*, 77, 111, *123*
Chiefs, 163
Chinatown, 125
Choreography for Camera, 189
Chromophobia, 97
Cinema verité, 150, 160-65, **161**
Citizen Kane, 5, *13, 18, 45, 121*
City, The, 154
Clay, or The Origin of Species, *174*, 176
Clockwork Orange, A, 139
Close-up lenses, 206-7
Close-up shot, **8**-10, 13, 45, 47, 63, *181*, 207
Clowns, 93
Collins, Judy, 132, 161
Color, 91-103, 193-94; activities, 102-3. *See also* Color film
Color as Seen and Photographed, Eastman Kodak book, 102
Color film: early use of, 91-92; hand-colored, 91, 92, 179, 193, 209; "speeds" of, 205; *vs.* black and white, 94-101, 205. *See also* Color
Compilation cutting, **64**-65
Compilation films, **185**, 196
Computer filmmaking, 189-91
Confession, The, 173
Conner, Bruce, 194
Conrad, Tony, 194
Continuity cutting, **65**
Coppola, Francis Ford, 65, 80, 138
Corman, Roger, 98, 123-24, 137, 143-44
Corral, 5, 8, 26, 83
Corrida Interdite, *30*, 31, 58
Costa-Gavras, 138, 172-73
Counterpoint, 109
Cover shots, **67**
Cozny, Tamas, 111
Crane (boom) shots, **19**, 43
Critic, The, 111
Cul de Sac, 125
Curtiz, Michael, 143
Cut-away shot, **67**, 165
Cut-in shot, **65**-67
Cuts, **64**-67; activities, 73; *vs.* dissolves, 68-69. *See also* Intercutting

Dali, Salvador, *187*, 188
Dassin, Jules, 128
Daunant, Denys Columb de, 31, 57-58
Day after Day, 62
Day the Earth Stood Still, The, *139*, 144-45
Death of One, The, 63
Defeat of the German Armies Near Moscow, 155
Dell, Jeff, 65, 67
Demonstrative shot, **10**
Depth of field, **12**, 86
Deren, Maya, 189
De Sica, Vittorio, 83, *129*
Dialog. *See* Sound
Diaphragms, **203-4**
Diary of Anne Frank, The, 115
Directors, 121-33; activities, 132-33; freedom of, 128-31, 149; and genre films, 140-43; "messages" of, 124-28; role of in editing, 45, 128; special audiences of, 131; styles of, 28, 79, 121-24; women as, 133
Disney, Walt, 124, 173-74
Dissolve, **68**-69, 73
Dr. Heidegger's Experiment, 101
Dr. Jekyll and Mr. Hyde, 139
Documentary, 149-67; activities, 36, 166-67; cinema verité as, 150, 160-65; definitions of, 149-50; early history of, 150-52; editing of, 162-65; personal, **151**; propaganda, **153**-57; social, 150, **152**-53; use of light in, 83; use of on television, 154, 157-60, 163-65, 166-67
Dolly shot, **19**, 41, 43, 86
Donald Duck, 173
Dots, 115, 176
Downhill Racer, 107, 115
Dracula, 138
Dream of the Wild Horses, 31, 57-58
Dutch-angle, **18**
Dynamic cutting, **65**
Dziga-Vertov, 150-51, 155

Earthquake, 139
Earth Shakes, The, 83
Easy Rider, 3, 130
Eat, 1, 34
Eclair NPR camera, 86, 88, 202, *203*
Edison, Thomas, 1, 34, 150
Editing, **45**-55, 61-63, 207-9; activities, 54-55, 72-73; in cinema verité, 162-65; intercutting, 49-51; juxtaposition, 48-49, 54, 57; montage, 51-53, 57; role of director in, 45, 128; rough cutting, **207**; for rhythm, 57, 61-63, 72-73; selecting and arranging shots, 46-48, 52-53; sound, 116, 118-19, 209. *See also* Splicing
8mm cameras, 201, 202
8mm film, 201, 202
Eisenstein, Sergei, M., 51, *52*, 92, 111, 129
Elegy, 177
El-Trip, 195
Empire, 1, 34
Endless Summer, The, 201
End of Summer, The, 63
Enrico, Robert, 5, 7-9, 10, 11-12, 13-14, 18, 19, 26, 186; and film editing, 45, 46-47, 49, 64-65; general style of, 123; and use of light, 77-79; and use of sound, 111, 112
Ersatz, 177
Essene, 163
Establishing shot, **3**
Eternal Jew, The, 155
Execution of Mary, Queen of Scots, The, 150
Exorcist, The, 139
Experiential (non-linear) films, **186**
Extreme long shot, *3*, **5**-7
Extreme close-up shot, **10**

Fades, **69**-70, 73
Fall of the House of Usher, The, 144
Fantasia, 173, 174
Farber, Manny, 195
Fast motion. *See* Speeded motion
Fat and the Lean, The, 122-23
Fearless Vampire Killers, The, 125, 130
Felix the Cat, 173
Fellini, Federico, *17*, *61*, 93, 131, 140
Fill light, **85**, 86
Film, **203**-5; black and white, 94-101, 205; color, 91-92, 94-101, 102, 205; cost of, 185, 201-3, 210; 8mm, 201, 202; emulsion side of, **178**; fast, **204**; removing pictures from, 179; sepia, 94; 70mm, 201; 16mm, 72, 178, 182, 201, 202; slow, **205**; sound tracks for, 115, 176, 196, 209; "speeds" of, 203-5; Super 8, **202**-3, 205; 35mm, 201
Filmmaking, 199-211; activities, 210-11; cameras, 201-3; film, 203-5; film idea, 199-200; planning, 200-1; sound track, 209; technique, 205-7
Film projectors, 207, 209; speed of, 29, 179, 182, 211
Film scripts, 36, 54-55, 73, 116, 146, 200-201; reverse, 54, 72-73
Filters: camera, *204*, 205; light, 88
First Foundation, The, 14, 69
Fischinger, Oscar, 174
Fish-eye lenses, **13**
Flag, **43**
Flaherty, Robert, *151*-53, 161
Flash Gordon serials, 18
Fleisher, Max and David, 173
Flicker, The, 194
Flowers on a One Way Street, 162-63
f-numbers (f/stops), 203-5
Focal length, **21**
Follow pan, **18**
Ford, John, 128, 135, 136-37
Foreman, Carl, 111, 145
Forsberg, Rolf, 24
400 Blows, The, 35
Fox, Donald, *193*
Fragments of a Day, 69
Frankenstein (1932), 138
Frankenstein (Warhol), 143
Frankenheimer, John, 131
Free Fall, *184*, 185
Freeman, Jim, 15, *24*
Freeze frames, 35, 36
French Connection, The, 61
Funnel-like order, **47**

Gangster films, as genre, 137-38, 142
Generator noise, 38
Genre films, **135**-47; activities, 146-47; as art films, 143-45; and the director, 140-43; gangster, 137-38, 142; horror and science fiction, 138-39, 143; musicals, 146; stereotyping in, 145; Western, 135-37, 142, 143, 145
Gertie the Dinosaur, 173
Gimmie Shelter, 162, 165
Gladwell, David, 46
Glass, 112
Godard, Jean-Luc, *80*, *83*, *137*, 200
Godfather, The, 65, 80, 131, 138
God is Dog Spelled Backwards. *See Art*
Godzilla, 135
Golden Fish, The, 65
Goldman, Les, 109
Gone with the Wind, 7
Good Night, Socrates, 109
Goofy, 173
Gospel According to St. Matthew, The, 165
Graduate, The, 12, 27, 107, 112, 130, 169, 170
Granton Trawler, 153
Great Train Robbery, The, 27
Great White Hope, The, *108*
Greed, 129
Gregoriev, Roman, 155
Grierson, John, 58, 152-53, 154, 161

Griffith, David Wark, 5, 65, 70, 92, 96, *105*
Gunfighter, The, *140*, 145
Gunsmoke, 136, 140
Gypsy Moths, The, 34

Haanstra, Bert, 112
Hagmann, Stuart, 109-11
Halas and Batchelor, *173*
Hand-colored film, 91, 92, 179, 193, 209
Hand-held camera shots, *19*, 123, 165, 205, 206, *207*
Hand, The, *172*
Hangman, The, 109, *111*
Harvest of Shame, 158, *160*
Hatari, 140
Hat, The, 170, 171
Hawks, Howard, 125, 128, 135, 137, 140-42, 186, 195
Hearts and Minds, 165
Help! My Snowman's Burning Down, *188*
Henson, Jim, 64
High-angle shot, **16**, 38, 51
High-key lighting, **76**, 84
High Noon, 19, 142
High School, 163
Hill, George Roy, 65
Hippler, Fritz, 155
Hiroshima Mon Amour, 28
Hitchcock, Alfred, 65, *75*, 128, 189, 200-201
Hole, The, 170
Horror films, as genre, 138-39, 143
Horseman, The, 131
Hospital, 163
Hubley, Faith, 170; John, 170, 171
Hughes, Ken, 137
Hunchback of Notre Dame, The, 67
Hustler, The, 68
Huston, John, 156-57
Hydraulic lifts for dollies, 43

Iconic graphic films, **182**
If, 32, 46, 98
I. F. Stone's Weekly, 161
Iliad, The, 183
Including shot. *See* Long shot
Inheritance, The, 111-12
Intercutting, **49-51**
In the Year of the Pig, 153
Intolerance, 5, 65, *105*
Is It Always Right to Be Right?, 98
Ivens, Jorris, 154

Jane, 161
Jaws, 7, *91*, 131, 139
Joe Macbeth, 137
Johnny Got His Gun, 70, 108
Jules and Jim, 71, *130*

Jump cut, **67**
Juvenile Court, 163
Juxtaposition, 48-49, 54, 57

Kaczender, George, 27, 48-49
Kael, Pauline, 28, 144
Kaleidoski, 31, 34
Katzenjammer Kids, The, 173
Kaufman, Denis. *See* Dziga-Vertov
Kazan, Elia, 16, 17, 27, 108
Key light, 84
Keystone Kops, 30
Kinestasis films, **183**-84
King, Henry, *140*, 145
King Kong, 17, 138
Kino-Eye series, 151
Kino-Pravda series, 151
Kiss, The, 1, 34
Knife in the Water, 125, 131
Know Your Enemy—Japan, 145
Kubrick, Stanley, 19, 46, 75, 114-15, 139, 186
Kurosawa, Akira, 70

Labyrinth, 176
Ladies and Gentlemen, The Rolling Stones, 162, 165
La Jetee, 34, *35*
Lamorisse, Albert, 10, 57, 69-70, *101*, 176
Lapis, 191
Last Picture Show, The, 96
La Strada, 17
Last Year at Marienbad, 28
Law and Order, 163
Lawrence of Arabia, 112, 115
Leacock, Richard, 163
Lean, David, 115
Left-Handed Gun, The, 79, 126
Legion of Decency, 173
Lelouch, Claude, 61, 94
Lenica, Jan, 176
Lenny, 94
Lenses: close-up, 206-7; filters for, 204, 205; fish-eye, **13**; f-numbers, 203-5; focal length, **21**; macro, **207**; normal, **10**, 11, 21, 206; telephoto, **10**-12, 13, 21, 26, 86, 205, 206; wide angle, **12**, 13, 21, 26, 205; zoom, **13**-15, 21, 41, 86, 206
Le Roy, Mervyn, 137
Les Astraunautes, 176
Les Escargots, 67, 68, 176
Les Mistons, 24
L'Homme Vite, 34, 61
Light, 38, 43, 75-85, 205; activities, 84-85; angles of, 84-85; in black and white *vs.* color films, 101; fill light, 85, 86; high-key, **76**, 84; for indoor shooting, 86-88; key light, 84; low-key, **77**, 84;

main light, **86**; "painting with," 75-9; "realistic," or documentary, 83, 97
Light meters, 86, 202
Linear films, **186**
Lines Horizontal, 176
Lines Vertical, 176
Lipsett, Arthur, *184*, 185, 186
Listen to Britain, 154
Little Big Man, *53*, 79, 126, 137
Little Caesar, 137
London Can Take It, 154
Loneliness of the Long Distance Runner, The, 30, 35
Long-focus lens. *See* Telephoto lens
Long shot, **3**-7, 13, 47, 63, 152, 207
Loops, 115, 176
Lord of the Flies, 18, 35
Lorenz, Pare, 109, 154
Lovin, J. Maynard, 67
Low-angle shot, **17**, 26, 46, 140
Low-key lighting, **77**, 84
Lucas, George, 65
Lumiere, Louis and Auguste, 1, *2*, 34, 149, 150

Macbeth, 125
Machine Gun Kelly, 144
Macro lenses, **207**
Main light, **86**
Mammals, 122-23, 124-25
Mamoulian, Rouben, 91
Man and a Woman, A, 61, 94
Man for All Seasons, A, 68
Marker, Chris, 34-35
Married print, **118**
Mask, **70**-71
Matte box, **41**
Mayseles, David and Albert, 161, *162*
McKay, Winsor, 173
McLaren, Norman, 115, *174*, 175, 176, 177, 186
McLaughlin, Dan, 182-83, *184*, 186
McLuhan, Marshall, 158, 166
McTeague, 129
Medium Cool, 165
Medium shot, **3**, 7-8, 47
Meet Me in St. Louis, 146
Méliès, George, *4*, 67, 149, 150
Memorandum, 28
Meshes of the Afternoon, 189
Mickey Mouse, 173
Mickey One, 126
Microphones, 38, 46, 88, *165*
Minimalist cinema, **197**
Miracle Worker, The, 126
Moana, 152
Mockingbird, 78, 111, 112, *123*
Montage editing, 51-53, 57
Moods of Surfing, 29
Morrissey, Paul, 143

MOS, 88
Moscow Strikes Back, 155
Motion, 23-37; activities, 36-37; audience movement, **33**-34; camera movement, 27-28; camera speed, 29-32; little or no movement, 34-35; subject movement, 24-27
Moving camera shots, 27
Munro, Grant, 114
Murnau, F.W., 68
Music. *See* Sound
Mutt and Jeff, 173
My Darling Clementine, 136-37

Nanook of the North, *151*-52, 153
Narration. *See* Sound
Naturally cinematic objects, **57**, 72
Negro Soldier, The, 145
Neighbors, 175
Nelson, Robert, 195
Neutral density filter, 205
Nichols, Mike, 12, *27*, *107*, 112
Night and Fog, 28
Night Mail, 58, 109, 153, 154
Night Moves, 126, 128
Night on Bald Mountain, 173
Nights of Cabiria, 61
1984 (George Orwell), 2
Nine Years in Nine Minutes, 183-84
Nobody Waved Goodbye, 165
No Reason to Stay, 5, 12, 26, 61, 69, 107, 163
Normal-angle shot, **15**
Normal lens, **10**, 11, 21, 206
Nosferatu, 68
Not as Yet Decided, 65
Now-film, **181**-97; activities, 196-97; compilation films, 185, 196; computer films, 189-91; iconic graphic, **182**; kinestasis, 183-84; minimalist cinema, **197**; non-linearity of, 186-88; personalist cinema, 184-85; psychedelic films, **191**-94; underground films, **195**
Noyes, Elliot, *174*, 176
Nyby, Christian, 140

Occurrence at Owl Creek Bridge, 69, 111, 186; editing techniques in, 45, 46-*47*; shotmaking techniques in, 5, 7, 8, 10, 11-12, 13-14, 18, *19*, 27; use of lighting in, 77, 79; use of music in, *112*, *123*
Odyssey, 200
Off-On, 193-94
Oh Dem Watermelons, 195
Olympia, 31, 34, *58*
Omega, *193*

Omega Man, The, 139
On Film Technique, V.I. Pudovkin, 1
On the Waterfront, 16, 17, 27, 108, 112
Opening Speech, 175
Optical printer, **176**, 177
Orange and Blue, 176
Orr, Bob, 14
Ousmane, Sembene, 80
Overexposure, **204**
Overture/Nyitany, 111
Owen, Don, 165
Ozu, Yasujiro, 124

Pacific 231, 58
Palazzolo, Tom, 184-85, 186
Pan shot, **18**
Paper Moon, 96
Parable, The, 24
Parallel cutting, **65**
Pas de Deux, 177
Pasolini, Pier Paolo, 165
Passenger, The, 129
Peckinpah, Sam, 31, 135, 142
Penn, Arthur, 31, *53*, 58, 79, 124, 126, 128, 133
Pen Point Percussion, 115, 176
Permutations, 191
Personalist cinema, 184-85
Phenakistoscope, **178**
Phoebe, 26-27, *48*-49, 67, 69
Pit and the Pendulum, The, 144
Pixillation, **175**
Planet of the Apes, 139
Play it Again, Sam, 143
Pluto, 173
Point Blank, 138
Polanski, Roman, 92, 94, 96-97, 98, 121-23, 124-26, 130, 131
Pontecorvo, Gillo, 83, 111, 165
Popeye, 173
Porter, Edwin S., 27
Power and the Land, 154
Powers of Ten, 15
Praxinoscope, 178
Primate, 163
Princess or the Tiger?, The, 101
Projectors. *See* Film projectors
Psychedelic films, 191-94
Psycho, *75*, 200-1
Public Enemy, 137
Pudovkin, V.I., 1, 50

Rainshower, 83
Ransen, Mort, 5, 12, 61
Ray, Nicholas, 98
Rebel Without a Cause, 98
Red Balloon, The, 10, 69, *101*, 105, 176
Renaissance, 175
Report, 194
Repulsion, 125
Requiem for a Heavyweight, 19

Resnais, Alain, 28, 124
Reverse scripting, 54, 72-73
Rhythm, **57**-73; activities, 72-73; editing for, 61-63; motion within a shot, 57-61
Richardson, Tony, 30, 35
Riefenstahl, Leni, 18, 31, 34, 51, 57, *58*, 69
Rim lighting, **84**
Rink, The, 58
Rio Bravo, 140, 142, 186
River, The, 109, 154
Rollerball, 139
Rolling Stones, 132, *162*
Rome, Open City, 83
Rosemary's Baby, 125
Rosselini, Roberto, 83
Rossen, Robert, 68
Rough cut, **207**
Roullet, Serge, *80*
Runner, 25, 109

Safety Last, 1
St. Matthew Passion, 111
St. Valentine's Day Massacre, The, 138, 144
Salesman, 161, 165
Sanders, Terry and Denis, 170-71
Scarface, 137, 140
Schiappacasse, Robert, 14, 195
Schoedsack, Ernest, 17
Science fiction film, as genre, 138-39
Sechan, Edmond, *15*, 65, 94
Selling of the Pentagon, The, 154, 163
Sepia, **94**
Sergeant York, 140
Servais, Raoul, 97
Seventh Seal, The, 8, 24-25, 26, *58*, *76*-77, 94-97, *106*, *125*, 144-45
70mm film, 201
Shane, 136
Shoeshine, 83
Short-focus lenses. *See* Wide-angle lenses
Shotgun mike, **38**
Shot, **1**-21; activities, 20-21; close-up, 8-10, 13, 45, *47*, 63, **207**; cover, **67**; crane (boom), 19, 43, *86*; cut-away, **67**, 165; cut-in, **65**-67; demonstrative, **10**; dolly, **19**, 41, 43, 86; Dutch-angle, **18**; effects of camera hand-held camera, **19**, 123, 165, 205, 206, *207*; indoor, angles on, 15-18, 26, 46, 51, 86; effects of camera movements on, 18-19, 27-28, 34, 124; effects of lenses on, 10-15, 26; effects of subject movement on, 24-27, 34, 36; establishing, **3**; extreme long, **3**, 5-7; freeze-frame, 35-36;

86-89, 204-5; length of, 63, 207; long, **3-5**, *7*, 13, *47*, 63, 152, 207; medium, *3*, *7*-8, 47, 62; pan, **18**; preparing for, *38-43*; rhythmic motion in, 57-61, 109; "slating" of, *88*; subjective camera, **19**; tilt, **18**-19; tracking, **19**, *41*; zoom, **13**-15, 21, *41*, *86*, 205-6

Silent Running, 139
Singin' in the Rain, 146
Siskel, Gene, 98
16mm cameras, *43*, *86*, 182, 202
16mm film, 72, 178, 182, 201, 202
Ski the Outer Limits, *23*, 31, 34
Sky, 30, 105, 186
Sky Capers, 34
Slating of shots, *88*
Sleep, 1, 34
Slow motion, 29-32, 36
Smothers Brothers Comedy Hour, 182, 183
Soldier Blue, 137
Sound, *38*, 105-19, 118-19, 209; activities, 116-17; camera noise, *88*; dialog, 105-8, 116, 121-22; editing of, *118-19*; effects, records of, 117; generator noise, *38*; lip-synchronized, 209; music, 111-14; narration, 64, 109-11, 118, 209; noise, use of, 108, 114-15, 122-23; silence, use of, 115; sound track, making of, *118-19*, 209; use of in cinema verité, 160-61. *See also* Microphones; Tape Recorders
Soylent Green, 139
Speeded motion, 29-32, 36-37
Splicing, 116, 207, *208-9*
Sporting Life, This, 106
Stagecoach, 136
Stevens, George, 115
"Stock" shots, **51**
Strawberry Statement, The, 109
Stringbean, The, *15*, *94*, 105
Stroheim, Erich von, 129
Subjective camera shot, **19**
Subject movement, 24-27, 34, 36; activities, 36-37
Sullivan, Pat, 173
Summer We Moved to Elm Street, The, 79
Super 8mm cameras, 14, 185, 202-3, 205, 206, *207*, 209
Super 8mm film, *202*-3, 205

Tabor, Michael, *165*, 184

Takes, **46**
Tales of Terror, 144
Talkies, 105, 106
Tape recorders, *38*, *41*, *88*, 116, *118*, 132, 160-61, 209
Tape splicers, **207**-209
Target for Tonight, 155
Telephoto lens, 10-12, 13, 21, 26, 205, 206
Television, activities, 166-67; censorship of *Bonnie and Clyde*, 32; documentaries, 154, 157-60, 163-65; filming techniques, 20, 36, 73, 106, 133
Televisionland, *183*
Tenth Victim, The, 139
They Also Serve, 154
Thing, The, 140
35mm film, 201
Three Little Pigs, The, 173
Threshold, 67
Tilt shot, **18**-19
Time-lapse photography, 30
Time Out of War, A, 171
Timepiece, 57, 64, *93*
Titicut Follies, 163
Towering Inferno, 139
Toys, *114*, 115
Tracking shot, **19**, *41*
Train Comes into Paris, 34
Train Coming into the Station, 149
Treatment, **200**
Tripods, *203*, 205, *206*
Trip, The, 144
Trip to the Moon, A, *4*, 149-50
Triumph of the Will, The, 17-18, 51, 57, *58*, *69*
Trnka, Jiri, *172*
Truffaut, Francois, 25, 35, *71*, 80, *96*, 115, *130*
Trumbo, Dalton, 70, 108
21-87, 185
Two Men and a Wardrobe, *122*, 124, 125
Two Rode Together, 137
Two-shot, **8**
2001: A Space Odyssey, 7, 19, 46, 75, 112, 114-15, 139, 186

Un Chien Andalou, 187, 188
Underexposure, **204**
Underground films, **195**
Untouchables, The, series, 137
Ustinov, Peter, 94

Vadasz, Janos, 111
Van Dyke, Willard, 154
Varlamov, Leonid, 155

Vertigo, 189
Very Nice, Very Nice, 185
Victors, The, 111
Vigo, Jean, *31*, 32
Visconti, Luchino, 83

Wall, The, 80, *174*
War Game, The, 83, *98*
Warhol, Andy, 1, 34, 143
Watkins, Peter, 35, 83, *98*
Watt, Harry, 153
Welfare, 163
Welles, Orson, 5, *13*, *45*, 96, *121*, 130, 149
Wellman, William, 137
Western films, as genre, 135-*36*, 142, 143, 145
Wet splicers. *See* Cement splicers
When Angels Fall, 92, 94, 96-97, 98, 122-23, 124
White Mane, 57, 101
Whitney, James, 191; John, 189-91; Michael and John, Jr., 191
Why Man Creates, *169*-70, 176
Why We Fight series, 156
Wide angle lenses, **12**, 13, 21, 26, 205
Wild Angels, The, 144
Wild Bunch, The, 31, 142
Wild Child, The, 71, 80, *96*, 115
Willard, 70
Wipe, **70**, 73
Wise, Robert, *139*, 144
Wiseman, Frederick, 163
Woodstock, 33, 162, 165, 201
Workers Leaving the Lumiere Factory, 149
Work print, **118**
World of 68, 182-83
Wright, Basil, 153

XL (Kodak) cameras, 204, 205

Yellow Submarine, 174
Yojimbo, 70
Young Frankenstein, 142
Yourself, 184
Yust, Larry, 101

Z, 26, *138*, 172-73
Zabriskie Point, 128-29
Zagreb, *174*, 177
Zardoz, 139
Zero for Conduct, *31*, 32
Zinnemann, Fred, 19, 68, 142
Zoetrope, 178
Zoom lens, **13**-15, 21, *41*, *86*, 206